By the same author:

A Century of Judaism in New York
   (New York, Congregation B'nai Jeshurun, 1930)
Toward a Solution
   (New York, G. P. Putnam's Sons, 1940)
Shanah be-Yisrael, an account of Dr. Israel Goldstein's year of service as
   Treasurer of the Jewish Agency
   (Jerusalem, World Confederation of General Zionists, 1950)
Brandeis University—Chapter of Its Founding
   (New York, Bloch Publishing Co., 1951)
American Jewry Comes of Age: Tercentenary Addresses
   (New York, Bloch Publishing Co., 1955)
Transition Years, New York–Jerusalem, 1960–1962
   (Jerusalem, Rubin Mass, 1962; published in Hebrew as *Shenot Ma'avar,*
   1963)
Israel At Home and Abroad
   (Jerusalem, Rubin Mass, 1973)

Festschriften:

Two Generations in Perspective: Notable Events and Trends 1896–1956, essays
   dedicated to Dr. Israel Goldstein on the occasion of his sixtieth birthday
   (New York, Monde Publishers, Inc., 1957)
Studies in the History of Zionism (Pirké Mehkar be-Toledot ha-Tziyyonut),
   essays presented to Dr. Israel Goldstein on the occasion of his eightieth
   birthday by the Hebrew University's Institute of Contemporary Jewry
   (Jerusalem, World Zionist Organization, 1976)

Jewish Justice and Conciliation

Israel Goldstein

JEWISH JUSTICE
AND CONCILIATION

History of the Jewish Conciliation Board of America, 1930–1968

and a Review of Jewish Juridical Autonomy

With a Preface by
Dr. Simon Agranat,
President of the Israel Supreme Court, Retired

HERZL PRESS

New York

DEDICATED

To my Revered Parents of Blessed Memory

David L. and Fannie Goldstein

Who Taught Me

Just and Peaceful Ways

and to

All My Fellow Jews

Whose Faith and Confidence

Helped Our Tribunal

To Administer Justice and Conciliation

"Administer true justice, and show kindness and compassion to one another"

Zechariah 7:9

Contents

List of Illustrations

Preface

by DR. SIMON AGRANAT
President of the Israel Supreme Court (Retired)

Execute the judgment of truth and peace in your gates
ZECHARIAH 8:16

The reading of this book has been for me a fascinating and educational experience. I am therefore glad of this opportunity—and indeed grateful for the privilege—to make the following observations about its contents.

Jewish Justice and Conciliation is divided into two major parts. Its thrust, the initial and main purpose which actuated the author to write it, is reflected in Part II, which consists of a comprehensive account of the work of the Jewish Conciliation Board of America in the years 1930–1968, during which it acted as a voluntary tribunal for the arbitration and settlement of the many disputes and quarrels which arose between the "little men" among the Jewish population in the City of New York. In performing this function the Board filled a vital social need of the persons belonging to this sector of the Jewish community, since they looked askance on applying to the civil courts for relief against the infringement of their alleged rights by their Jewish opponents.

This was so for a variety of reasons pointed out in the author's account. For example, many of them were immigrants who were still encountering the difficulties involved in the process of their "Americanization," including the fact that their sole vehicle of communication was the Yiddish language, to which they had been accustomed in their countries of origin. They were thus overawed by the thought of having to ventilate their grievances in what appeared in their eyes as the strange and formalized atmosphere of the civil courts, with whose procedure they were unfamiliar. They were also discouraged from seeking a judicial resolution of their disputes because of what others told them about the "law's delays." Then, too, the expense of securing legal aid was, for many of them, prohibitive, due to poor economic circumstances.

Perhaps the most important reason for their inhibition from going to the courts for the vindication of their grievances was their lack of confidence that non-Jewish judges were possessed of the ability to understand in a meaningful way—to pierce through the "veil" of—the peculiarly Jewish character or background of the subject matter which was the core of their differences with the other party to the controversy. Finally, those among them who were strictly observant Orthodox Jews felt themselves bound by the Talmudic prohibition against resort to a non-Jewish court, which was based on the idea that to do so is to commit *Hillul Hashem* (desecration of God's Name), i.e. to discredit an integral part of the Jewish religious heritage.

I offer no apology for repeating at some length the author's specification of the motives on account of which Jews who were at loggerheads with their spouses or other members of their family, their neighbors, business rivals, governing committees of the synagogues or officers of their fraternal lodges, etc., did not appeal to the ordinary courts for redress of their grievances. My object in doing so is to bring out in full relief the singular social importance which, in my estimation, must perforce be attributed to the service rendered them by the Board in providing the facility of a free arbitral forum to which they could turn for the resolution and settlement of those conflicts—a forum where they were able to argue their case in person, without the necessity and expense of hiring a lawyer to represent them, and in which they found the proceedings to be informal and the atmosphere sympathetic and congenial. They could expect the panel of arbitrators selected to deal with the dispute and which, in accordance with Jewish tradition, invariably consisted of three members, to give them—in the author's phrase— a "listening ear"; to comprehend fully their Yiddish speech; and to display, when such was pertinent, a proper understanding of the Jewish element that colored the subject matter of the litigation. The arbitrators on each panel were always a rabbi, a lawyer or civil judge and a person experienced in business affairs; all of them served voluntarily, without pay, and purely as a matter of Jewish community spirit.

Having regard to the advantages—convenience and suitability to their economic and social circumstances—which, it soon became evident to this class of Jewish disputants, could be derived from applying to the Board for the litigation and settlement of their controversies, it is not surprising that there was increasing readiness on the part of both the claimants and their opponents to appear and air their differences before its arbitral panels. Yet, for myself, I cannot but be impressed by the fact that, during the period of nearly forty years covered by the author's account, these volunteer arbitrators, although they could devote to this purpose only the late hours of the afternoon or early hours of the evening, disposed of no less than 15,000 cases.

It is patently clear, and indeed hardly necessary to point out, that the experience of Dr. Israel Goldstein, resulting from his presidency of the Board throughout that period as well as from his frequent service on its arbitral panels, easily assures his special competence to tell the success story of this unique tribunal. As could be expected, he has done so in pellucid and concise language, which of course, notwithstanding the wealth of the material, makes for very easy reading. Moreover, I am confident that other readers will perceive (as I have) the discerning thought and immense labor he has invested in selecting and classifying the many "typical" cases which he describes; in reciting their pertinent facts and summarizing the adjudicatory decisions reached therein or the compromises which the litigant parties were persuaded to accept; and in adding, in many instances, his personal comments on the significance of the decisions and compromise solutions to the adjustment of the particular social or economic problems which often beset some of the claimants and defendants, and which the ventilation of their disputes brought to the surface.

From the author's introduction to this part of the book we learn that the Jewish Conciliation Board had a precursor, namely the "Jewish Arbitration Court" which was established in 1919 as a voluntary tribunal for ministering to the litigious needs of immigrant Jews on the Lower East Side of New York City. As from 1920, when the New York State Arbitration Act came into force, the awards of this tribunal were enforceable, provided the party-litigants signed in advance an agreement to abide by them, in the same way as the judgments of the civil courts were enforced. This was also, it may be stated parenthetically, the structure of authority by virtue of which the arbitral panels of the Board subsequently functioned. The detailed story of the activity of the former body has been related elsewhere. I have, however, found it proper to refer to the author's mention of this forerunner of the Board for the following reason.

In January 1930, Dr. Goldstein was invited to become President of the Jewish Court of Arbitration, an invitation which he felt impelled to accept "out of deep concern for social justice and for Jewish dignity." Shortly after entering upon this office, he arranged for the change of its name to that of "The Jewish Conciliation Court," under which it was then incorporated. Later, in 1939, there took place a final alteration of the name to "The Jewish Conciliation Board of America." Although arbitration had been this court's foremost principle from 1930 onward, its final change of designation was motivated not by some new policy, but by the concern which Dr. Goldstein felt for a more accurate indication of the Board's objectives and terms of reference. The stress was on conciliation, i.e. persuading the contending parties to accept a compromise or otherwise reconcile their differences so that peaceful relations between them might be restored and they would then walk away from the hearing with a mutual feeling of friendship rather than of enmity. As the author has put it, the primary role which the Board's arbitrators filled throughout the period in question was that of "voluntary conciliators."

It hardly needs to be added that when, from time to time, their efforts for conciliation in a given case were non-productive, the members of the panel were left with the sole recourse of adopting a purely adjudicative approach to the solution of the dispute. In such cases, their decisions were guided by what they conceived to be standards of common sense, justice and fairness (rather than by legal niceties), as well as by the spirit of Jewish ethics. However, after the disposition of the case by an announcement of the decision reached therein, the arbitrators or one arbitrator often "took time out" to explain to the losing party the reasons on which it was based, in order to convince him of its justifiability and thereby diminish, if possible, any sudden untoward feeling on his part regarding his opponent, which the thought of the latter's legal victory may have engendered. It is, I think, true to say that this "post-adjudicative" practice also reflects, in a certain sense, an attitude in the direction of conciliating and making peace between the rival disputants which was the hallmark of the Board's activity of "social engineering" in this field.

I turn now to Part I of the book, a valuable monograph wherein the author reviews the history of Jewish juridical autonomy as a feature which, for the most part, characterized the life of the Jews in the various countries of their dispersion during the nearly two thousand years following their loss of independent, territorial statehood and extending, in some measure, down to modern times. This also includes a treatment of the nature of that autonomy in Eretz Yisrael, both when the land was under Roman control (after the destruction of the Temple) and in the succeeding periods during which it was under Arab, Turkish and British rule. (The period since 1948, when the State of Israel was established, is outside the scope of the survey.)

One of the main facts brought out in this historical account is that the exercise of juridical autonomy by the Jews was usually dependent, certainly in Western Europe until the Emancipation, on the will and consent of the reigning sovereign or ruling authority of the region in which the Jewish community was settled. In other words, permission for the Jews to adhere to their own jurisdiction for the adjudication of their internal disputes—which meant going to their own courts of law *(Batei Din)* for this purpose or to Jewish courts of arbitration—was in the nature of a privilege. This was so, given the fact that Jews played virtually no role in the political institutions of the country. Thus it happened that the prevailing political authority in their locality at times denied juridical autonomy to the Jews; at other times, they were privileged to enjoy it; and there were also times when the privilege was abrogated owing to whim or caprice. On the other hand, there were situations in which, notwithstanding official disapproval or withholding of the privilege, there was passive toleration on the part of the ruler in regard to the prevalence of that phenomenon. Nor does the author fail to point to those cases wherein the ruler (because of policy considerations) even obligated the Jewish population to rely on its own legal system for the ventilation of its internal disputes. One of the useful things in the author's account, which reflects the precarious nature of the exercise of Jewish juridical autonomy in different places and periods, is his painstaking enumeration of the decrees and legislative instruments which were the legal sources of the above edicts and which gave them force.

So far I have touched upon an external legal factor, relating to the possession of juridical autonomy by Jewish communities in the relevant times and regions. In addition, however, the author also singles out the cruel tribulations to which Jewish communities were intermittently subjected—persecution, massacre, expulsion, and the hardship involved in enforced wandering to other lands and in building a new life. These grievous sufferings and privations, which were due to official fiat, antagonism on the part of Gentile neighbors and the pressure of church prelates, inevitably had a repressive influence on the existence here and there of Jewish juridical autonomy and led to its deterioration. Nevertheless, this institution of Jewish Diaspora life was not, in general, extinguished and, indeed, it eventually even came to life again in some of the very countries where the cruelties had been perpetrated (e.g. England). It is interesting to quote, in this connection, a passage from the judgment given at the end of the eighteenth century by a famous English judge, Lord Stowell, in a case where he had to decide on the validity of a marriage celebrated according to Jewish law. Lord Stowell made the following sympathetic allusion to Jewish juridical autonomy:

> This is a question of marriage of a very different kind between persons governed by a peculiar law of their own, and administered, to a certain

degree, by jurisdiction established among themselves—a jurisdiction competent to decide upon questions of this nature with peculiar advantage. . . . If I am to apply the peculiar principles of Jewish law, I may run the hazard of mistaking those principles, having a very moderate knowledge of that law.

I think, however, that the more important factor which gave impetus to the cementing of Jewish juridical autonomy (I have in mind here particularly the period of the Middle Ages, when political emancipation had not yet reached the Jews) was the internal Jewish one. I mean by this the willingness of the Jewish disputants, with a few exceptions, to seek the aid of their own courts of law and courts of arbitration rather than accept an alien jurisdiction, a fact which is also indicated by the author. No doubt they were influenced by the religious ban on the appeal by Jewish litigants to the Gentile courts, which could only be relaxed if the other Jewish party refused to appear before the *Beth Din* or abide by its decree. It is evident, however, that apart from the moral influence of this prohibition, the Jewish court had no sanctions at its disposal for enforcing obedience of the ban or compliance with its decisions in other respects. It could only threaten the recalcitrant party with *Herem* (excommunication) which, because of its harsh character, was not often put into effect.

It is true that, according to the author's account, Jewish courts were in some places empowered by the political authority to impose on criminal offenders sentences of imprisonment, flogging and even capital punishment; but it is not clear to what extent such sanctions were applied (I am myself highly doubtful if the last of these penalties was ever imposed or, at any rate, implemented). It would, I think be a fair inference from the author's account that the Jewish courts functioned by virtue of their religious and moral authority and because of the freely given consent of the disputants to adhere to the Jewish legal system. One should add to this the contributing factor of the wisdom and ingenuity with which the Talmudic sages and the great Rabbinic commentators and codifiers of later generations developed the Halakhic principles so that they might conform to the changing needs of Jewish Diaspora society and thus ensure their vitality within it.

It is noticeable in this monograph that the author has not raised the question as to whether, when circumstances required, Jewish courts or jurists allowed elements of alien origin to penetrate the Jewish legal system. My surmise is that this was by design and that one reason for the omission was that, given the wide ambit of this survey of Jewish juridical autonomy, it would be going too far afield to pursue this interesting and broad topic, particularly since it has already exercised other scholars. For example, in Chapter V of his book, *Exclusiveness and Tolerance* (1961), Professor Jacob Katz—discussing Jewish juridical autonomy in the Middle Ages—expresses the conclusion that "in theory the Jewish legal system was regarded as self-sufficient, but in practice the Jewish courts and jurists (i.e. the halakhists) did not entirely disregard legal rulings and enactments emanating from non-Jewish sources."

The omission of this topic in no way detracts from the author's monograph on that phase of Jewish history. Nor would I have mentioned it at all, but for my desire to accentuate the principal aim which he envisaged would be achieved by his review. This was to paint a broad canvas portraying to the reader the very prevalance, to a greater or lesser extent as the case may have been, of Jewish juridical autonomy over nearly two millennia and in almost every country or region where an organized or semi-organized Jewish community existed. This object has indeed been accomplished and, to my mind, in an admirable and exhaustive fashion. The tireless and extensive research work involved is apparent from the copious footnote references to the supporting sources. To my mind, the historical value of the author's finished product lies in the fact that it serves to reinforce, and give added justification to, the well-known inference that the continuous and widespread persistence of that remarkable and unique phenomenon—Jewish juridical autonomy—has played a major part in preserving the separate existence and identity of the Jewish people as a religio-national entity.

It will, I hope, not be thought extraneous if, at the end of these remarks, I note Dr. Goldstein's explanation of why this comprehensive historical narrative—a self-contained monograph which could easily appear as a separate book—came to form Part I of the present volume. His reason, we are told, was that it may serve as background to the chapter of Jewish social history which constitutes Part II. In this, I think, he was right. Clearly, in functioning during close to half-a-century as a voluntary tribunal for the resolution and pacific settlement of the internal conflicts which arose among members of the largest Jewish community in the United States, the Jewish Conciliation Board epitomized in a sense the whole idea of Jewish juridical autonomy and worked within the spirit of Jewish tradition.

Jerusalem   SIMON AGRANAT
June 1980

Foreword

For a period of more than half-a-century, the Jewish Conciliation Board of America—a voluntary agency of arbitration, adjudication, and conciliation serving the largest Jewish community in the world—fulfilled a vital Jewish, civic, and human purpose.

The author's experience with the Board, which he served as President for thirty-eight years, impels him to leave a permanent record of this tribunal and its significance, as it functioned during the period of his active association with it. That experience has also stirred his interest in the history of juridical autonomy among Jewish communities in the Diaspora.* The introductory section of this volume is therefore intended to provide some detailed historical background to illuminate the subject. For the benefit of readers who may wish to check the source material, footnotes are provided at the end of Part One. Against such a background study, the proceedings of the Jewish Conciliation Board of America can be evaluated more meaningfully.

This volume, in which, it is hoped, the reader will find considerable human interest, is intended primarily to relate the history of the Board during the nearly four decades of my association with it. The major section of the book presents a number of typical cases which have come before the Board and which have received its good offices, describes the manner in which they were handled at the hearings, and suggests the value of this unusual social-service agency to the largest Jewish community in the Diaspora.

During my own career and program of activities, this particular work has occupied a special place in my heart, because it combined humanitarian endeavor with concern for Jewish justice, Jewish dignity, and Jewish conciliation. May I add that it has also played a part in the Americanization process of many Jewish immigrant families.

This activity made a special appeal to me, because it gave me an opportunity of being helpful not only to *Klal Yisrael,* the Jewish community, but also to "Reb Yisro'el," the Jewish individual, as a Jew and as a human being.

There was an additional factor which attracted me to this area of service. The synagogue which I had the privilege of serving for more than four decades, Congregation B'nai Jeshurun of New York, was an upper-middle-class *Kehillah*. Hence, I felt the need of ministering also to *Amkha*, the Jewish masses. Engagement in the work of the Jewish Conciliation Board offered this enriching opportunity.

I am deeply indebted to Dr. Simon Agranat for his important preface to this book. His vast legal knowledge, his distinguished career as a member and then as President of the Israel Supreme Court, and his understanding of the American Jewish scene from which he emanated, endow his comments with special value.

Generous acknowledgment is due to Mr. Esriel Hildesheimer, for his painstaking and valuable research assistance in preparing the introductory section of this volume on the history of Jewish juridical autonomy; to Rabbi Professor Louis Rabinowitz, for having provided an insightful evaluation of the Jewish Conciliation Board's handling of the cases in the spirit of Jewish tradition; to Mr. Shmuel Gorr, for his helpfulness in the selection and classification of the cases; and to Rabbi Ilene Schneider and to Mrs. Shirah Twersky-Cassel, for their valuable assistance in the organization and preliminary editing of the material.

For the final redaction of this volume I am deeply indebted to Dr. Gabriel Sivan, whose experienced editorial eye, seasoned judgment, and broad scholarship have contributed greatly to the end result.

To my beloved wife, Bert, I am obliged, as ever, for her interest, encouragement, and helpfulness, and for the reading of the manuscript.

My thanks are extended to my secretary in Jerusalem, Mrs. Pauline Cooper, for typing portions of the manuscript and for handling administrative details in connection with the work, and to my long-time faithful secretary in New York, Mrs. Mimi Solomon, for having handled my New York files in order to make them available in Jerusalem.

Appreciation is due to the Altman Foundation of New York and to its former President, the late John S. Burke, of blessed memory, for having provided the initial funds for the publication of the book, and to his son, John S. Burke, Jr., for his ongoing interest and encouragement.

ISRAEL GOLDSTEIN

Jerusalem, Sivan 5740
      June 1980

---

*For an earlier, and brief, treatment of the subject, see "Modern Courts of Arbitration and the Jewish Historical background," in *Toward a Solution* (New York: G. P. Putnam's Sons, 1940), pp. 303–321. This essay was republished more recently in *Justice, Justice Shalt Thou Pursue*, papers assembled by Ronald B. Sobel and Sidney Wallach on the occasion of Dr. Julius Mark's seventy-fifth birthday (New York: KTAV Publishing House, 1975), pp. 49–69.

Part One
JEWISH JURIDICAL AUTONOMY IN THE DIASPORA

I

Introduction

The principal purpose of this volume is to discuss the background, history, cases, and drama of the Jewish Conciliation Board of America. It is, however, important to realize from the outset that the Jewish Conciliation Board (hereinafter JCB) had not been established in a vacuum: it was a continuation of the long history of juridical autonomy granted to Jews in the lands of their dispersion during the two millennia when they were denied political autonomy in a state of their own. Beginning with the central internal authority set up in Eretz Yisrael immediately following the fall of Judea in 70 C.E.,[1] to the Exilarchate of Babylonia during the second century C.E., from the community leadership of the elected officials of the Jewish communities in Central and Western Europe during the Middle Ages, then onward to the authority of the Council of Four Lands in Eastern Europe during the modern era, some form of self-government and self-adjudication was permitted to the Jews wherever they organized their own community life.

The extent of the autonomy granted to the Jewish communities varied from country to country, and was often dependent upon the whims of the secular governmental authorities. Those governments which were eager for the Jewish communities to organize themselves under their own leadership considered such autonomy a means to further their own aims, such as tax collection.[2] Often, particularly in Europe, Jews were permitted the same degree of self-government as other ethnic groups. But even when there was an existent policy of self-government for ethnic groups, Jews were unique in being allowed their own system of law courts.

A major factor in the development of Jewish courts of law (*Batei Din*) in the Diaspora was the Talmudic ban on Jews voluntarily presenting cases to the Gentile courts.[3] This was later reaffirmed by the ensuing Rabbinic authorities. It is of interest to note that the early Christians prohibited dealings with the Roman courts[4] and that the early Karaites in Egypt, during the Geonic period (6th–11th cent.), did not allow their members to use Muslim courts.[5]

There were several reasons for Rabbinic authorities of the Geonic period to reaffirm the Talmudic ban on Jews utilizing the Gentile courts: one, a general lack of confidence in non-Jewish courts; two, the fact that Jewish trials conducted before Gentile judges were regarded as undermining the authority of Jewish law and the Rabbinic courts. Moreover, a Jew who accused another Jew in a Gentile court was considered to be an informer who had committed the major sin of denunciation.[6]

During the twelfth century, there was a further affirmation of the ban against bringing Jewish cases to Gentile courts by both Rabbi Isaac Alfasi (Rif, 1013–1103)[7] and Rabbi Solomon Yitzhaki (Rashi, 1040–1105).[8] At an even later period, the German rabbis of Speyer, Worms, and Mayence issued Responsa (legal opinions) to the effect that any judicial decision made by a Gentile which affected Jewish matters was null and void in the eyes of Jewish law.[9]

It is obvious, however, even from the time of the *Geonim,* that the prohibition was not, and perhaps could not be, enforced. As early as the ninth century, there were Geonic opinions that permission could be received from a Jewish court *(Beth Din)* for a case to be heard in a Gentile court, if the defendant refused to appear before the Jewish court.[10]

A similar opinion was voiced by Maimonides (Rambam, 1135–1204) at a later period. He wrote that a Jew who brings a case before a Gentile court, even when the court decision is the same as under Jewish law, has behaved "as if he had raised his hand against the Torah." Maimonides added, however, that if a Gentile defendant refused to be tried before a Jewish court, the Jewish plaintiff must ask permission of the latter to bring suit in a Gentile court, to insure that he (the plaintiff) "would rescue whatever was due to him through [a hearing in] the Gentile tribunal."[11]

Another example of what may be considered growing tolerance[12] was exhibited by the French rabbis who composed the Rabbinic Council of Troyes, held around 1160, under the leadership of Rabbi Jacob ben Meir (Rabbenu Tam, ca. 1100–1171), a leading Tosaphist, and the grandson of Rashi. Although the Council invoked the penalty of *Herem* (excommunication) against any Jew bringing a case before a Gentile court, the rabbis further decreed that the penalty not be invoked in cases where both parties agreed, in the presence of proper witnesses, to bring the case before the Gentile court.[13]

A further indication that the ban against the use of Gentile courts was not strictly adhered to, or adequately enforced, is its frequent renewal in later centuries.[14]

The courts themselves were of several different types, depending to a large degree on the amount of autonomy allowed by the local authorities. By the fourth and fifth centuries, Roman law had already recognized the Jewish Court of Arbitration, composed of three members. Decisions of this court were enforced by the Roman government.[15]

At a later time, courts were set up for special occasions, such as fairs. These fairs were of great importance to merchants, who would flock to them in order to conduct their business with other merchants and tradespeople. They also afforded an excellent opportunity for settling lawsuits, and for this reason *Batei Din shel ha-Yeridim* ("law courts of the fairs")[16] were frequently held in those East European communities which enjoyed a large measure of self-government.

Another example of special courts was the establishment of internal courts to handle the affairs of specific professional groups. Thus, we hear of the special courts established in various countries for tradespeople, laborers, and communal societies.

In certain countries which did not permit Jewish autonomous adjudication, there were special government-appointed judges for the Jews,[17] who were not necessarily always Jewish.[18] In addition, there were occasions when non-Jews sat as members of a *Beth Din,* and other instances when Jews were not allowed their own courts at all and were forced to use the official government courts. It is interesting, however, to note that there are examples of Gentiles bringing suit among themselves before a *Beth Din,* because such trials were shorter and less costly.[19]

In addition to the different types of Jewish courts allowed to function by the various governments, there was unanimity regarding the number, selection, and qualifications of the judges. Before the destruction of the Temple, there were three different kinds of Jewish courts: the Great Sanhedrin of seventy-one members; the Minor Sanhedrin of twenty-three members; and the local courts with three members. The judges were all obliged to be experts in *Halakhah* (Jewish law) and to have received their ordination *(Semikhah)*. After the destruction, outstanding scholars were nominated to serve as judges by either the *Nasi* (president), the *Resh Galuta* (exilarch), or the Geonic High Court,[20] all of these scholars being recognized and elected leaders of the community.

Semikhah was not permitted by the governments of some countries, nor was it always possible to find three experts in Jewish law qualified to act as judges. Therefore, it was ruled that civil suits could be tried before a court of *Hedyotot* (laymen). Such courts are mentioned in the Palestinian Talmud [21] and in Roman law.

During later periods, judges were no longer nominated, but were elected by the *Kahal* (general community), either directly or through representatives. Even then, the selection was "by authority handed down from the Sages in Eretz Yisrael." In those lands which had Councils or Synods of Rabbis,[22] such as Spain and Poland, the judges were chosen not by the community as a whole, but by a special election committee. The members of these committees, as well as the community leaders themselves, were often called *Berurim*, "the elected."

In many communities which did not have a permanent or official *Beth Din*, the communal rabbi would personally deal with disputes arising between members of his *Kehillah*. He would sometimes enlist two additional rabbis or laymen to serve with him as a court, but if this was not possible he would hear the case alone. Although the rabbi almost always held the title of *Av Beth Din* or *Rosh Beth Din* (head of the court), there were communities which specifically exempted their rabbis from being members of a court.[23] Generally, however, especially in those countries during the last 150–200 years where Jews were not allowed their own courts, the local rabbi would decide how and before what kind of tribunal a case should be heard.

Even though, according to *Halakhah*, judges were not to receive remuneration (indeed, their verdicts were declared void if they did accept money),[24] payment was allowed them as compensation for time spent in the court. During the Geonic period, these payments were taken out of community funds. At a later period, in Germany and Poland, the disputants generally paid a voluntary sum, called *Demei Kenas* (penalty fee).[25]

There was also no unanimity as to whether or not the litigants were permitted to appoint representatives to appear on their behalf.[26] In accordance with *Mishnah Avot* (I,8), "act not the counsel's part," some scholars prohibited the use of an agent *(Shali'ah)*. Often, however, it was necessary to permit such representation,[27] as in the case of women who did not wish to appear, or were advised not to appear, before an all-male court. Also, a plaintiff suing for payment of a debt was often allowed to appoint a representative by means of *Kabbalat Kinyan* (transfer of ownership).

Generally, Jewish authorities prohibited the use of representatives. There was concern that litigants appointing agents might feel themselves exempt from having to appear personally, thereby invalidating the court proceedings. In addition, it was often necessary that one of the disputants take an oath, which could not be done by a representative.

Another area of dispute was the question as to whether or not a verdict should be handed down in writing. Since no verdict was final, the parties always had the option to reappeal with new witnesses or evidence. Verdicts were generally returned verbally.[28] According to Ḥai Gaon (ca. 1000), the verdict must be written,[29] whereas such authorities as Maharam of Rothenburg[30] and Maimonides[31] decreed in favor of a written verdict in the case of a litigant requesting the same. Rabbi Ḥaim Or Zaru'a of Vienna (mid-13th cent.) went further in declaring that any God-fearing judge would commit his verdict to writing in order to substantiate his opinion at a later date. (It is worthy of note that, in the case of a judicial error, the judge had to pay the fine imposed on the defendant out of his own pocket.[32])

In addition, judges in medieval Spain handed down written, detailed verdicts[33] in important cases only, while seventeenth-century Moravian judges did so in every case.[34]

There would have been no justification, of course, for the existence of Jewish courts had they not been allowed to enforce the penalties upon the guilty party. These penalties took many forms, from capital punishment to the payment of fines, depending on the permission of the governmental authorities.[35]

It is interesting to note that, although both capital punishment and flogging had been formally suspended in Judea just prior to or immediately following the destruction of the Temple, particularly outside of Eretz Yisrael, both were still widely practiced in later times, "when it was necessary," to punish "informers."[36] For example, Spanish Jews were permitted by the authorities to inflict capital punishment almost until the period of the expulsion from Spain in 1492,[37] and certain East European communities retained this right even after that date. Flogging, too, was frequently inflicted, usually in the presence of the members of the community, as a means of discouraging others from committing similar offenses.

There were also many other forms of punishment, such as the levying of fines or the foreclosure of a debtor's property. In addition, there were provisions for several forms of corporal punishment, including even the severing of hands, nose, or tongue. These severe penalties were, however, rarely enforced. Certain communities maintained their own prisons, supervised by Jewish wardens,[38] although in earlier times sentence of imprisonment had been imposed only rarely by Jews.

In addition to imprisonment, the *Batei Din* decreed several other penalties which had been unknown or rarely used by Jews prior to that time. The most common—and in some ways the most harsh—was *Herem*, excommunication. A decree of *Herem* meant the virtual expulsion of the person upon whom it was inflicted, and sometimes his family also, from the religious and social life of the community. In the closed society of an earlier era, the consequences of *Herem* were so severe that many Rabbinic authorities permitted its use only in the most serious cases, while some governments actually prohibited resort to *Herem* by the Jewish community.[39] Another severe penalty was exile from one's city, or even from one's country of origin.

There were two other forms of sanction which utilized the closed nature of Jewish society. One, *Ikkuv Tefillah*, permitted an unsatisfied plaintiff to delay the reading of prayers or of the weekly Torah portion, as a means of forcing the defendant to appear in court. A similar form of coercion, utilized for the same purpose, was locking a defendant out of the synagogue.[40] This latter sanction is mentioned only in the Palestinian Talmud[41] and was unknown in Spain. It was, however, often utilized in medieval Germany and France, and later in various European countries, including seventeenth-century Germany.[42] This coercive measure appears to have been often misused, and its utilization was therefore restricted by many Rabbinic authorities, including Rabbenu Tam at the Council of Troyes (1150 C.E.).

Generally, the enforcement of various penalties was left to the *Beth Din* or to the community leaders. In certain cases, however, particularly where capital punishment was involved, the Gentile authorities reserved the right to confirm and execute the judgment.[43]

II
Jewish Courts in
Individual Countries

As previously mentioned, the degree of autonomous adjudication permitted to Jews differed from country to country, although there was a degree of uniformity in terms of general principles. For a broader understanding of the subject, it may be helpful to examine the situation of each country separately, beginning with those in which Jews settled earliest—i.e., post-Destruction Eretz Yisrael and Babylonia—and continuing with those areas to which Jews migrated in later periods, such as Europe, North Africa, India, South Africa, Australia, and the Western Hemisphere. It should be noted that several European countries (including Belgium, Ireland, Rumania, and Scandinavia) are not discussed below, either because Jewish tribunals were not established or for lack of available information.

Eretz Yisrael

There are five distinct periods in the history of Eretz Yisrael during the nineteen centuries since the destruction of Judea. The first, during which Eretz Yisrael was under Roman control, has been mentioned previously. The following three are the periods of Arab, Turkish, and British domination, and they will be discussed below. The fifth, the period of Jewish statehood, which began in 1948, is beyond the scope of this present survey, which is concerned with Jewish autonomous adjudication under foreign regimes.

There is virtually no information about the existence of Jewish courts in Eretz Yisrael between the end of Roman domination in 476 C.E. and the Arab conquest of Palestine in the seventh century. Documentary evidence from the Middle Ages testifies to the existence of either Jewish courts or individual judges during the rule of Islam. In fact, some of the earlier documents even mention a Great and a Minor Sanhedrin. The earliest document, of the Rabbinical family of Ben Meir (1015), was signed by "members of a court and witnesses."[1] Other documents of the same family mention a *Beth Midrash* and its superior, the *Av Beth Din*.[2] It can be inferred from a *Get* (bill of divorce), written in Ramleh in 1027,[3] that a court existed in that town.

Many eleventh-century letters and documents mention individuals who acted in the capacity of judges or of members of the Sanhedrin. Thus, "Rabbi Jeshuah, member of the Great Sanhedrin,"[4] signed a letter from the community of Gaza; and a certain "Joseph ha-Mumḥeh, judge of Hebron," and his father, "Saadiah, member of the Sanhedrin," are both mentioned in an "Elegy on the Destruction of Communities in Eretz Yisrael."[5] There is a document from the latter half of the century which relates the story of "Rabbi Eliyyahu Gaon who went to Haifa in the last year of his life, 4843/44 [1083/84], to renew the Gaonate and the *Semikhah* in the *Beth Va'ad*," the seat of the Sanhedrin and the High Court.[6] In addition, a well-known Palestinian personality of the same period, Rabbi Daniel ben Azariah, "who administered justice even to those in distant places,"[7] was called *Nasi* and *Gaon*,[8] and as *Gaon* included the appointment of judges among his other duties.

There are documents dating from the second Crusade, in the twelfth century, which were written by or referred to judges. In the following century, around 1260, the famous Tosaphist, Rabbi Yeḥiel ben Joseph of Paris, founded an academy of several hundred pupils in the town of Akko (Acre).[9] He corresponded with important scholars in Europe, including Rabbi Solomon ben Adret and Rabbi Meir of Rothenburg, and discussed with them the numerous legal decisions which he made as head of a *Beth Din*. At a later date, Rabbi David ben Abraham Maimuni, grandson of Maimonides, acted in the same capacity in Akko.

Rabbi Obadiah of Bertinoro, who arrived in Eretz Yisrael in 1488, seems to have been a judge or head of a court.[10] From this period onward, regular courts appear to have existed in Eretz Yisrael, mainly in Jerusalem.[11] These courts, connected with the Sephardi community until the arrival of the Ashkenazim at the end of the eighteenth century, occasionally issued *Takkanot* (communal regulations), many of which are still in force today.

Two major controversies in the city of Safed, during the first half of the sixteenth century, demonstrate the importance of the *Beth Din* in that period. In the year 1538, Rabbi Jacob Berab (ca. 1475–1546), head of a Safed *yeshivah*, reinstituted *Semikhah* and ordained four rabbis[12] in an attempt to unite all Jews under one Rabbinical authority and to reconstruct the Sanhedrin "so as to hasten the Redemption and the Messiah." The leading scholar in Jerusalem, Levi ibn Ḥabib (ca. 1480–1545), opposed Berab's actions, which were supported by the other rabbis in Safed. During the violent controversy which ensued, Berab fled to Damascus. This concluded the argument.

At about this same time, a second controversy arose in Safed concerning the authority of the different communities which had settled there following the expulsion from Spain.[13] The two principal opponents, Rabbi Joseph Caro (author of the *Shulḥan Arukh*) and Rabbi Moses di Trani (Mabit, 1505–1585), disagreed, among other issues, over the composition of the *Beth Din* and the nomination of its judges.

Under the rule of the Turks, commencing in the sixteenth century, Jews together with all other Turkish subjects were allowed juridical autonomy under the doctrine of "personal status," a doctrine which disappeared in Europe after the Middle Ages.[14] According to Muslim law, the individual religious and national communities under Turkish dominion were allowed to follow their own laws in regard to matters of personal status—marriage, divorce, guardianship, and succession. Accordingly, in countries of the Ottoman Empire, including Palestine, Muslims were under the jurisdiction of the *Sharia* (the Muslim religious courts) and Koranic law, Christians were subject to the laws and courts of their own churches, and Jews were under the jurisdiction of *Halakhah* and the Rabbinical courts. All persons who were not Turkish subjects, such as Europeans residing in the Ottoman Empire, were subject to the jurisdiction of their national laws and consular judges.

According to the doctrine of personal status, full juridical authority was vested in the ecclesiastical head of the community. In the case of the Jewish community, this meant that the *Ḥakham Bashi* (Chief Rabbi) was authorized by Turkish law to delegate his powers to local Rabbinical courts. This custom was maintained by the British military government when General Allenby and his troops occupied Palestine at the end of World War I.

In addition to the Rabbinical courts which operated during the period of Ottoman rule, courts of arbitration called *Batei Mishpat ha-Shalom ha-Ivri* were established by Jews trying to avoid litigation in Gentile courts.[15] There were practical reasons for the establishment of these courts, including the inadequacy and corruption of the Turkish court system and awareness of the role which such courts could play in the development of a national character for the still unformed Jewish commonwealth.

The first of the *Batei Mishpat ha-Shalom ha-Ivri* was established in 1909 by several leading personalities of the Jewish community in Palestine, including Meir Dizengoff, Mordecai ben Hillel Hacohen, Bezalel Jaffe, Dr. Arthur Ruppin, and Dr. Ya'akov Thon, and on the initiative of the Palestine Office of the Zionist Organization.[16] This court, which traveled from settlement to settlement as the need arose, "paid honor to faith and religion, but it regarded Jewish law as something unique, available equally to all, be they religious or not."[17]

Even though the tribunal's decisions were not based on *Halakhah,* but rather on general principles of justice and equity, and despite the fact that its three to five members were of the laity, many of its decisions were approved by Rabbi Avraham Yitzhak ha-Kohen Kook, who was at that time Chief Rabbi of Jaffa and the settlements. In fact, Rabbi Kook himself presided at a session of the court when a particularly complex case arose. The tribunal continued to function until the first years of World War I, when, like so many other Jewish institutions in Palestine, it was dissolved.

During the era of the British Mandate, the power of both the Rabbinical courts and the reestablished *Batei Mishpat ha-Shalom ha-Ivri* was strengthened. It was a principle of the British governors not to interfere with established institutions of an occupied or conquered land. Thus, the doctrine of "personal status" was maintained for former Ottoman subjects.[18] In 1923, the Mandatory officials approved the jurisdiction of the respective religious courts.

Three important events which shaped the course of Jewish self-adjudication during the period of the Mandate took place in the 1920s. These were the convening of a special Rabbinical Assembly, the reestablishment of the *Batei Mishpat ha-Shalom ha-Ivri,* and the establishment of internal courts of arbitration within various groups and organizations, especially those affiliated with the Histadrut, the General Federation of Labor.

In February 1921, a special committee appointed by Sir Herbert Samuel, first High Commissioner for Palestine, convened a Rabbinical Assembly in Jerusalem composed of sixty-eight rabbis and thirty-four laymen.[19] This Assembly established a Rabbinical Council comprising two Chief Rabbis (Ashkenazi and Sephardi) elected by the Assembly and a number of other rabbis from both communities. The Council itself was divided into two sections: local Courts of the First Instance composed of three members; and a Court of Appeals composed of seven members, including one of the Chief Rabbis who would act as presiding judge. Because of the ambiguity of *Halakhah* in respect of courts of appeal, the Chief Rabbinate issued a *Takkanah* authorizing its establishment.[20]

Shortly after its foundation, the Rabbinical Court was formally recognized by the Mandatory government as the highest religious authority of the Jewish community and as a Court of Appeals from local Rabbinical courts. Moreover, any *Beth Din* sanctioned by the Rabbinical Council would be recognized as the sole authority in matters of Jewish law, and the decisions of both the *Batei Din* and the Court of Appeals of the Rabbinical Council would be implemented by civil courts.

In 1922, the Palestine Order in Council defined the powers of the Rabbinical courts:[21]

. . . inclusive jurisdiction in matters of personal status shall be exercised . . . by the Courts of the religious communities . . .
(Article 51)

The Rabbinical Courts . . . shall have (I) exclusive jurisdiction in matters of marriage and divorce, alimony and confirmation of wills of members of their community, other than foreigners . . . ; (II) jurisdiction in any other matter of personal status of such person, where all the parties to the action consent to their jurisdiction over any case as to the constitution or internal administration of a Wakf or religious endowment constituted before the Rabbinical Court according to Jewish law.
(Article 53)

In addition, the Order in Council defined the powers of the civil courts in Palestine and gave them jurisdiction over all matters of personal status not covered by the religious courts of the communities, "in conformation with the Ottoman law in force . . . and in conformity with the substance of the common law and the doctrines of equity in force in England . . ."

Despite practical difficulties, such as the problems of applying *Halakhah* to modern developments and the lack of Halakhic knowledge among many of the lawyers appearing for the litigants, the Rabbinical courts functioned continuously during the years of the Mandate, particularly as courts of arbitration in civil cases. In 1943, Chief Rabbi Isaac Halevi Herzog published procedural regulations for the Rabbinical courts, covering everything from the initiation of proceedings to the payment of court fees and from the rules of evidence to the modes of appeal. The publication of these regulations greatly improved the functioning of the Rabbinical courts.[22]

In the winter of 1918, a society called *Ha-Mishpat ha-Ivri* was established in Moscow with the intention of founding an institution in

Jerusalem to conduct research on important and practical problems of Jewish law, in preparation for the establishment of a Faculty of Law at the envisaged Hebrew University. The founders, including such experts in Jewish law as S. Eisenstadt and A. Gulak, who later left their mark in Israel, also intended to publish a quarterly, but only one issue ever appeared. [23]

During the same year, Va'ad ha-Tzirim, the Organization Conference of Jewish Settlement Institutions, adopted a resolution calling upon all Jewish citizens of Palestine to bring their litigations only before Batei Mishpat ha-Shalom ha-Ivri. [24] These reestablished courts of arbitration, which functioned along with the Mandatory courts and the Rabbinical courts (just as earlier they had functioned in conjunction with the Ottoman and Rabbinical courts), were set up in the major cities of Jerusalem, Tel Aviv, and Haifa, as well as in the outlying districts, with a Supreme Court located in Tel Aviv. The regulations, which were amended in 1922, 1928, [25] and 1936, [26] allowed for judges and lawyers, as well as laymen, to serve as members. The work of these arbitration courts, which were very active during the years 1920–1925, was recognized by the (Mandatory) Arbitration Ordinance of 1926, [27] which allowed for disputes to be brought before tribunals as well as before individual arbitrators.

In the years following 1925, the leaders of the Batei Mishpat ha-Shalom ha-Ivri tried to extend the powers of their courts to include public and official cases as well as private litigations, [28] but since their legal authority was in the framework of boards of arbitration and, as such, having no real power of compulsion, their efforts failed and their activities declined. Despite the opposition of the Rabbinical courts, which objected to decisions not based solely on Halakhah, and despite the lack of a fixed system of Jewish or general law, [29] the Batei Mishpat ha-Shalom ha-Ivri continued to function until 1949, when they were replaced by the civil courts of the new State of Israel.

In addition to the Rabbinical courts and the Batei Mishpat ha-Shalom ha-Ivri, there were also internal courts of arbitration, called Mishpat Haverim (Courts of Colleagues), set up by various communities and organizations. Shortly after the establishment of the Histadrut, the General Federation of Labor, in the 1920s, it was decided that all Histadrut members must bring their internal litigations before the Mishpat Haverim of the Histadrut. In addition to the Courts of the First Instance, composed of one to three members, there was also a High Court in most of the local Histadrut branches, composed of three members. [30] The Secretariat of the Mishpat Haverim of the Histadrut published rules of procedure, the results of important cases dealt with in the High Court, and an information bulletin. Special courts for the various

Histadrut affiliates were set up, such as the courts of the Cooperative Villages Movement, established in 1926.[31] Similar courts also existed in other workers' organizations and in some of the Jewish ethnic groups, such as the Yemenite community.

Babylonia (Iraq)

From the time of the Babylonian Exile, brought about by Nebuchadnezzar's conquest of Judea in 586 B.C.E., organized Jewish communities have existed in Bavel, or Babylonia (modern Iraq and parts of Syria). There is no historical record of Jewish law courts during the Babylonian Exile, although some statements in the Talmud indicate that even a Sanhedrin existed there at that time.[1] The Talmud also states that Ezra, on resettling the Jews in Judea by permission of Cyrus II, after the Persian capture of Babylonia in 539 B.C.E., set up law courts in Judea which met every Monday and Thursday.[2] Whether these courts were indigenous to Judea, or based on a Jewish Babylonian model, is unknown.

It is certain, however, that Jews living in Babylonia under Parthian rule after 240 B.C.E. did have the right to their own law courts. This period was one in which Babylonian Jewry flourished. Indeed, some towns—such as Nehardea, Nisibis, and Maḥoza—seem to have had predominantly Jewish populations.[3] In addition, some of the most famous centers of Jewish learning where the Babylonian Talmud was compiled by the *Amoraim* during the years 200–500 C.E., were established during this period. The head of Babylonian Jewry, entitled *Resh Galuta* (Exilarch), acted as head of the *Batei Din* and appointed the other judges for the community.[4] Many *Amoraim* of the later period also served as heads of various *Batei Din*, as well as of their respective academies.

The status of the Babylonian Jewish community depended upon the current rulers. During the third century C.E., the conquering Sassanids made Babylonia part of their new Persian Empire; their reintroduction of the ancient Persian religion, Zoroastrianism, led to a deterioration in the position of Babylonian Jewry. This regime continued from the fifth to the seventh century, when the area was conquered by the Arabs and subsequently renamed Iraq. In general, the Jews fared well under Arab rule. There were exceptions, such as in 850, when one Caliph issued a decree denigrating Jews and other non-Muslims. The office of Exilarch was maintained until it was abolished by the fanatical Shiite dynasty, which ruled Persia during the years 945–1055.

From the time of the Arab conquest until the mid-eleventh century, the *Geonim*,[5] leaders of the two major academies then located in Sura and Pumbeditha, also enjoyed the privilege of nominating judges and acting as judges themselves or as heads of the *Batei Din*.[6] The *Geonim* were opposed to decisions being made by a single judge,[7] and therefore every judge, after being nominated, had the right to choose two other scholars to assist him as *Dayyanim*.

Following the dissolution of the academies in the eleventh century, smaller academies continued to function, especially in Baghdad.[8] The heads of these academies, sometimes nominated by the Caliphs, used the title *Gaon*, but did not enjoy official recognition by the Jewish community. One of the most famous Baghdad *Geonim* was Rabbi Samuel ben Ali Halevi (d. 1194), who, in addition to heading an academy, authorized rabbis in the various cities to act as *Dayyanim*.[9] The well-known Jewish traveler of the thirteenth century, Benjamin of Tudela, recounts in his book that *Dayyanim* also functioned in the communities of Mosul and Basra, two major centers of Jewish life in Iraq.

The position of the Jews in Iraq continued to fluctuate according to the whims of the current rulers. Thus, conditions improved after the Mongol conquest in the second half of the thirteenth century, but soon deteriorated again after the Mongols converted to Islam and introduced discriminatory laws against the Jews. The status of the Jews did not improve until the Turkish conquest in 1534. In fact, records from another period of Persian rule (1508–1534) indicate that many *Dayyanim*, including Rabbi David Thabat (or Thabit), were forced to give up their posts as *Dayyanim* and *Ḥakhamim*.[10]

The Turkish rulers allowed the *Nasi,* the head of the prominent *Kehillot* (communities), to act as Chief Rabbi, with the power to try members of his community, to impose fines and punishments, and to appoint and dismiss *Dayyanim*. In the middle of the eighteenth century, a *Nasi*, Rabbi Tzedakah Ḥutzin, dismissed a *Dayyan* who tried cases as a single judge. In his place Rabbi Ḥutzin nominated a *Beth Din* of three *Dayyanim*.[11]

Batei Din existed in the larger Iraqi cities, such as Baghdad, Basra, and Mosul, well into the twentieth century. These *Kehillot* were officially recognized in 1931 by the "Law of the Jewish Community," which allowed for the appointment of a Chief Rabbi only in those cities which had a *Beth Din*. As in other Muslim countries (including Palestine under Turkish rule, mentioned earlier), the *Batei Din* were empowered to handle cases of personal status.[12]

The existence of officially recognized *Batei Din* during most of the periods of Jewish residence in Iraq negated the necessity for lay courts of arbitration. Such courts are not mentioned in the Babylonian Talmud.[13] The first known court of this type was not set up in Iraq until 1896.[14] The function of this court, styled *Hevrat Ahavat Shalom* (Society of the Love of Peace), was to arbitrate between litigants in civil cases and, thereby, assist the *Beth Din*. Because of the permanence of the *Batei Din*, Jewish litigants rarely had to turn to Gentile courts. In fact, only when a defendant did not accept its verdict did the *Beth Din* itself then turn the case over to the civil courts.[15]

Italy

The first evidence of Jewish settlement in Italy, and indeed in Europe, is of a Jewish community in Rome in 139 B.C.E.[1] There appear to have been additional communities at a somewhat later period in the neighborhood of Rome, as well as in Sardinia, Sicily, Milan, Genoa, Bologna, and Ravenna. Following the Roman conquest of Judea and the destruction of the Second Temple, Jewish captives were brought to Italy and more communities were established.

As in many other lands, the fate of the Italian Jews varied according to the predilections of the current rulers. The status of the Jews declined in 313, when the Emperor Constantine the Great proclaimed Christianity the official state religion, but the situation improved under the Ostrogoths and the Lombards. Pope Gregory I (590–604) granted the Jews certain protection and rights, but their status again deteriorated in the southern parts of the country, under the Byzantines. Soon Jews in all regions of Italy suffered this fate, as the influence of the Roman Church and the clergy grew. Nevertheless, new communities continued to be founded, particularly in the northern towns of Turin, Modena, and Verona.

During the thirteenth century, Jews began to play an important role in business and finance. Many Jews who had been expelled from Spain (1492) and Portugal (1497) settled in Italy. Although their prominent role in business and finance continued during the sixteenth century, they were expelled from some towns for brief intervals, for example from Venice in 1527 and from Naples in 1541. During the mid-sixteenth-century Counter-Reformation period, and until the late nineteenth century, most Italian Jews were forced to live in ghettos. (The word "ghetto" derives from Italian; the first ghetto was established in Venice in 1516.) Despite these restrictions, the Jewish arts flourished, and on the whole, the sixteenth century was a Golden Age for Italian Jewry.

At the end of the eighteenth century, Italian Jews were emancipated, and they were granted the same rights as the rest of the population during the French Revolution. Later, some of these rights were rescinded, but in the middle of the nineteenth century there was a general improvement in status, accompanied by a far-reaching and expanding trend toward assimilation.

It is important to note that the name "Italy" was not applied to that country until its unification in the late nineteenth century. Until that time, various sections of the country were governed by different rulers. Hence, the condition of the Jewish population differed from province to province, and often from town to town. When reviewing Jewish autonomous adjudication in Italy, therefore, every major city must be discussed separately.

Rome and the Roman Empire

Jews came under Roman jurisdiction in many parts of Rome's far-flung empire. One of the first references to Jews under Roman rule outside of Eretz Yisrael is a report by Josephus that Julius Caesar (100–44 B.C.E.) had extended many civil rights to the Jews of Alexandria, Egypt, including the right to be judged in civil cases by their own courts and according to their own laws.[2] Caesar extended similar rights to the Jews of Cyrene (part of modern Libya),[3] and these rights were later reaffirmed by the Emperor Claudius (41–54 C.E.).[4] Even Vespasian and Titus, the conquerors of Judea, did not rescind the civil rights of the Jews of Antiochia (Syria), despite a plea to the contrary from the non-Jews of that country.[5]

During this early period, the office of judge was held by the *Parnas*, or leader, of the *Kehillah*.[6] The first Talmudic reference to a *Beth Din* in Europe tells how Rabbi Matyah ben Ḥarash (or Ḥeresh), an important *Tanna*, left Eretz Yisrael for Rome at the time of the Bar-Kokhba Revolt in 132–133 C.E. In Rome, he established the first Rabbinical academy of Europe, and became leader of that *Kehillah* and consequently head of a noted *Beth Din*.[7]

The Roman law which allowed Jews jurisdiction over civil cases in their own courts, and according to their own laws, had been written into the Codices of Theodosius and Justinian and was renewed by Theodoric, King of the Ostrogoths (489–526), who practiced similar tolerance toward all the peoples under his rule.[8]

From the thirteenth century, when Jewish courts of arbitration were set up, until the seventeenth century, when *Yeshivot* (academies) were established in Padua and Venice, laymen often acted as judges.

Since few Italian rabbis were learned enough to act as judges, Jews often turned to Gentile courts, which they respected more than their own lay courts of arbitration. It was not until the founding of the *Yeshivot* that scholars were once again found to head the Rabbinical courts.[9]

Beginning in the fourteenth century, a *Judex Judaeorum* ("Judge for the Jews") was appointed.[10] As distinct from the situation in other localities, the Roman "Judge for the Jews" was himself always a Jew. In 1342, a committee of ten *Berurim* was elected to manage the affairs of the Roman *Kehillah*, to appoint judges, and to serve as judges themselves.[11] The situation altered in 1402, when the Jews, who were full-fledged citizens of Rome, were ordered to bring their cases only before the Curia, the Papal legal authorities, rather than before their own courts.[12]

In 1536, the bankers of the Sicilian Jewish community in Rome, who were important financiers during the Renaissance, decided to bring all their own lawsuits concerning business affairs before their own internal courts of arbitration,[13] with Jewish judges volunteering to act as arbitrators.[14]

The Papal authorities agreed to allow the financial disputes of the Jews to be judged by Jewish courts, but decreed that all other cases, including appeals, had to come before the Vicariate, the Papal office in charge of legal jurisdiction in Rome. This decision, which was renewed by Pope Clement XIII (1758–1769) and again in the early nineteenth century,[15] in effect ended organized Jewish autonomous adjudication in Rome.

Ferrara

Even though the Jewish community of Ferrara, established in the late thirteenth century, was one of the most important centers of Italian Jewry during the Renaissance, little is known about its courts. There is evidence that in 1402 the Jews of Ferrara, like their coreligionists in Rome, were allowed to present their cases to the Curia only.[16] A Rabbinical Synod, in 1554, renewed the ban on Gentile courts, yet was cognizant of the fact that the Jews utilized them at this time.[17] The Synod further decreed that a plaintiff who was dissatisfied with the verdict of a Gentile court might not bring the same case before a Jewish court.[18]

At a later period, the Jews of Ferrara again enjoyed a measure of autonomous adjudication, but after 1708 this jurisdiction was restricted to religious matters only.[19]

Florence (Firenze)

An organized Jewish community was not established in Florence until the middle of the fifteenth century, when a group of Jews was invited to establish loan-banks for the poor. There is, however, a report dated 1324 regarding a Jewish doctor living in Florence who was allowed to bring a civil case before a general law court, "like all other people in the city."[20] Despite occasional outbreaks of violence, and even expulsion (as in the years 1495 and 1527), the Jews of the city flourished, particularly under the Medicis, who maintained extensive connections with Jewish bankers and financiers.

During the fifteenth century, the "Eight Guardians" who managed *Kehillah* affairs supervised Jewish jurisdiction and directed cases to the relevant courts. By mutual consent of the litigants, Jews could appear before courts of arbitration, composed of two or three Jews, with one of the "Guardians" acting as judge. Cases of a religious nature could, by mutual agreement, be referred to a Rabbinical court. Owing to the occasional lack of rabbis in Florence, these cases were sometimes tried in another city. It is noteworthy that cases tried by the official Gentile courts were known to be decided, at times, according to *Halakhah*.[21]

The situation of the Jews in Florence deteriorated during the next century with the establishment of the ghetto, in 1571, by Grand Duke Cosimo I of the House of Medici. One year earlier, all supervision of Jewish tribunals, including Rabbinical courts, was taken over by the authorities.[22]

The Inquisition, which had been active in Italy, although in a less organized manner than in Spain and Portugal, was abolished in Tuscany and its capital, Florence, in 1787. Eager to show their appreciation, the Jews asked and were allowed to submit all their cases to the official courts.[23]

Leghorn (Livorno) and Modena

The Jewish communities of Leghorn and Modena became two of the most important centers of Jewry in Italy and, indeed, in all of Western Europe. Jews settled in Modena in the late fourteenth century and established loan-banks there, as well as in Leghorn, where they were invited to settle by the Grand Dukes of Tuscany in the late sixteenth century. No ghettos were set up in Leghorn, but after 1638 they did exist in Modena. During the seventeenth and eighteenth centuries, both communities flourished, enjoying complete internal autonomy in both civil and criminal areas, with the secular authorities responsible for enforcement of the Jewish court rulings. Appeals could be made only to the Grand Dukes.[24]

Mantua

Although there are no records of an organized Jewish community in Mantua until the end of the fourteenth century,[25] Rabbi Isaac ben

Moses of Vienna (Or Zaru'a, ca. 1180–1260) mentioned a *Beth Din* there,[26] a century earlier, as being the only institution of its kind in Italy at the time.[27]

The Mantua community flourished during the Renaissance, but the ghetto system was enforced at the beginning of the seventeenth century. The Germans who occupied the city in 1630 expelled the Jews, allowing them to return in 1632, after which this *Kehillah* again became one of the most important and thriving Jewish communities in northern Italy.

Generally, the Mantua *Kehillah* enjoyed a communal and legal autonomy unparalleled in the other Italian communities. Its *Batei Din*,[28] with few exceptions, were recognized by the authorities. They functioned as courts of arbitration in addition to the official, non-Jewish courts, but only in cases where both litigants were Jews. Thus, a document from 1562 relates how three members of the community were nominated to act as arbitrators in a litigation between certain moneylenders and the *Kehillah*.[29] If they could not reach a decision, the case would then be turned over to the *Va'ad ha-Klali*, a General Council comprising the leadership of the Jewish community.

Cases between Jews and Gentiles were handled by the official courts, and occasionally by a special court, the *Commissario degli Ebrei*. The Gentile courts executed the sentences passed by the *Batei Din*. In 1542 and again in 1590, the clerical and secular authorities both granted permission to the Jewish courts to impose a ban on Jews who did not follow *Halakhah*.

Owing to the large number of inheritance cases that resulted from the deaths of many Mantua Jews during a plague in 1577, permission was granted for the *Kehillah* to elect a Rabbinical committee to function as *Dayyanim*. The court's jurisdiction was extended at the end of that year to cover personal-status issues, in addition to financial affairs, and in 1578 this authority was extended for one year. In 1590, the Duke of Mantua officially recognized the jurisdiction of the Jewish court of arbitration, whose sentences would be executed by a special Gentile commissary and "Judge of the Jews," nominated by the Duke.

During the seventeenth century, the Jews retained the right to nominate their own arbitrators, sometimes chosen from a prepared list of rabbis. In 1632, the Jews renewed the ban on Gentile courts and, in 1647, the Duke recognized the ban for civil cases, decreeing that only appeals could be tried in the official courts. This privilege was annulled in 1659 but was renewed in 1661, when the Jewish court's authority was extended to include all civil cases up to a certain monetary value. The *Kehillah* was responsible for the composition and procedures of the court during this period.

In 1677, Rabbi Moses Zacuto (ca. 1625–1697), the Kabbalist and poet who was then a rabbi in Mantua, published *Shudei de-Dayyenei*,[30] *Takkanot* for *Batei Din shel Borerut*. This work, published by consent of the delegates from other Italian communities, included decisions of *Dayyanim*, regulations for the nomination of arbitrators, rules of procedure, and the functions of the judges. It provided for legal representation of both plaintiff and defendant, and for the waiving of appeal privileges. If the right to appeal had not been waived by means of a signed and sworn deed of arbitration *(compromissus)*, then the appeal could be made within eight days to the High Court of *Ba'alei Yeshivah*, Heads of the Academy.

The Hapsburg emperors ruling Mantua during the early eighteenth century did not change the autonomous status of the Jewish courts. The Jews themselves, however, were dissatisfied with the dilatory processes of their own courts, and although the *Kehillah* renewed the *Takkanot* of Rabbi Moses Zacuto, they increasingly submitted cases to the Gentile courts. Jewish-Gentile suits were handled by a special commissary, a senator nominated by the Hapsburgs, and the Senate, the governing body of the city, sat as a court of appeal. The Empress Maria Theresa (1740–1780) renewed Jewish court autonomy, but her son, Joseph II (1765–1790), disbanded all separate religious courts in 1782. He did, however, make provision for rabbis to appear as experts before the public courts to insure that cases between Jews would be handled according to *Halakhah*. In 1791, the situation again changed when Leopold II (1790–1792) allowed the *Kehillah* a certain measure of juridical autonomy, with the provision that the nomination of the arbitrators be renewed annually.

The *Kehillah* retained its juridical autonomy during the period of Napoleonic occupation, as well as during the Austrian reoccupation in 1799–1801. The Jewish courts were finally abolished in 1804, principally by the Jews themselves, who were no longer interested in maintaining their own tribunals.

Padua

The Padua Jewish community was established in the fourteenth century, but the earliest and scant information on record concerning its court system is dated 1601. This states that before Jews were confined to the ghetto of Padua, a court of arbitration, composed of two judges, was established to fix rents for dwellings being evacuated by the Jews. The case was to be turned over to the secular authorities if the arbitrators could not come to a decision.[31]

Sicily and Southern Italy

According to some sources, Jews lived in Sicily as early as Roman times. The first documentary source is the eleventh-century chronicle of Ahimaaz ben Paltiel (ca. 1017–1060),[32] who wrote that one of his ancestors in the Adriatic coast town of Oria had established a *Beth Din* which was authorized even to impose capital punishment.[33] Since much of Ahimaaz's family chronicle is interwoven with legend, the authenticity of his account is doubtful.[34] It is probable, nevertheless, that autonomous Jewish law courts did exist in southern Italy (Oria and Bari) as early as the tenth century, and most definitely in the eleventh and twelfth centuries.[35] In the thirteenth century, Jewish courts came under the jurisdiction of the king, who recognized Jewish law as authoritative in cases among Jews. Matters of personal status were adjudged by the ecclesiastical courts of the different religious communities, including those of the Jews.[36]

When King Martin of Aragon (1395–1410) united Sicily and Aragon around 1400, the Jews were granted a single judge to supervise all lawsuits of the Sicilian Jews. This judge, entitled *Judex Universalis* or *Dienchele* (a corruption of *Dayyan Klali*),[37] also functioned as an administrator and approved regulations enacted by the *Kehillah*. According to one source, this post was occupied by a succession of five Jewish doctors who functioned close to the king.[38] The post was abolished in 1447, ending Jewish juridical autonomy in Sicily.

Venice

The first permanent settlement of Jews in Venice dates from the eleventh century. Though segregated in the ghetto after 1516, the Jews were an important factor in Venetian finance and trade. The *Parnasim* of the Venice community acted as judges in the Jewish courts,[39] and a special court for tradesmen, mentioned in Rabbinical literature of the sixteenth century, was established in the ghetto.[40]

Jewish juridical autonomy was restricted in the late seventeenth century, when the Republic of Venice recognized Jewish jurisdiction only in cases involving the religious or internal affairs of the *Kehillah*, although courts of arbitration were allowed for civil cases. At this time, the heads of the *Yeshivah* served as *Dayyanim*, but subsequently the courts of arbitration were composed mainly of laymen.[41] After the French Revolution, the fully emancipated Jewish community dwindled, and by the late nineteenth century, it had become assimilated.

The Iberian Peninsula

As in Italy, the Status of the Jews in the Iberian Peninsula, particularly in Christian Spain, varied under the rulers of different localities.[1] Following a discussion of the general conditions under which Jews lived in Spain, the areas of Castile, Aragon, Majorca, and Portugal will be treated separately.

Spain

The first group of Jews to settle in Spain probably arrived during the era of the Roman Empire. The community grew rapidly, and at the beginning of the fifth century, under Visigothic rule, Jews were allowed their own courts of arbitration as prescribed by the *Codex Theodosianus*.[2] The Visigoths sometimes forced Jews to convert to Christianity, and while many Jews were baptized, albeit nominally in most cases, many others chose to leave Spain.[3]

When the Muslims conquered Spain in 711, they found very few openly professing Jews. Many of the secret Jews *(Anusim)* welcomed them and, as a reward for their military aid, they were permitted to establish their own garrisons in several towns, including Córdoba, Granada, Toledo, and Seville. The Jews were also treated well by the Omayyads, who in 755 established the Moorish Empire in a large area of Spain. Jewish scholarship and culture flourished, and many Jews held important positions in the spheres of medicine, trade, and the crafts. Thus, Ḥasdai ibn Shaprut (ca. 915–970), Chief Rabbi and head of a Córdoba *yeshivah*, also served as court physician and diplomat.

Some cities, such as Lucena and Granada, had largely Jewish populations during this period. Spanish Jews were dependent on the Babylonian *Geonim* in matters of self-adjudication, and often asked their opinions on matters of *Halakhah* and concerning internal disputes.

The rule of the Omayyads began to decline in 1013, but the Arabs who replaced them in Spain, such as the Berbers from North Africa, had a favorable attitude toward the Jews and often assigned them to prominent posts. Samuel ha-Nagid served as vizier to the king of Granada in the early eleventh century; Rabbi Isaac Alfasi (Rif, 1013–1103), set up a *yeshivah* in Lucena after being forced to leave his home in Fez; and Maimonides (Rambam, 1135–1204) lived in Córdoba for a short time. Seville, Saragossa, Toledo, and Huesca also became important centers of Spanish Jewry.

The position of the Spanish Jews deteriorated after the establishment of the Almohad dynasty in 1146. A fanatical Berber dynasty from Morocco, the Almohads forced the Jews to convert to Islam, although many of these conversions were only formal. Nevertheless, many important Jewish communities in Andalusia, the southwestern part of Spain, ceased to exist.

Under Muslim rule, the *Kehillot* established their own *Batei Din*, composed of one or three *Dayyanim*, depending on the size of the community. Some of the smaller communities used the *Batei Din* in the larger towns.[4] Many famous Rabbinical scholars lived in Spain during this period. The *Dayyanim* were mostly well-versed in *Halakhah*. Styled *Berurim* ("chosen ones"), the *Dayyanim* were selected by the *Kahal*,[5] and in some communities, such as late eleventh-century Denia, on the Gulf of Valencia, they were appointed as professional judges.[6]

As in other Muslim countries, the Jews of Spain had judicial autonomy, and their *Batei Din* were permitted to deal with civil and certain criminal cases, as well as with matters of personal status. The verdicts, which were handed down according to *Halakhah*, sometimes had to be signed by the *Parnasim*, the heads of the *Kehillot*. Lawsuits between Jews and Muslims were brought before Muslim courts, since the Muslims often did not recognize Jewish law. Nevertheless, there are instances of Muslims being tried before Jewish courts[7] and of Jews turning to Muslim courts, particularly in cases regarding transfer of property. The Spanish rabbis often renewed the ban on Gentile courts.[8]

Beginning in the eleventh century, parts of Spain were reconquered by the Christians, who ordered the Muslims to leave the towns, while simultaneously granting many privileges to the Jews, whose cooperation they sought. The focus of Jewish settlement moved away from the Muslim areas in the south to the Christian states, where, joined by kinfolk from oriental countries and southern France, the Jews settled in such towns as Toledo, Zamora, Valladolid, and Burgos in Castile; Tudela in Navarre; and Barcelona, Saragossa, and Huesca in Aragon. Under royal protection, many of the Jews gained important positions in commerce and industry. In some areas (for example, Barcelona), they became landowners. From the late eleventh century, under King Alfonso VI of Castile (1072–1109), almost until the Expulsion of 1492, important Jews became courtiers and, while remaining loyal to their own faith, exercised considerable authority over the general population.

The twelfth century was the "Golden Age" of Spanish Jewry. During this period, Jewish influence in various fields of trade, commerce, and Spanish culture was strongly felt. As the *Reconquista* proceeded, Jews employed in the Christian armies settled in cities evacuated by the Muslims, and organized Jewish communities were established there as independent units with royal privileges and charters. These charters defined the juridical relations between Jews and Christians, and between Jews and Muslims, but did not always imply the recognition of political or social equality of Jews with Christians. According to Spanish custom, these privileges were granted to all sections of the population as members of separate religious and national groups, but not as common citizens of one nation.[9]

The situation of Spanish Jewry worsened, however, in the early thirteenth century, mainly because of the influence of the Dominicans and other Catholic orders. The first blood libel occurred in 1250, and the famous dispute between Rabbi Moses ben Naḥman (Naḥmanides or Ramban, 1194–1270) and the apostate Dominican priest, Pablo Christiani, took place in 1263 at Barcelona. Subsequently, the first Inquisition in Spain against converted Jews (1265–1268) was initiated by Pope Clement IV. Nevertheless, many Jews in both Castile and Aragon still held important economic and cultural positions, and the *Kehillot* (or *Aljamas*) flourished with the renewal of their privileges by the kings. Many famous scholars, whose influence extended not only to their own communities but to the Christian world and the royal courts as well, lived during this period. Two such were the "Rabbi of Spain," Rabbi Solomon ben Abraham Adret of Barcelona (Rashba, 1235–1310), and Rabbi Asher ben Jehiel of Toledo (Rosh, 1250–1327).

During the fourteenth century, some of the Jewish communities in Spain began to decline, especially in the wake of the Black Death (1348–1350), when Jews were accused of poisoning wells. Nevertheless, many Jews were still allowed to retain their authority over organized *Kehillot*, and certain rulers tried to counteract the Church-instigated Inquisition and persecutions.[10] In general, the situation continued to deteriorate, and in 1391 severe persecutions inspired by the clergy were experienced by the Jews in the cities of Madrid, Burgos, Córdoba, and Valencia. The Talmud was censored, and many Jewish communities ceased to exist as a result of forced conversions.

Although some Jewish communities were able to reorganize and many Jews kept their preferred positions at court, the general situation was exacerbated during the fifteenth century. In 1483, the Jews were expelled from Andalusia and the notorious Inquisitor-General, Tomás de Torquemada, instituted the Inquisition against the *Conversos*, or New Christians, in all Spanish provinces. Finally, on the last day of March, 1492, King Ferdinand II of Aragon and Queen Isabella of Castile, having united their two kingdoms by marriage, signed the edict of expulsion which drove all professing Jews from Spain.

Despite the changing conditions under which Jews lived in Christian Spain, there were certain general principles concerning their courts of law which obtained during the entire period. The Responsa literature, initiated in the thirteenth and fourteenth centuries, often dealt with *Batei Din,* notably the Responsa of Rabbi Solomon Adret of Barcelona, Rabbi Asher ben Jehiel of Toledo, and Rabbi Isaac ben Sheshet Perfet (Ribash, 1326–1408), the last of whom left Spain and settled in Algiers. According to these Responsa, the *Batei Din* had jurisdiction over criminal as well as civil cases, and were also authorized to impose capital punishment, particularly in the case of informers *(Malshinim).* The *Batei Din* generally were made up of three *Dayyanim* styled *Berurim,* as in the Moslem period, a title also given to those in the community who chose the *Dayyanim.*[11] There were, however, cases in which only two *Dayyanim* presided. During the earlier period, the communal rabbi was a member or the head of a *Beth Din.* Later on, cases were tried by the *Parnasim,* known in Spain as *Mukadamim,* independently of the Rabbinical courts. Sometimes, limitations were set on the jurisdiction of these two courts. Thus, the *Parnasim* dealt mainly with financial and tax cases, though more in accordance with state rules than with *Halakhah.* Although they were not usually Jewish scholars, the *Parnasim* often did take it upon themselves to deal with cases which should have been under Rabbinical court jurisdiction.[12]

Appeals could be submitted to the king himself or to one of his *Alcaldes* (judges), but more often they were addressed to the court rabbi, styled *Rab de la Corte* or *El Rab,* who was appointed by the king for each city or province. Also known as *Dayyanei Sillukin,* "*Dayyanim* who disposed of cases," these appeal judges were appointed not by virtue of their scholarship, but rather because they enjoyed the king's favor.

Even when a king or court official heard an appeal, they often tried the case according to the principles of *Halakhah.* Occasionally, they referred the case back to a Rabbinical court. King Pedro II of Aragon (1196–1213) had the legal code of Maimonides translated into Spanish in order to personally examine the Halakhic decisions.[13]

Although the Jewish courts were authorized by Spanish kings to decide all litigations in their communities, the kings did not relinquish any of their royal prerogatives. The establishment of Jewish courts under the king's sanction did not indicate the complete transfer or surrender of the king's supreme judicial powers. Indeed, the Jewish courts were often restricted in their functions by rival government agencies, particularly when the dividing lines between local judiciaries and officials of the crown were not clearly defined. Consequently, there were often overlapping and contradictory tribunals, and the Jewish courts had to contend with the royal judges and functionaries who were concerned with common fields of jurisdiction.[14] In some parts of Spain, an appointed official, known as a *Bedin* (a corruption of *Beth Din*), functioned alongside the *Batei Din*, serving as public prosecutor and chief of the police force which supervised the Jewish communities.[15]

It is not clear whether Jewish courts of arbitration existed in Christian Spain. The Responsa literature does mention the fact that Spanish Jews brought some cases to *Batei Din shel Borerut*, which functioned alongside the organized Jewish law courts.[16]

The Jewish courts usually met in synagogue buildings, on fixed days, excluding evenings, Fridays, eves of holidays, and the months of Nisan and Tishri. Written records of the verdicts were generally kept, except in the most elementary cases, and decisions were generally in accordance with *Halakhah*, even if it contradicted Spanish law. For example, Halakhic rules governing the pronouncement of death sentences varied greatly from both the secular and the clerical laws of Spain.

In addition to fines, the Jewish courts handed down various punishments, such as detention in special Jewish prisons. Some scholars, for example Adret, allowed the plaintiff to be represented by a lawyer,[17] although most *Batei Din* did not usually permit this. The Spanish *Batei Din* functioned not only as courts of law, but also as regulating agencies overseeing the communal life and spiritual well-being of Jews in the various communities.[18]

Castile

The central and northwestern section of the Peninsula, Castile, included those provinces reconquered by Christian kings from the Almohads, together with the formerly independent kingdom of León. Information concerning Jewish law courts exists from the eleventh century, when Alfonso VI (1072–1109) enacted a legal code which provided for both civil and criminal cases between Jews to be tried either by rabbis or by *Adelantados* (lay leaders). It also decreed that a case between a community member and an *Adelantado* must be tried by a rabbi, while a lawsuit against a rabbi had to be brought before the king or his delegate. The king also dealt with appeals, which he often decided according to Halakhic advice from a rabbi.[19]

Appeals could also be brought to the *Rab de la Corte*, who was not necessarily a scholar versed in Jewish law. More of an administrator than a rabbi, the *Rab de la Corte* supervised the administration of the *Kehillah*, including its finances, taxes, and courts of law. The judges chosen by him to decide lawsuits by general consent of the *Kahal* were not always learned men.[20] The *Rab de la Corte* who was appointed to a particular province would travel around the various *Kehillot* and hear appeal cases.

The situation regarding Jewish-Christian cases was otherwise. Alfonso VII (1127–1157) decreed that such cases must be tried by a Christian judge, even if the Christian party agreed to have the suit come before a Jewish court. The Christian judges were sometimes delegates of the king and, on occasion, were local magistrates. It is interesting to note that Christians often preferred the Jewish courts not only for litigations with Jews, but also for disputes among themselves.[21]

Alfonso X (1252–1284) renewed the edict that Jews, like other religious groups, be permitted their own courts. Actions between Jews were to be adjudicated by the rabbi and the community elders, while appeals could be brought either to the king or to the *Rab de la Corte* A special *Beth Din* was also authorized to hear appeals. For example, the *Beth Din* of Burgos, the capital of Castile, served as court of appeals for a neighboring city as well. This city had been removed from the king's jurisdiction and placed under that of a monastery.[22]

Alfonso X also authorized the elders of Toledo to appoint lay leaders with judicial authority in both civil and criminal cases. Often, he personally intervened in Jewish lawsuits and had them transferred to his own tribunals. Even in these cases, however, the palace judges were directed to receive advice from the *Kahal* rabbis and leadership.[23]

Alfonso's successor, Sancho IV (1284–1296), abolished Jewish court jurisdiction over criminal cases, which henceforth were heard by Christian judges. This rule, however, was not adhered to in all the provinces.[24] His successor, Ferdinand IV (1296–1312), abolished Jewish jurisdiction in capital cases involving Christians, at the insistence of his courtiers.[25] This indicates that neither the law forbidding Christians to use Jewish courts nor that abolishing Jewish jurisdiction over criminal cases was observed. During the reign of Alfonso XI (1312–1350), around the year 1320, Jewish jurisdiction over criminal cases was renewed.[26] In the years that followed, Jewish jurisdiction over criminal (and sometimes civil) proceedings was occasionally abolished, but it was again restored in most cases.

Although the *Batei Din* generally used their jurisdiction over capital offenses only against informers, there was a debate among the scholars as to whether a *Beth Din* in the Diaspora could try capital cases at all, since there was no longer a Sanhedrin. For example, Rabbi Asher ben Jehiel, who had arrived in Spain from Germany in 1303, expressed surprise at this function of the *Beth Din*.[27] His son, Judah ben Asher (1270–1349), who served as deputy to the Rosh in Toledo and later succeeded him, believed that *Batei Din* had the right to try criminal cases in order to save the life of a Jew who might be sentenced to death by a Gentile court for a crime which was not a capital offense according to Jewish law.[28]

Despite the worsening conditions for the Jewish community following the Black Death libel, and in spite of forced conversions and persecutions, certain communities were able to preserve their autonomy and were sometimes even granted new privileges.

During the late fourteenth and early fifteenth centuries, conditions improved somewhat. In 1395, the Archbishop of Toledo nominated his personal physician, a converted Jew, to act as chief justice over all Jewish lawsuits, a position which this physician had held before his apostasy.[29] Juan II (1406–1454) abolished Jewish jurisdiction for a short period, but soon restored it, even including certain capital offenses.[30] In 1432, he appointed Don Abraham Benvenisti, his financial agent, as *Rab de la Corte*.[31] The situation of Castilian Jewry so improved during the reign of Juan II that, according to some sources, no other contemporary Jewish community had a centrally organized *Kehillah* which could compare with that of Castile.[32]

Soon after his appointment, Don Abraham convened a Rabbinical Council in Valladolid, one of the most important *Kehillot* in Castile. This Council renewed the ban on Gentile courts and, among other regulations concerning the life and organization of the Jewish communities, enacted rules for the functioning of the *Batei Din* and the nomination of their judges by the electors of the community.[33]

Even Ferdinand II and his wife Isabella, in the early years of their reign, appointed a *Rab de la Corte*, Don Abraham Seneor (ca. 1412–ca. 1495), to function as tax collector, Chief Rabbi, and supreme judge for all the *Kehillot* in their kingdom. Shortly after Don Abraham's appointment, courtiers demanded the abolition of all Jewish criminal jurisdiction. Despite the courtiers' demand and violent anti-Jewish outbreaks in many parts of the country, Don Abraham retained his post until the termination of Jewish life in Spain in 1492, at which time he became a convert in order to avoid expulsion.[34]

Aragon

Aragon, with its capital in Saragossa, included the northeastern portion of the Iberian Peninsula. Catalonia, with the communities of Barcelona and Gerona, was joined to Aragon in 1137, while Valencia was annexed in the mid-thirteenth century.

The Jews, who had resided in Aragon since its establishment as an independent kingdom in the tenth century, were granted royal charters for the regulation of their community life. One of these, granted to the Jews of Teruel in the twelfth century, provided for a mixed court of arbitration, composed of one Jew and one Christian, chosen by the parties, to deal with litigations between Jews and Christians. Appeals could be made to a higher court of arbitration, composed of two Jews and two Christians. Execution of the verdicts was handled by the city judges, and differed for Jews, Muslims, and Christians.[35]

The Jewish communities of Aragon flourished, particularly under James I (1213–1276), who conferred many privileges on them, including the rights of self-determination and jurisdiction. Thus, the Jews of Saragossa and Barcelona were entitled to elect two or more *Dayyanim*, who could adjudge civil (and sometimes criminal) cases. The Jews of Calatayud enjoyed the privilege of appointing a rabbi and four directors to control the affairs of the *Kehillah*. They were entitled to pronounce *Herem* and to impose the death sentence on informers. The Jews of Majorca were granted one of James's charters in 1229.[36]

James I and his two successors, Pedro III (1276–1285) and Alfonso III (1285–1291), retained exclusive jurisdiction over "their" Jews. They also appointed a *Rab de la Corte*, as well as lower judges who served as agents of the king, functioning as financial secretaries, advisors, or diplomats. These agents seldom had rabbinical qualifications.[37]

During the thirteenth century, the Jews of Aragon, particularly the *Kehillah* of Saragossa, appointed a council which in turn appointed *Berurim*. A distinction was made between *Berurei Averot*, judges who tried criminal cases, and *Berurei Tevi'ot*, judges of civil and monetary suits.[38] At this time there was also a *Bedin*, who served as public prosecutor and supervisor of public order, and was authorized to impose fines.

The general situation of the Jews of Aragon did not alter significantly during the fourteenth century. In 1327, new *Takkanot* for the Barcelona community were approved by King James II (1291–1327). He abolished all former privileges and entrusted the administration of the *Kehillah* to a Council of Thirty, which included judges who always acted in the framework of courts of three. Among this council's members were Hasdai ben Abraham Crescas (ca. 1340–1410), one of the most important Rabbinical scholars of the period, and Isaac ben Sheshet (Ribash, 1326–1408). The Ribash indicates that this council became the most important institution of the Spanish *Kehillot*. It has also been said that its establishment was an attempt to unite all the Spanish Jews under one governing body, although it did not succeed in this function.[39]

There is little information available regarding Jewish autonomous jurisdiction in Aragon during the last century of Jewish life in Spain. It is recorded that different regulations were enacted from time to time concerning litigations between Jews and Christians. These suits were handled either by a royal bailiff or by a member of the clergy. In 1429, King Alfonso V (1416–1458) renewed an edict permitting litigations between Jews and Christians to be tried by mutually agreed arbiters. A similar edict is recorded in a city of Aragon as early as the twelfth century.[40]

Majorca

The conditions under which Jews lived in Majorca, the largest of Spain's Balearic Islands, were similar to those on the mainland. Persecutions in Castile and Aragon were emulated by similar disasters in Majorca. It is evident, however, from contemporary Rabbinic literature—particularly from the Responsa of Rabbi Isaac ben Sheshet—that Jewish autonomous jurisdiction was very different in Majorca. The Majorcan Jews themselves, in the early fourteenth century, voluntarily abandoned autonomous administration of civil law, and decided to bring all their litigations before Gentile courts only. These courts, though not permitted to consult Jewish scholars, nevertheless often acted in accordance with Halakhah or Spanish-Jewish tradition.[41]

Portugal

Although the first signs of Jewish settlement in Portugal date from the year 300 C.E. (and there was also a tradition that Jews lived there during the Roman period),[42] little is known about the Portuguese Jews before the twelfth century, by which time regular communities had been founded.

Independent Kehillot, established by charters issued by the monarchs, existed from the reign of Alfonso II (1245–1279). These Kehillot appointed a Chief Rabbi, the Arrabi Mor, who in turn nominated a local rabbi for each community consisting of at least ten Jewish families. The local rabbis were authorized to adjudicate all civil affairs, and appeals could be presented to the rabbis appointed by the Arrabi Mor for each of the seven provinces. The Arrabi Mor himself toured the provincial capitals and acted as the highest instance of appeal, in conjunction with his chancellor and secretarii—who were not necessarily Jews. Appeals could also be dealt with by the king. Except in matters related to royal finances or hearings to be tried by a royal judge, litigations between Jews and Christians were also conducted by the local rabbi.[43]

Despite the worsening conditions of the Portuguese Jews under Alfonso IV (1325–1357) and following the Black Death plague, João I (1385–1433) and Alfonso V (1433–1481) renewed the charters which the Jews had held previously. From that time onward, Jewish jurisdiction remained as it had been in the thirteenth century, and sometimes included criminal cases.[44]

When the Jews were expelled from Spain in 1492, they were at first allowed to settle in Portugal. Following the marriage of the daughter of Ferdinand and Isabella of Spain to King Manoel I of Portugal (1495–1521), the Jews were expelled from Portugal in 1496–97. This expulsion included some of the wealthiest and best-educated Jews of Portugal. Others were forcibly baptized. Many thousands of the New Christians, or *Conversos,* who secretly practiced Judaism, were martyred in the following decades, especially after the Inquisition against Judaizing *Conversos* was established in 1536. The Inquisition continued in force until the second half of the eighteenth century, forcing many *Conversos* to emigrate, but Jews were permitted to resettle in Portugal in 1800. They were granted certain rights in 1868 and again in 1912. A small *Kehillah* exists in Lisbon today, and there are indications that crypto-Jews, or *Marranos,* still live in Portugal.

Central and Western Europe

Despite territorial and boundary changes during the Middle Ages and modern times, the fate of the Jews in Central and Western Europe generally followed a similar pattern, and regulations for Jewish self-adjudication were often identical. There are even parallels between the history of the Jews in England and on the European mainland. Nevertheless, the status of Jews did differ from nation to nation, from province to province, and even from one city to the next. The various regions will therefore be discussed according to countries: Germany and Austria-Hungary, Switzerland, France, the Netherlands, and England.

Germany and Austria-Hungary

According to some sources, Jews had settled in Western Europe by the first century C.E., but the earliest records of organized Jewish life in Germany date from the fourth century. Until the eleventh century, the Jewish communities in Germany were centered mainly in the Rhineland and Lorraine, the cities of Regensburg and Prague, and the three communities of Speyer, Worms, and Mayence (known acrostically in Hebrew as *Shum*). From the second half of the eleventh century, and especially during the era of the Crusades, German Jews were often the target of persecution. After the Thirty Years' War

(1618–1648), local rulers became interested in Jewish financial skills and permitted the Jews to set up banks, especially for commerce with Spain and Portugal. They were also allowed to participate in the annual Leipzig Fair. Polish Jews fleeing the massacres of 1648–49, perpetrated by the Cossacks of Bogdan Chmielnicki, sought asylum in the now-flourishing Jewish communities of Germany.

During the period of absolutism in the seventeenth and eighteenth centuries, monarchs became increasingly interested in Jewish trade and finance, improved the economic position of the Jews, and appointed some of them to court. These rulers, however, sometimes interfered with the autonomy of Jewish communal life.

The publication of works by Moses Mendelssohn (1729–1786) on Judaism and philosophy inaugurated a new age for German Jewry. Some Gentiles, such as Mendelssohn's friend, the poet and dramatist Gotthold Ephraim Lessing (1729–1781), favored Jewish emancipation. During the French Revolution, Jews were granted equal rights in some of the German states. Despite regressions during the first half of the nineteenth century, the assimilation of German Jewry had begun, and the Jews themselves increasingly emphasized their German nationality at the expense of their Jewishness.

The situation of the Austrian Jews resembled that of the Jews in Germany. It is believed that Jews arrived in Austria with the Roman legions, but the first reliable evidence of a permanent Jewish settlement in Austria dates only from the eleventh century. Like their German kinfolk, the Austrian Jews were ravaged by persecution during the Crusades.

The first synagogue in Vienna was built in 1204, by which time the city had become a center of Jewish learning. A charter was granted to the Viennese Jews in 1238, and to all Austrian Jews in 1244. Despite the renewal of these rights, the Jews of Austria during the late thirteenth and early fourteenth centuries suffered periodically from high taxes, restrictions on trade and commerce, and confiscation of their property, apart from being targets for anti-Jewish riots. Following a "ritual murder" libel in 1421, many Viennese Jews were killed, and others fled to Bohemia and Moravia, where they likewise experienced persecution and expulsion.

An era of improvement eventually ensued, however, and many new *Kehillot*—especially in small towns—were protected by the local rulers. These communities were enlarged in 1648 by Jews fleeing the Chmielnicki massacres. The situation further improved under Rudolf II of Hapsburg (1576–1612) and his successors, who appointed privileged court Jews. The Jewish position again deteriorated under Leopold I (1657–1705), however, but improved during the reign of

Empress Maria Theresa (1710–1780), who regulated all aspects of public and private life among Austrian Jews in the General Police Law of 1754. The Jewish communities in some parts of her realm were granted almost full judicial autonomy, and the office of *Landesrabbiner* was renewed. The office of *Landesrabbiner,* rabbi of the entire region of Moravia, along with a Council of Moravian Jews, had existed since 1651. Although Maria Theresa also was known to discriminate against Jews, her son and co-regent, Joseph II (1741–1790), published the famous *Toleranzpatent* (Edict of Tolerance) in 1782. Although it attempted to integrate the Jews as useful citizens, the Edict limited many elements of Jewish autonomy. This autonomy was finally abolished in 1784.

The situation of Austrian Jewry again deteriorated during the first half of the nineteenth century, especially during and immediately following the 1848 Revolution. Thereafter, however, many Jews of wealth and status gained influential roles and were admitted to state and army service. The lifting of economic restrictions and closer contacts with the Gentile population led increasingly to almost total assimilation.

The rules and regulations laid down for Austrian Jews were operative in Hungary only after the unification of the two states in 1683. Before that time, the two communities had not shared the same conditions.

Individual Jewish graves dating from the second century C.E. have been found in Hungary. Organized Jewish communities date from the ninth century. Despite occasional persecutions and expulsions, the Jews who had settled in Hungary during the reign of King Bela IV (1235–1270) enjoyed generally good relations with their neighbors. The fifteenth and sixteenth centuries were marred by restrictions and recurrent "ritual murder" charges. When the Ottoman Turks occupied the capital, Buda, and the southern parts of Hungary during the early sixteenth century, the Jews were granted a large measure of civic and religious liberty. Severe economic restrictions were again imposed with the restoration of Hungarian sovereignty in the latter part of the seventeenth century.

It must be kept in mind that, for many centuries, Germany, Austria, and Hungary were divided into hundreds of small states, known as *Länder.* These *Länder* were ruled by kings, princes, dukes, or other nobles and sometimes by bishops, certain cities remaining under the autonomous control of the municipal authorities. Many of the Jewish communities had their own special regulations, but seldom were unified legislatively. The local rabbi often served as head of a local *Beth Din,* a post to which he had not always secured formal appointment, and he assisted the *Parnasim* in managing the *Kehillah.* Smaller

Kehillot, without their own rabbi, were under the jurisdiction of a larger, neighboring community.[1]

A rabbi or.*Dayyan* of one *Kehillah* could rarely decide the cases of another, and there rarely was a Chief Rabbi. Nevertheless, certain scholars were considered the highest Rabbinical authority, such as Rabbi Meir ben Barukh (Maharam) of Rothenburg. In the few instances where Gentile rulers attempted to appoint Chief Rabbis, mostly to serve as tax collectors, they were opposed by the *Kehillot.*

Most communities had their own *Beth Din.* Verdicts were handed down by a solitary judge, or by a judge assisted by other Rabbinical or lay leaders of the community. Though not appointed to act as *Dayyanim,* certain rabbis took it upon themselves to impose fines, bans, and even corporal punishment, even if, in the latter cases, they were rarely entitled to do so. If a rabbi was not prepared to serve as *Dayyan,* a *Kehillah* would sometimes appoint special *Dayyanim.*[2]

The various rulers granted differing degrees of autonomy to the Jews. According to several sources, Charlemagne (768–814) gave the Jews certain rights of jurisdiction among themselves.[3] His son, Louis the Pious (814–840), who was very much under the influence of the clergy, himself assumed jurisdiction over the Jews under his protection.[4] In subsequent generations, the Jews appear to have utilized Gentile courts to a large extent, as is indicated by the fact that Rabbi Gershom ben Judah of Mayence (Me'or ha-Golah, ca. 965–1028) found it necessary to renew the ban on Gentile courts.[5]

In 1084, Bishop Rüdiger granted the Jews of Speyer exclusive jurisdiction in internal disputes, and extended the jurisdiction to cover certain cases between Christian plaintiffs and Jewish defendants. In the same year, similar privileges were granted to the Jews of Meissen in Saxony and to all Jews living in Bohemia and Moravia. The same privileges were granted in 1090 to the Jews of Speyer and Worms by Emperor Henry IV (1056–1106), who decreed that Jews should be judged according to their own laws and by their own judges. Difficult cases had to be brought before a "bishop" and appeals heard by an imperial court. These regulations also applied to each of the individual ethnic and national groups living in Germany—a common practice in the Middle Ages. [6] There is also a reference at this time to special Jewish courts for the fair in Cologne.[7]

From the thirteenth to the fifteenth century, there was a different phase of jurisdiction over the Jewish communities. The German emperors, local rulers, and heads of the clergy often considered the Jews living in their areas to be their personal property. As a consequence, the regulations concerning jurisdiction over the Jews varied from state to state, from province to province, even from city to city. Sometimes an emperor would sell the rights over "his" Jews to a local ruler. At other times, the emperors appointed representatives to act as judges over the Jews, while maintaining their own jurisdiction. The emperors also often permitted local rulers or bishops to decide independently how to organize jurisdiction over the Jews.

Despite some differences, there were certain similarities in the methods utilized to arrange this jurisdiction. For example, many rulers nominated a special Jewish court, the *Judengericht*. These tribunals, which occasionally decided cases according to *Halakhah*, often met in synagogue courtyards. Their judges, who were mainly Gentiles, could sometimes be nominated only with the consent of the Jews.[8] The office of *Judenrichter, Judenmeister,* or *Judenbischof* was also known to be held by Jews. Thus, there is a reference to an *Archisynagogus*, one of the *Kehillah* leaders having jurisdiction over his community similar to that of a Christian judge in his community. Isaac, a Moravian *Judenbischof*, lived in the middle of the fourteenth century,[9] and in 1407 Israhel of Worms was appointed "master over all Jews in German countries."[10] Emperor Frederick II (1440–1493) appointed a Jew, Moshe, as *Magister Judaeorum* in 1473, and a Gentile, Thomas Pucher, to the corresponding post in another city in 1492.[11]

It is not clear whether all these "Judges for the Jews" had judiciary powers. Some may have exercised purely administrative functions, such as tax collecting and the execution of royal rules and regulations, as was the case in the cities near the Rhine—Speyer, Worms, Trier, Cologne, and Frankfurt; in Bavaria—Nuremberg, Augsburg, Bamberg, and Würzburg; and in parts of Austria.

Despite the *Judenrichter* and special Jewish courts administered by the rulers, internal Jewish courts also existed during this period. Some of these courts, which often acted as arbitration tribunals, were recognized by the authorities and could hear certain cases between Jews and Gentiles. Such courts existed in Nuremberg, Nördlingen, Ulm, Frankfurt, and Halberstadt.

Until the fourteenth century, many famous Jewish scholars lived in Germany. Although some of these scholars refused to act as members or heads of courts, others did serve in these capacities.[12] There was no one rule concerning recognition of the Rabbinical courts by the authorities. Some courts were given far-reaching jurisdiction and could impose bans or punishments, while others had no authority even to impose fines or to handle monetary cases.

Many of the Jewish arbitration courts were composed of laymen, with a rabbi acting as *Shalish*, the third judge. Often, however, the lay leaders took broad judicial authority upon themselves, and this led to disputes with the Rabbinical leaders over the issue of competence. The

Takkanot Shum of Speyer, Worms, and Mainz (1220) decreed that the functions of the *Parnasim* be curtailed, and that they no longer be entitled to impose bans.[13].

After the twelfth century, Jews in some German towns, as well as in many other cities of Western and Central Europe, were subject to the Magdeburg *Stadtrecht* (Municipal Law), which provided for a high court. The far-reaching influence of this court's judicial decisions extended also to the Jews, although the Magdeburg jurors often used Jewish courts, even in cases involving Christian defendants. The Rabbinical court of Magdeburg seems to have had authority over the Jews, similar to the authority exercised by the high court over the Gentiles, while other Rabbinical courts, such as that of Goslar in the thirteenth century, turned to the rabbis of Magdeburg for advice.[14]

From the scant information available concerning Jewish courts in the sixteenth century, it seems that the position remained static. There were still a few special courts for the Jews, although in some areas there were independent Jewish judges as well. For example, in 1579, Emperor Rudolf II (1576–1612) gave the Jews of Prague a *Patent* (privilege) which extended for a three-year period, allowing them to elect the elders and judges of the community.[15] Emperor Ferdinand II (1619–1637) decreed that Austrian Jews should have their own tribunals and even their own appeal court, designated *Oberjuristen Collegium* (high court), under the jurisdiction of a district rabbi.[16] This privilege was renewed by Ferdinand's successors; and a special Jewish prison existed in Prague. The *Kehillot* of Bohemia enacted detailed *Takkanot* for the functioning of the Jewish courts.[17] The *Beth din* of Prague published its protocols during the years 1682–1779,[18] and in addition to this *Beth Din*, a court of arbitration operated in Prague. The literature of the period called each of its *Dayyanim "Dayyan Shaveh"*, and styled the *Beth Din* itself *"Mishpat Shaveh"* (or *"Mosh"*), which seems to indicate that all three judges were "equal," i.e. of the same rank.[19] The Jews of Vienna had also been granted their own jurisdiction by Archduke Mathias in 1601. This privilege, which was renewed several times by Emperor Ferdinand III, declared that only the court Jews had to be judged by the Emperor's own high court.[20]

There are other examples of independent Jewish jurisdiction in Germany during the seventeenth century. A Rabbinical council held at Frankfurt-on-Main in 1603 established Jewish district courts in the larger cities of the province, including Frankfurt, Worms, and Fulda.[21] The council also prohibited the members of one *Kehillah* from bringing their litigations to another *Kehillah* court. During and following the Thirty Years' War, the Jews of Frankfurt and Cologne, as well as other cities, were allowed jurisdiction only over religious and ceremonial matters. They were, however, permitted to establish courts of arbitration.[22]

Since there were almost no Jewish appeal courts in Germany during the eighteenth century, litigants agreed, as a precondition, to abide by the decisions of the Courts of the First Instance.[23] In contrast to this situation, courts of appeal did exist in Austria. Maria Theresa, in her General Police Law for the Jews of Moravia, provided in 1747 for the nomination of district rabbis, as well as a general rabbi, to act as judges of appeal with authority to impose even corporal punishment. Some jurisdiction was left in the hands of the annually elected Elders of the *Kehillah*. These Elders sometimes functioned in rotation for one month at a time, and so were given the designation of *Parnasei ha-Ḥodesh*.[24]

Maria Theresa's son, Joseph II, in his famous *Toleranzpatent* of 1782, abolished the autonomy of the Jewish communities and decreed that henceforth all Jewish trials be handled by the general courts. [25] Nevertheless, many unofficial *Batei Din* continued to function in the German and Austrian *Kehillot*, under the guidance of famous scholars such as Rabbi Jacob Emden (1697–1776) of Altona, Germany, and Rabbi Moses Sofer (Ḥatam Sofer, 1762–1839), in Pressburg.

Jewish courts also existed in Prussia during the eighteenth century. Generally comprising the rabbi of the *Kehillah* and its *Parnasim*, these courts only had jurisdiction over religious and ceremonial affairs and could impose small fines.[26]

The era of Enlightenment and Emancipation, which began in the second half of the eighteenth century, changed the legal position of the German Jews.[27] The Jews themselves, as well as the government, wanted to abolish all legal and civic differences between Jews and the Christian population. One of the first measures of the Emancipation, therefore, was the abolition of separate courts of justice for the Jews. Moses Mendelssohn himself opposed any special jurisdiction for religious groups as being a form of religious coercion.[28] One of the first regulations abolishing separate Jewish courts was enacted in Prussia (1797), where the General Jews' *Réglement* decreed that "the rabbis shall have no jurisdiction whatsoever, neither in civil nor in religious-ritual or even ecclesiastical-disciplinary matters."[29] Although Bavarian Jewish communities still had officially recognized courts of arbitration in 1806, King Max Joseph I of Austria (1806–1825) declared that no "Rabbi and *Barnossim* [*Parnasim*]" should have any jurisdictional powers.[30]

King Frederick William III of Prussia (1797–1840) decreed, in the emancipationist *Judenedikt* of 1812, that "in no case should rabbis or elders of the Jews have any jurisdiction." Jurisdiction over the Jews of Berlin was entrusted to the general courts of the city. The decree was renewed from time to time in Prussia, and also enacted in Baden (1809), Sachsen-Weimar (1823), and Württemberg (1828). A law of the German Reich abolished all separate ecclesiastical jurisdiction in 1873, and allowed only disciplinary cases against members of the clergy to be tried by ecclesiastical authorities. Rabbis and other officials of the Jewish communities were not included in this exception.

Despite all these regulations, nearly every *Kehillah* with its own rabbi also had a *Beth Din* until the destruction of the German Jewish communities under the Nazi regime. In the smaller communities, the rabbi alone acted as judge or was assisted by the elders of the community, while the larger communities had at least one Rabbinical court composed of three *Dayyanim*. These courts were never officially recognized by the government. In 1927, a prominent German Jewish lawyer in Berlin proposed the establishment there of an official Jewish Court of Arbitration, but his suggestion was never put into practice.[31]

The Jews who returned to Germany after World War II reestablished courts of arbitration, at least in the West German Federal Republic. These courts, often composed of rabbis from different cities, are entitled to handle matters of personal status, as well as civil affairs, by mutual consent of the litigants. Their verdicts are recognized by the general courts.[32]

Switzerland

As in many other states, the position of the Jews in Switzerland was dependent on the wishes of the different rulers. Thus, by the eleventh century, Jews had received permission to settle in certain localities and to maintain jurisdiction over religious matters, whereas in the municipality of Zurich, during the same period, Jews had to submit all their litigations to the Burgomaster.

More *Kehillot*, such as that of Basle (founded in 1213), were established during the thirteenth century. During this and the following two centuries, no special jurisdiction was allowed for any religious community. Zurich prohibited all independent Jewish jurisdiction in 1383.[33] The municipality of Fribourg, on the other hand, decreed in 1413 and again in 1457 that "Jewish people of good reputation or their teachers" could act as judges in internal Jewish matters. Only criminal or difficult cases had to be tried by the municipal court.

During the seventeenth and eighteenth centuries, Jews in some parts of Switzerland were allowed jurisdiction through Rabbinical courts. Only when a rabbi could not reach a decision did the case have to be heard by the governor of the canton.

In 1803, the canton of Aargau established a "moral court" for the

Jews, to deal with quarrels between husband and wife, children and parents, or teacher and teacher. Similar laws were enacted in other cantons in 1825. In 1824, however, after the emancipation of the Swiss Jews had already begun under the influence of the French Revolution, a proposed law for the organization of the Jewish communities, with rabbis acting as arbitrators, was proposed but was not adopted by the government of the Helvetian Republic.

The Federal Constitution of 1866, which granted Jews absolute freedom of residence and civic and legal equality, did not provide for Jewish juridical autonomy.

France

The areas lying within the borders of modern France were not always under French rule. Much of what has already been stated concerning *Batei Din* in Germany and Spain, therefore, applies also to France.

Despite a tradition that individual Jews reached some parts of Gaul by the first century C.E., the earliest reliable evidence of Jewish settlement there dates from the fifth and sixth centuries. The Visigoths, who often expelled Jews or forced them to convert, sometimes granted them the right to try religious and civil cases in their own courts and according to their own laws. Cases between Jews and Gentiles, and penal cases against Jews, were tried according to Roman law in the south, and old Frankish law in the north.[34]

Attempts were made by various church councils from the ninth century onward to counteract the privileges granted to the Jews of France, but the situation during the Carolingian period (9th–11th cent.) was favorable. Although Archbishop Agobard of Lyons (d. 840), "the father of medieval anti-Semitism," had appointed a Gentile "Master of the Jews,"[35] *Batei Din* existed in France until the tenth century. Composed of three *Dayyanim* in the larger cities, and of one rabbi in the smaller towns, these courts relied heavily on the Halakhic decisions of the Babylonian *Geonim*.[36] The jurisdiction of the *Batei Din* was gradually limited, until even the most simple matters of synagogue administration had to be brought before Gentile courts.

The position of the French Jews deteriorated during the Crusades, although not to the same degree as in Germany. Blood libels, persecutions, and massacres occurred, yet Jewish courts were maintained, particularly special tribunals during the Paris and Troyes fairs.[37] During the twelfth century, however, Jews often used the Gentile courts, and Rabbi Jacob ben Meir (Rabbenu Tam, ca. 1100–1171) renewed the ban on Gentile courts in the *Takkanot* of the Council of

Troyes (1160).[38] During this same period, the famous traveler Benjamin of Tudela mentioned Jewish courts in various French cities. These courts handled personal offenses and matrimonial problems, as well as religious matters.

The situation of the French Jews worsened during the thirteenth century. In 1240, the Jews were expelled from Brittany. During that same year, a notorious disputation took place in Paris as a result of which the Talmud was initially condemned and, two years later, burned. Jews were burned in the Dauphiné province in 1257, and they were expelled from Poitou in western France in 1259. Yet in 1288 and 1302, King Philip IV (1285–1314), in a move against the Papacy and the Catholic Church, refused to allow the French clergy the right to establish the Inquisition. He retained personal jurisdiction over the Jews, mainly so that he could extract more money from them.

The fourteenth century was characterized by further expulsions, until finally, in 1394–95, the Jews were forbidden to live in the Kingdom of France. Nevertheless, even during the fourteenth century, there were instances of internal jurisdiction and of the functioning of special Jewish courts, comprising the rabbis and representatives of the *Kehillot*. Cases between Jews and Gentiles were tried either by regular courts or by special *Judices* or guardians.[39] In 1364, King Charles V (1364–1380) appointed Mathatias ben Joseph Treves Chief Rabbi of Paris and judge of all the *Kehillot* in France.[40]

In 1558, the *Kehillah* of Avignon was allowed to enact a *Takkanon* (ordinance) which permitted the appointment of four members of the *Kehillah* as judges in all Jewish civil cases.[41] After 1595, the rabbi of Metz and two assessors were allowed to function as a court of arbitration with limited jurisdiction over civil affairs.[42]

Some Ashkenazi communities existed in Alsace and Lorraine, which came under French rule in 1648. During the eighteenth century, Jews were again allowed to settle in Paris, and in 1709 they were granted legal jurisdiction in courts of arbitration. In his *Lettres-Patentes*, King Louis XVI (1774–1792) allowed the Jews to try all internal disputes in their own courts.[43]

The Jews of Alsace were also permitted to establish their own courts during the eighteenth century, the verdicts being executed by regular courts. In 1765, Jews were given the right to stand trial before a regular court,[44] and in 1787 the provincial assembly of Strasbourg abolished all Rabbinical jurisdiction.[45]

The French Revolution inaugurated a new era for the Jews of France. In 1798, they requested the right to maintain Rabbinical courts.[46] In 1806, however, the Assembly of Jewish Notables—

preparatory to the Napoleonic Sanhedrin of 1807—informed the Emperor that rabbis had only ceremonial functions.

Although no official recognized Jewish courts have existed in France since the Emancipation, some *Kehillot*, including that of Paris, have maintained Rabbinical courts of arbitration up to the present day.

The Netherlands

During late medieval times, the Jews living in what is now Holland shared the fate of their brethren in Germany. The history of Dutch Jewry, as such, begins in the late sixteenth century, when refugee *Marranos* began to settle in Amsterdam.

Information about Jewish courts in the Netherlands is not readily available. It is known, however, that in 1605 the authorities decreed that Spanish and Portuguese Jews living in Haarlem would be subject to the city courts. The authorities did not curtail the right of the *Parnasim* to impose a ban on religious transgressors. [47]

In 1640, the *Parnasim* of the Amsterdam Sephardi community assumed sole authority over the *Kehillah*, including the Rabbinical right to pronounce *Herem*. They retained their authority during the following century. [48] Before this, the trial of Uriel da Costa (ca. 1585–1640) had been held before a Rabbinical court, and even after the action of the *Parnasim* one famous case is known to have been heard by a Rabbinical court. In 1656, Benedict (Baruch) de Spinoza (1632–1677) was tried by a *Beth Din* under the jurisdiction of Rabbi Saul Levi Morteira (ca. 1596–1660), and Spinoza was subsequently excommunicated. It should be noted that the Amsterdam City Council, which granted the Jews a certain degree of independent jurisdiction, had greatly influenced the Rabbinical courts to excommunicate both Da Costa and Spinoza. Despite the juridical autonomy of the Amsterdam *Kehillah*, appeals had to be brought before the general courts. [49]

During the seventeenth century, Ashkenazi Jews, mostly from Germany, established *Kehillot* in Amsterdam, The Hague, and Rotterdam, and the supremacy of the Sephardi communities came to an end. Dutch Jewry was formally emancipated with the occupation of Holland by the French Revolutionary armies. Since that time, only Rabbinical courts have existed in Holland.

England

Despite reports about Jewish settlements in England during the Roman and Saxon periods, the first authentic evidence of Jewish settlement in considerable numbers dates from the time of William the Conqueror (1066–1087).

By the middle of the twelfth century, *Kehillot* had been established in the larger cities, such as London, Lincoln, York, and Oxford. Even though the English kings and other rulers asked rich Jews for financial aid, there were instances of anti-Jewish feelings at the time, including the imposing of discriminatory fines and taxes. There were even blood libels and, at the end of the century, massacres of Jews in certain towns, notably York.

The monarchs of this period, Henry II (1133–1181), Richard I (Coeur-de Lion, 1180–1199), and John Lackland (1199–1216), granted charters to the Jews of their realm. These charters stated that a Christian bringing a civil complaint against a Jew had to be heard by Jewish jurors. If he refused, the case would come before a mixed jury, composed half of Jews and half of Christians.[50]

From the end of the twelfth until the end of the thirteenth century, several titled Jews are mentioned in the official documents of medieval England. It is unclear who held these titles, but it seems probable that they were wealthy Jews. What exactly their function was is also uncertain. According to one view, they were concurrently members of a Jewish court administering justice in the communities and officials of the Royal Exchequer responsible for the allocation and collection of various taxes.[51] Another view is that the titles refer to different groups of officials: "Presbyters" or "Wardens" had secular functions, such as the collection of taxes; "Bishops" or *Eveskes* were *Kohanim* exercising certain ecclesiastical, but not judicial, functions. According to this opinion, "judges" were Gentiles who functioned as members of a special court for Jews, called the "Jews' Chapter."[52]

Although the general situation of the Jews in England during the thirteenth century worsened, Jews did have a certain measure of autonomous jurisdiction, but no permanent courts. Ad hoc Jewish courts, composed of laymen, had been formed in Norwich between 1243 and 1267.[53] King Henry III (1216–1272) granted London's Jews a "Patent Roll" in 1250. According to this document, the "Masters of the Law of the Jewish Community" were permitted to excommunicate any Jew who refused to contribute to the upkeep of the community's cemetery.[54] In 1268, the Jews of Northampton were given the right to be tried by justices appointed by their own community.[55] Commercial lawsuits between Gentiles and Jews had to be tried before a jury of twelve Jewish businessmen.[56]

The general position of the Jews in England continued to worsen, and on July 18, 1290, King Edward I (1272–1307) signed an order banishing all Jews from the realm. By the beginning of November of that year, no Jews remained in England.

They were not permitted to resettle until 1656, when Manasseh ben Israel (1604–1657) persuaded Oliver Cromwell, Lord Protector of the Commonwealth, to declare that there was no statute excluding Jews from England. In his petition, Manasseh ben Israel also asked Cromwell to allow the Jews to settle their own internal disputes. This petition was granted, and from that time onward, Jewish courts of arbitration existed in England.[57] King Charles II (1660–1685) allowed Jews to swear on the Pentateuch in Gentile courts. He also laid down that no trial in which a Jew was involved could be held on a Saturday.[58]

In 1664, the Jewish community of London received a formal promise of protection by the crown, and in 1671, it was guaranteed freedom of worship. The Jewish population in England grew, and in 1790 the Sephardi and Ashkenazi communities cooperated for the first time. This joint move led to the founding of the Board of Deputies of British Jews, the recognized representative body of all Jews in the British Commonwealth. It was in this century as well that important London rabbis, such as Tzvi Hirsch Levin (Hart Lyon), David Tevele Schiff, and Solomon Hirschel, presided as heads of an Ashkenazi *Beth Din* in London, whose authority was accepted by all British Jews. It dealt essentially with personal matters and only rarely with civil cases.[59]

The London *Beth Din*, which exists to this day, was established in the early nineteenth century. Its first records have been preserved in the *Proceedings of the London Beth Din, 1833–1885*. The first two Chief Rabbis of the British Empire, Nathan Marcus Adler (1803–1890), appointed in 1844, and his son, Dr. Hermann Adler (1839–1911), were instrumental in giving the London *Beth Din* its definitive shape and in gaining governmental recognition. Functioning as an ecclesiastical court, and dealing mainly with matters of personal status, the London *Beth Din* exerted an authority that was long accepted in the distant United States. Halakhic questions were often referred to it by the American Jewish community in the nineteenth century.[60]

The London *Beth Din* also functions in civil cases as a voluntary court of arbitration whose legal power was strengthened by the Arbitration Act of Britain's Parliament in 1889. It deals mainly with marital disputes and cases between parents and children and among neighbors, who are often advised by English magistrates to apply to this tribunal. The *Beth Din,* assisted by experts in the areas of trade and industry, also deals with cases involving employer and employee, landlord and tenant, and vendor and consumer, as well as with commission and inheritance claims and breach of promise suits. Actions involving *Shadkhanut* (marriage brokerage), not accepted by ordinary British courts, are often brought before the London *Beth Din*.

Approximately three hundred cases are heard annually by the London *Beth Din*, which also serves as the highest Rabbinical authority in religious matters for English Jewry. Its cases are usually decided by a combination of *Halakhah* and *Yosher*, Jewish law and a sense of justice.

In addition to the above, there are also Anglo-Jewish arbitration courts which are affiliated with various nonreligious public bodies. Thus, a Trades Advisory Council was established under the auspices of the Board of Deputies in 1940. While its principal object has been to combat anti-Semitism in trade and industry, another was "to arbitrate between disputants, whether members or otherwise, where difficulties are encountered and arbitration is acceptable to the parties concerned."[61] The Trades Advisory Council, which was particularly active during World War II, maintains panels of lay and legal arbitrators to deal with commercial disputes whose repercussions might bear a communal aspect. In recent years, it has especially concerned itself with the Arab boycott of British firms trading with Israel.

There are provincial *Batei Din* in Manchester, Leeds, and Glasgow. They work in close cooperation and consultation with the London *Beth Din*. Similarly, in Ireland, matters are usually referred to the London *Beth Din* for adjudication.

Eastern Europe

Poland and Lithuania

The first reliable evidence of organized Jewish communities in Poland dates from the twelfth century, and in Lithuania, from the fourteenth century. The Mongol invasion in 1240–41 caused an upheaval in the Polish economy, and the king and princes encouraged German merchants to immigrate to Poland. Many Jews settled in Poland at that time, bringing with them their German-Jewish vernacular, which later was transformed into Yiddish. Prince Boleslav V the Pious (1227–1279) decreed in the Statute of Kalisz (1264) that Jews were to be tried either by the Princes or by their own representatives, and not in the general municipal courts. Usually, the *Voivoda*, a nobleman who administered the various provinces on behalf of the king, functioned as *Judex Judaeorum* (Judge of the Jews).[1]

In 1334, King Casimir III the Great (1333–1370) permitted Jews to appoint their own judges to decide civil cases according to Jewish law.

Criminal cases had to be tried by the Grand Dukes or the local *Starosta,* an official similar to the *Voivoda.*[2] In 1364, these privileges were extended to the Jews of White Russia and Lesser Poland, and, in 1386, to Lithuania, which was then united with Poland. Vladislav V Jagello (1386–1434), under the influence of the anti-Jewish German traders and clergy, refused to reconfirm Jewish privileges. Casimir IV Jagello (1447–1490) renewed some of the privileges in 1453 and exempted the Jews from ecclesiastical-court jurisdiction. A year later, however, under pressure from the clergy, he rescinded the privileges. Despite recurrent persecution from the period of the Black Death until the end of the fifteenth century, Jews continued to play an important part in Polish trade and commerce.[3]

In 1494, Jan Albert (1492–1501), a son of Casimir IV, established the first Jewish quarters. This move was strengthened by his brother, Grand Duke Alexander I Jagello of Lithuania (1501–1506). Due to their unique situation in their enclaves, the Jews maintained their own communal and cultural life.

In 1503, Alexander I Jagello appointed Rabbi Jacob Pollack (1470– after 1522) Chief Rabbi of Polish and Lithuanian Jewry. He was authorized to function as the highest authority and judge in all inter-Jewish disputes.[4] In 1514, Alexander's brother and successor, Sigismund I Jagello (1506–1548), King of Poland and Grand Duke of Lithuania, appointed Michael Ezofovich "elder of all Lithuanian Jews," with the right to dispense justice according to Jewish law. Since the latter had no Rabbinical or even general religious knowledge, the Jews did not recognize his authority.[5] Four years later, the same king confirmed the appointment of two leading Posen rabbis as provincial judges for all the Jewish communities of Great Poland.[6] In 1531, he also granted extensive judicial functions to Rabbi Mendel Frank of Brest-Litovsk.[7]

After 1551, Sigismund II Augustus (1548–1572) allowed the Jews of Great Poland to nominate their own judges. Along with the elders of the *Kahal,* these judges had wide judicial powers, even in certain criminal cases. Any Jew who refused to be tried by their tribunals was to be delivered to the king's own courts and could be punished severely. Jewish elders were present at any trials heard by the *Voivoda.* Jews living on independent estates *(Szlachta)* were not subject to the *Voivoda,* but to the hereditary owner of the *Szlachta.*[8]

One of the most important periods of Jewish autonomy in Eastern Europe began in the middle of the sixteenth century.[9] With the growth in importance of the different provinces where Jewish populations were concentrated, and the establishment of new *Kehillot,* the communities in each province united and appointed an *Av Beth Din* to head each of the provincial courts. These courts generally met during the two major fairs, that of Lublin in the spring (before Passover) and that of Jaroslaw in the late summer (before the High Holy Days). In these two locations, as well as in Posen and at smaller and less-frequent fairs, *Batei Din shel Yeridim* (Fair Courts) functioned as the highest tribunals of the land.[10] Not only merchants but Jews from all social strata attended these fairs. Rabbis, accompanied by their students and even by entire *yeshivot,* came to discuss and to solve difficult Halakhic problems. Many marriage negotiations were also finalized at these fairs.

Out of these meetings of the leaders of the different communities and their courts there developed an autonomous, central governing body for the Jews of Poland.[11] Beginning around 1580, the *Va'ad Arba ha-Aratzot* (Council of the Four Lands) was composed of representatives from five provinces—Great Poland, with Poznan (Posen) as its center; Lesser Poland, with Cracow and Lublin as its centers; Red Russia, Podolia, and Galicia, with Lemberg (Lwow) as their center; Volhynia, with Ostrog and Kremenets as its centers; and Lithuania, which separated from the Council in 1623. The Council was divided into two sections, with the secular heads of the provinces acting as a kind of autonomous Jewish parliament, and the recognized Halakhic scholars, styled *Dayyanei ha-Aratzot,* elected to serve as the highest court of the land. The Council was the most important institution of Jewish life in Poland for almost two hundred years.

Although the protocols of the Council have not been found, detailed reports of its functions have been collected from various sources and documents, and these have been compiled as the *Pinkas Va'ad Arba ha-Aratzot.*[12]

The *Batei Din shel Yeridim* of Lithuania may have predated the similar courts of Poland.[13] After splitting away from the *Va'ad Arba ha-Aratzot,* Lithuanian Jews formed their own Council—the *Va'ad Medinat Lita,* often referred to as *Va'ad ha-Medinah.* This was composed of representatives from the *Kehillot* of Brest-Litovsk, Grodno, Pinsk, Vilna, and Slutsk. The records of this Council have been preserved and published.[14]

These two sets of records give us a complete picture of the different activities of the two Councils, their rules and regulations, their legal decisions, their procedures, the composition of the courts, and the election of their judges. For example, a judge would normally be reelected at the end of his term, unless notified otherwise at least half-a-year in advance.[15] The tribunals sometimes functioned as courts of appeal, usually with the consent of the head and the members of the lower courts.[16] Judges were not paid for their services, but received *Pesharah-gelt*, service fees, and the money received from the fines was divided among the poor.[17] Initially, the courts only dealt with cases directly connected with the fairs, but later they began to deal with general civil and monetary cases.[18] Some of the courts even had the right to impose capital punishment on informers.[19]

The Councils continued to function until 1764. During this period, certain *Kehillot* retained their individual autonomy and their *Batei Din*. Many of the Council's decisions referred to rulings of local or provincial courts.

In 1595, the community of Cracow decided to establish three "grades" of tribunals—lower, middle, and high courts—which divided cases according to the amounts of money involved. Similar courts existed in other communities, along with courts of arbitration. The arbitration courts were usually composed of three, five, or seven members, with one of the leading rabbis of the community acting as the deciding judge. If a permanent court existed in a locality, however, a defendant could not choose to use the arbitration court instead.[20]

According to some regulations, the secular leaders of the *Kahal* were allowed to participate only in communal matters, such as the collection of taxes and fees, and were not permitted to take part in court proceedings.[21] Other regulations did allow the lay leaders to participate in trials, either as judge or as counsel for the defendant.

During and after the era of the Councils, different occupational groups established guilds in certain *Kehillot*. Some of these guilds, in turn, established their own courts, as was the case with the guild of tailors.[22]

Many courts, mostly those for arbitration, continued to function in the *Kehillot* after the Councils were abolished. The situation of Polish Jewry changed considerably, however, following the three partitions of Poland in 1772, 1793, and 1795. In addition, the influences of *Haskalah* (Enlightenment) and of the Reform movement began to be felt. These changes also influenced the existence and functions of Jewish courts. For example, Jews who became Prussian citizens were at first granted the same rights as other Jews in Prussia, but these privileges, including the right to establish separate Jewish courts, were abolished in 1802.[23] In Vilna, on the other hand, the impetus to abolish the tribunals came from the Jews themselves.

In 1789, a *Darshan* (preacher) named Shim'on ben Wolf or Shimel Wolpovitz asked for the abolishment of the *Kahal* as part of a wider program of reforms. He also called for the functions of the Rabbinical courts to be curtailed, limiting their jurisdiction to religious and ceremonial affairs. Three years later, also in Vilna, a Dr. Solomon Polonius demanded that all litigations between Jews be tried in the regular courts, with the assistance of two Jewish advisors.[24]

Russia

The first regulations referring to separate Jewish courts in Russia date from the era of Empress Catherine II the Great (1762–1796), who gave judicial functions to the District *Kehillot* and to the *Kehillot* of the different "governments" or territories. The latter functioned as courts of appeal for all litigations between Jews. Cases between Christians and Jews were tried by the general magistrate courts, with Jews being allowed trial by a jury composed of Jews. In 1782, Catherine restricted the jurisdiction of the Jewish courts to "spiritual" affairs only, and she eventually deprived the *Kehillot* of all social and judicial functions.[25] At the same time, the leaders of the *Kehillot* often abused their power. For this reason, Jews often preferred to approach the Gentile courts, despite the prohibition against their use.[26]

Czar Alexander I (1801–1825), in his Jewish Constitution of 1804, placed the Jews under the sole jurisdiction of the general courts. From that time onward only Rabbinical arbitration courts functioned in Russia, although at certain periods they exercised more power and authority than they had been granted officially.[27] Many civil and monetary cases continued to be brought before them and, even at the beginning of the twentieth century, Justices of the Peace in the general courts often transferred certain cases to the Rabbinical tribunals. Some *Kehillot* even employed a permanent *Borer* (arbitrator) to deal with minor cases and to act as the deciding factor in arbitration courts.[28]

For a short time following the Revolution of 1917, the Jewish community of Moscow had its own arbitration court, composed of nine members representing the different Jewish political parties and the *Mishpat ha-Ivri* Society.[29] Dealing mainly with monetary affairs, the court litigated as many as 250 cases a month until 1918, after which its functions were restricted and it was finally abolished.[30] No officially recognized Jewish courts existed in Soviet Russia after this time, and the members of any Rabbinical court which dealt with other than strictly religious affairs were penalized by heavy fines and imprisonment.

During the 1920s and 1930s, the Soviet authorities established courts with Jewish judges in some of the larger Jewish communities. Even though their official language was Yiddish, these courts functioned according to Soviet law and so could not be considered Jewish courts.[31]

Bulgaria

Jews have lived in Bulgaria since Roman times, and often under favorable conditions. Theodora (Sarah), a queen in the mid-fourteenth century who had great influence on state affairs, was of Jewish origin.[32]

Until the end of Ottoman rule in 1878, Bulgarian Jews had their own courts, comprising one or more rabbis or *Dayyanim*, who decided matters of education and trade, as well as religious affairs, according to *Halakhah*.[33] A new law was enacted in 1880, entitling the *Batei Din* to deal with religious matters only. In 1900, a high court of appeals was established by a committee of the *Kehillot* of Bulgaria. Based in Sofia, the capital, and in three other cities, the high courts functioned until the Nazi occupation and were reestablished in 1949.[34] Once Bulgaria entered the Soviet orbit, however, all religious courts were abolished.

The Ottoman Empire

Established by a Turkish tribe in the early fourteenth century, the Ottoman Empire eventually spread through Asia Minor, North Africa, Yemen, and some parts of southeastern Europe. In 1326, the community of Bursa (Brussa) in Anatolia (Turkey) became the first Jewish settlement to come under Ottoman protection. According to tradition, Romaniot (Byzantine) Jews had lived in that city since the beginning of the ninth century. The Ottoman rulers soon extended to the Jews of Bursa and other cities the right to build synagogues and to engage freely in business. They were also subject to poll taxes, to be collected by the elders of the community.

In the second half of the fourteenth century, the Ottoman Empire expanded into Europe, with the capture of Gallipoli and Adrianople (Edirne), which later became the largest Jewish community in the Balkan Peninsula. The empire then engulfed parts of Greece, Bulgaria, Rumania, and Albania. In 1453, the real founder of the Ottoman Empire, Sultan Muhammad II (1451–1481), conquered the Byzantine city of Constantinople, which he declared his capital. Many Jews from other cities in Turkey, as well as from other Ottoman provinces, soon came to Constantinople, where the Sultan permitted them to settle. He appointed a Romaniot, Rabbi Moses Capsali (1420–ca. 1496), as Chief Rabbi and head *Dayyan* of the entire empire.[1] Until that time, the Jewish courts had mainly been composed of laymen, styled *Nivharim* ("elected ones"), rather than of rabbis or Jewish scholars.[2] Rabbi Elijah Mizrahi (ca. 1450–1526) was Capsali's successor, and the last Chief Rabbi of the empire until that office was reinstituted three hundred years later.

Sultan Bayazid II (1481–1512) allowed many Jewish refugees from Spain and Portugal to settle in the empire. Though welcomed by the existing communities, these refugees often established their own settlements in cities all over the empire, including Safed and Jerusalem in Eretz Yisrael. From that time onward Jewish communities were often composed of as many as five different groups: the original Romaniots, North Africans, Ashkenazim, Italians, and Spanish-Portuguese. The Jews from the Iberian Peninsula frequently utilized Gentile courts until 1557, when the *Kehillot* of Constantinople and Salonika imposed a ban on any Jew who did so. Thereafter, no Jew in the Ottoman Empire resorted to the Gentile courts.[3]

Syria, Eretz Yisrael, and the Arabian Peninsula came under Ottoman rule during the reign of Sultan Selim I (1512–1520). The situation of the Jews under Selim was favorable, and many Jews held important positions in the cultural and economic spheres.

The greatest of the Ottoman rulers, Suleiman the Magnificent (1520–1566), who rebuilt Jerusalem and its ancient walls, granted Don Joseph Nasi (ca. 1524–1579), a Portuguese *Marrano* who reverted to Judaism, concessions of benefit to the Jewish community in Tiberias. Under Suleiman, the empire extended to Hungary and the Crimea, Egypt, Tunisia and Algeria, Mesopotamia, and Yemen. The Jewish communities developed, and many had both permanent courts and special courts of arbitration, including *Batei Din* of the five different Jewish groups living within them. These courts, designated *Batei Din Hashuvim* or *(Gedolim)* in the Responsa literature of the time, varied in size and composition.[4] As a rule, they comprised three rabbis or *Dayyanim-Mumhim* (experts in Jewish law), but there were also tribunals made up of one rabbi and two or more lay leaders of the *Kahal*, as well as courts of three lay leaders. The lay leaders did not necessarily decide cases according to *Halakhah*, but were guided by common sense and *Yosher*, and their decisions were not always accepted by the Rabbinic authorities.

Many Responsa also speak of courts of up to twelve members.[5] The latter were probably panels from which judges were selected to serve as members of regular courts of three *Dayyanim*. Some of these tribunals functioned in areas which had no permanent *Beth Din*, and others were special courts for specific kinds of cases. For example, in the sixteenth century, special courts were established to handle problems connected with the purchase and sale of immovable property involving newly arrived refugees from Spain and Portugal. The courts usually dealt with monetary and general civil affairs, and only occasionally with certain criminal cases.[6]

In addition to the *Batei Din Hashuvim*, courts of arbitration were frequently established. These, too, varied in size and composition. Sometimes one expert in *Halakhah* functioned as single arbitrator; at other times, three or more members made up the arbitration court. In some cases, the tribunal was headed by a rabbi of the community who appointed the other members of the court. In other cases, all the arbitrators were chosen by the litigants.[7]

Even though there was no Chief Rabbi of the empire for over three hundred years, Chief Rabbis were appointed in the various cities. These Chief Rabbis headed Jewish courts, which therefore functioned as high courts for the Jews of that city. Rabbi Samuel ben Moses de Medina (Maharashdam, 1506–1589) was Chief Rabbi and *Av Beth Din* in Salonika,[8] and his successor, Rabbi Ḥayyim Shabbetai (1555–1647), dealt with many civil and family disputes as *Av Beth Din*.[9]

The Ottoman Empire began its decline in 1567, and the situation of the Jews steadily deteriorated under the rule of Sultan Murad III (1574–1595) and his successors. Increasingly severe restrictions were placed on the private lives and business activities of Jews, and they were also compelled to wear special garments and to restrict the construction of their houses. Nevertheless, many influential, officially recognized Rabbinical courts continued to function in all parts of the empire, including Greece, Macedonia, Anatolia (Smyrna), Rhodes, Turkey,[10] Eretz Yisrael, Baghdad, Mosul, and Nisibis.[11] In the nineteenth century, under the rule of Sultan Mahmud II (1803–1839), every ethnic and religious community was authorized to administer its own affairs, according to the *Millet* system. This system required that the various non-Muslim groups appoint their own religious leaders. Around 1836, the Sultan confirmed the appointment of the *Ḥakham Bashi* (Chief Rabbi) as head of a grand court to settle the internal disputes of the *Kehillah*.

In 1840, during the first years of the reign of Abdul Mejid I (1839–1861), the Damascus Affair, one of the most notorious blood libels of modern times, occurred. It was settled only by the personal intervention of Sir Moses Montefiore and Adolphe Crémieux, the leading British and French Jews of the time, and of the orientalist Salomon Munk. The outcome was that the Jews of the Ottoman Empire were granted a *Firman* (imperial decree) according them the same rights and liberties as other non-Muslim inhabitants of the empire. They were guaranteed security of life and property, religious and personal freedom, and the right to hold government and military offices. The *Ḥakham Bashi* was given an authority in the Jewish community similar to that of the Imam among Muslims.

These privileges were renewed by Abdul Mejid and by his successor, Abdul Aziz (1861–1876). In 1865, Abdul Aziz confirmed the

"Organizational Regulations of the Rabbinate" of the Turkish *Kehillot*, according to which Jewish communal affairs were to be managed by a committee of sixty laymen and twenty religious leaders, who would elect seven rabbis to function as a Rabbinical court. Such courts existed in many cities of the empire, and each functioned as one of the most important institutions of the *Kehillah*. In Salonika, for example, the court acted not only in civil, family, and monetary disputes, but also in lawsuits between members of different organizations, such as merchants, craftsmen, and butchers.[12]

Courts were also established for handling special issues. In 1860, for example, an internal conflict troubled the community in Constantinople, and the authorities appointed a special tribunal, comprising the Chief Rabbis of Smyrna, Adrianople, and Salonika, to settle the dispute. In the late nineteenth and early twentieth centuries, a central High Court of Appeal functioned in Constantinople, Salonika, and Jerusalem.[13]

Abdul Aziz's successor, Abdul Hamid II (1876–1909), adopted a positive attitude toward the Jews at first, but later opposed Jewish national aspirations, proving hostile to Theodor Herzl and the early Zionists. Nevertheless, a certain measure of Jewish autonomy remained under his rule and continued until the fall of the empire at the end of World War I. Some *Kehillot* under present-day Turkish rule have retained their officially recognized Rabbinical courts, and an arbitration tribunal was still functioning among the Jews of Istanbul during the mid-1950s.

Yemen

The Jewish communities of Yemen, which formed part of the Ottoman Empire for almost four hundred years, were among the oldest outside of Eretz Yisrael. Even though Yemenite Jews occasionally held important posts, their general situation was unfavorable. After the Ottoman conquest, local rulers and tribes often accused the Jews of cooperation with the Turks.

During the twelfth century, the Jewish community in Yemen accepted the authority of the Jewish court of Aden, on the southwestern tip of the Arabian Peninsula. This court was itself dependent on the Rabbinical authorities in Egypt.[14]

Each of the small communities in Yemen had its own spiritual leader, the *Mori* or rabbi, who decided minor civil disputes. The highest authority for Yemenite Jews was the *Beth Din* of three *Ḥakhamim* in San'a, the capital. Although the authorities withheld official recognition from this court, they usually upheld its verdicts. By communal consent, the tribunal was empowered to litigate difficult cases between Jews from different communities. Members of the Yemenite Jewish communities rarely brought their disputes to Gentile courts, although cases between Jews and Muslims had to be tried by the Imam. The position of *Av Beth Din* was often handed down from father to son.[15]

In addition to the San'a *Beth Din*, the local *yeshivah* also functioned as a court, by consent of the litigants, even in appeal cases. Since this tribunal did not always decide cases in strict accordance with *Halakhah*, questions of competence often arose between the two institutions. At times, the leaders of the *Kehillah* took it upon themselves to make peace between litigants and to act as a civil judicial authority alongside the Rabbinical court.

North Africa

Tradition has it that Jews have lived in North Africa—the area comprising Egypt, Libya, Cyrenaica (Cyrene), Tripolitania, Tunisia, Algeria, and Morocco—since the era of the Second Temple. Jews often played an important role in the economic, cultural, and political life of these countries,[1] and famous Jewish communities and academies were established in a number of cities. Long before the destruction of the Second Temple, a populous and well-organized Jewish community was established in Alexandria, Egypt, where Jewish courts were active.

Nearly the whole of North Africa was conquered by the Arabs during the first half of the seventh century. Jews then began to settle in the seaports, maintaining their connections with Eretz Yisrael while forming strong links with the Babylonian *Geonim*. Saadiah Gaon was born in Egypt in 882, and studied there before moving to Babylonia.

In many cities, the Jewish communities were composed of three separate groups: Palestinians, Karaites, and Samaritans. The latter two groups, which did not accept the authority of the Oral Law, were opposed by the first group, known as the Rabbanites. Jewish courts were often established at this time, with *Dayyanim* from the Rabbanite community. Occasionally, the *Dayyanim* were appointed by the *Gaon* in Eretz Yisrael.[2]

Important *Batei Din* in Fostat (ancient Cairo) are mentioned in documents dating from the early eleventh century. They seem to have functioned occasionally as a *Beth Din ha-Gadol* (supreme court) for all Palestinian Jews in North Africa.[3] Litigants were entitled to appeal to the administrative heads of the *Kahal*, who, together with the spiritual leaders of the community, would render a decision.[4] A special court to deal with problems connected with immovable property also existed in Fostat.[5]

Kairouan, in Tunisia, was a main center of Jewish life and learning for over three hundred years, from the ninth to the twelfth century. During this period, it had an important *Beth Din,* a permanent court of three members who were not always experts in *Halakhah.* Some of the *Dayyanim* were important scholars, however, including Ḥananel ben Ḥushiel (d. ca. 1055) and Jacob ben Nissim ibn Shahin (d. ca. 1106), to whom Sherira Gaon addressed his famous Letter *(Iggeret)* of 987 C.E. regarding the compilation of the Mishnah. After Rabbi Jacob's death, this court lost its position, although it was still mentioned in the 1220s, when the *Kehillah* of Kairouan was already in a state of decline.[6]

In North Africa's smaller communities, Jewish courts were usually composed of a single judge, who was empowered to impose fines and punishments, including *Ḥerem* (excommunication) and flogging.[7]

Egyptian Jews of the period often brought their cases to Gentile courts, despite the opposition of the rabbis. According to some sources, the lack of expert *Dayyanim* was the reason why so many Jews utilized the Gentile courts.[8] Maimonides, in a letter to Rabbi Pinḥas, *Dayyan* in Alexandria, wrote that there was so little expert knowledge among the Jews of Egypt because in Muslim countries—unlike the lands of Christendom—many Jewish suits were adjudicated by Gentile courts.[9]

Until the fourteenth century, the Karaites in Egypt had their own courts. The verdicts of these tribunals were in some cases more stringent than those of the Rabbanite courts.[10]

The Fatimid dynasty, which rose to power in North Africa in the tenth century, appointed a *Nagid* as leader of the Jewish communities. His functions were similar to those of the *Nasi* in Babylonia.[11] According to the *Genizah* documents found in the attic of the Ben Ezra Synagogue in Cairo, two brothers named Judah and Mevorakh, sons of Saadiah, were the first *Negidim* (in the mid-11th cent.), although it has also been claimed that an Italian rabbi, Paltiel (969), was the first *Nagid.*[12] The *Negidim* were usually appointed by the Gentile authorities, on the recommendation of influential members of the Jewish community. The post became hereditary, however, for six generations following Maimonides' son, Abraham, in the early thirteenth century. A *Nagid* was appointed for the Jews of Tunisia and Algeria around the year 1000, and for the Jews in other parts of North Africa only from the sixteenth to the nineteenth century. The post was abolished in Egypt and Tunisia by Sultan Selim I in 1517.

Among the functions of the *Nagid* were the administration of justice to members of the communities on the basis of Jewish law, the appointment of judges in different communities, and the definition of their competence. The judges often also maintained law and order, served as arbitrators in cases of injustice, discrimination, and unfair economic competition, and confirmed communal decisions of the *Kahal*.

Not all the *Dayyanim* appointed by the *Negidim* were functioning rabbis or holders of Rabbinic ordination, but they were often elders of the *Kahal*. Some of the permanent *Batei Din*, however, were presided over by well-known Jewish scholars, such as Rabbi Simeon ben Tzemaḥ Duran (Rashbatz, 1361–1444) in Algiers[13] and Rabbi David ben Solomon ibn Abi Zimra (Radbaz, 1479–1573) in Cairo.[14]

The *Batei Din* in North Africa, under both the Fatimids and the Ottomans, always had jurisdiction over religious affairs and matters of personal status, as well as over some civil and monetary cases. The Muslim authorities did not interfere with the functioning of the *Batei Din* or of other non-Muslim courts, even during periods of persecution. However, the decisions of a Jewish or a Christian court were not fully recognized by the Muslims. For this reason, the Jewish tribunals were officially considered internal courts of arbitration.[15] Civil cases between Jews and Muslims had to be adjudicated by Muslim judges, who often turned Jews over to *Batei Din* for the administration of oaths.[16]

Under the jurisdiction of the *Nagid*, a central court was sometimes referred to, although it is doubtful whether Jewish courts of appeal existed in North Africa. Nevertheless, Rabbi Isaac ben Sheshet Perfet (Ribash, 1326–1408), who lived briefly in Algiers, mentions in certain of his Responsa a *Dayyan Sillukin*, "judge of the final verdict."[17]

In some localities, Jewish occupational groups maintained their own courts. For example, a *Kovetz Soḥarim* (league of merchants) had its own tribunal, recognized both by the government's law courts and by the *Beth Din*.[18] Nevertheless, Jews continued to bring their cases to Gentile courts, and they were even known to request that the Gentile authorities abolish the Jewish tribunals.[19]

In more recent times, courts in various North African countries began to develop independently. They will therefore be treated under separate geographical headings.

Egypt

During the seventeenth and eighteenth centuries, initially under the Turks and later under independent Egyptian rulers, the position of Egyptian Jewry was unfavorable. Turkish despotism, coupled with an economic recession, also led to a decline in the cultural level of Egyptian Jewry. Although eminent Talmudic scholars could still be

found, many *Kehillot* were no longer under the leadership of rabbis.
Occasionally, scholars coming from European countries acted as rabbis
and *Dayyanim*.

Despite internal friction during the nineteenth century, the situation of Egyptian Jewry improved. The reforms of Mehemet Ali, viceroy
of Egypt from 1805 until 1848, and the opening of the Suez Canal in
1869 brought new prosperity to the Egyptian economy, affecting all
spheres of life. The Jewish communities in Cairo and Alexandria grew,
and new *Kehillot* were established in other places. Included in these
Kehillot were many European immigrants, among them Rabbinical
scholars with a Western education who acted as rabbis and *Dayyanim*.
The only Jewish tribunals that existed were Rabbinical courts, which
functioned as internal courts of arbitration. Jewish-Muslim relations
remained fairly good during the nineteenth and twentieth centuries,
despite occasional cases of blood libel. The situation of Egyptian Jewry
deteriorated, however, after the establishment of the State of Israel in
1948.

Libya

In the seventeenth century, many Libyan Jews lived in special quarters
in the various towns, or in underground caves in some villages.
The only organized community existed in Tripoli, with approximately
one thousand Jewish families—one-third of the Jewish population.
According to the traveler Benjamin II (1818–1864), the community
maintained eight synagogues and four competent *Dayyanim*. These
Dayyanim, who constituted a Rabbinical court with the Chief Rabbi
as its president, received their salaries from the local authorities
and were officially recognized by the government. The court was
entitled to handle affairs of personal status and to act as an arbitration
tribunal in civil cases. After their conquest of Libya in 1911, the
Italians maintained this system and treated the Jews well until the
enactment of anti-Jewish legislation by the Fascists in 1938. Under
British rule, following World War II, the situation of the Jews improved, but it soon deteriorated as a result of Muslim riots following
the establishment of the State of Israel. Many of the wealthier Jews
then emigrated to Israel, leaving only the poorest members of the
community in Libya.[20]

Tunisia

The Jews of Tunisia (Ifriqiya), under Hafsid rule (1228–1534), participated in the economic development of the country and were generally treated well. Many Spanish Jews, following the severe persecutions of 1391, sought refuge in Tunisia, and a number of outstanding rabbis and *Dayyanim* settled there. The Jews, considered inferior by the Muslims, were obliged to pay heavy taxes and to wear special clothing or pieces of yellow cloth to distinguish them. Despite such discrimination, they were otherwise fully protected and enjoyed recognized administrative and cultural autonomy.

Many Tunisian Jews fled the country and settled in Italy, especially in the city of Livorno (Leghorn), following the Spanish invasion of 1535. After the Ottoman victory over the Spaniards in 1574, many of these Jews or their descendants eventually returned to Tunisia and established themselves in their own communities. This Spanish or Italian segment of the Jewish population, known as *Granas* or *Gornim* (from "Leghorn"), had many bitter disagreements with the native Tunisian Jews, the *Touansas*. The *Granas* maintained their own communal institutions and Rabbinical courts from 1710 until 1899, when, by a decree of the Bey of Tunis, the two rival communities were merged under one Chief Rabbi and one tribunal.

During the eighteenth and nineteenth centuries, the Jews of Tunisia engaged in trade with other countries, were appointed to diplomatic posts abroad, and became numerous in the arts and crafts. They had their own internal tribunals, comprising competent representatives of the various trade corporations, although these were supervised by the Muslim president of the corporations, in whose hands the final decisions lay.

In 1857, under French pressure, a declaration of human rights *(Pacte Fondamental)* was issued, repealing all discriminatory laws against the non-Muslim population. From 1861 onward, Rabbinical courts were organized by official decree of the Beys. Composed of the Chief Rabbi as honorary president, one rabbi as president, and two judges, these courts were entitled to deal with religious and personal cases, in accordance with *Halakhah*. Their decisions were usually final, although the Bey could annul them in "cases of judicial error," and they were executed by the administrative authorities, in the name of the government. The Jews also had the option of turning directly to governmental courts. A report of the functions and composition of the Jewish courts in Tunisia during the first two-thirds of the nineteenth century has been preserved as *Ma'aseh Beth Din*.[21]

The decree of 1861 was renewed in 1872 and, with minor changes, it was again renewed by the French authorities after Tunisia became a French protectorate in 1881.[22]

Algeria

The Muslim authorities established an organization of Algerian Jewish communities in the fourteenth century. At the head of each *Kehillah* was a *Zekan ha-Yehudim* ("Elder of the Jews"), who could administer punishment and had at his disposal a special Jewish prison and police force. The rabbis sometimes considered the *Zaken's* prerogative of carrying out the verdicts of the *Beth Din* an interference with their own authority. The Spanish Jews who settled in Algiers, the capital, after the persecutions of 1391 had their own Rabbinical courts for civil disputes and nominated their own leaders.

After conquering Algeria in 1830, the French allowed Rabbinical courts to function until the early 1840s, when jurisdiction over the Jews was transferred to the French courts. The office of Elder, or head of the community, was abolished, and one or two Jewish members of the municipal council or chamber of commerce replaced this communal leader. One of the primary functions of the French-appointed Chief Rabbis was the emancipation of members of their communities. Before long, widespread assimilation began to prevail among the Jews of Algeria.

Morocco

When Jews arrived in Morocco from Spain and Portugal, they were welcomed by the local rulers. Often, however, there was considerable friction between the refugees *(Megorashim)* and the local Jews *(Toshavim)*. In many areas, over a period of generations, the *Megorashim* had their own communities, synagogues, rabbis, and *Dayyanim*, maintaining their distinctiveness for centuries to come. Eventually, however, the two *Kehillot* merged.[23]

The fate of the Moroccan Jews varied. At times, they exercised wide influence on the economic and political life of the country, while at other times they underwent severe hardships. Thus, many Jews entered the service of Sultan Mulay Muhammad (1757–1790) and were entrusted with political and financial negotiations between Morocco and other countries. His rebellious son, Mulay al-Yazid (1790–1792), in revenge for the Jewish refusal to accept him as ruler, organized a wholesale massacre of the Jews and reserved particular fury for those who had been in his father's employ.

Despite the important role which Jews played in the economy of Morocco, they were not granted equal rights until 1864, when Sir Moses Montefiore visited Sultan Mulay Muhammad ben Abd-al Rahman (1859–1873). From that time onward, separate Jewish tribunals, similar to Muslim religious courts, were established. Cases between Jews and Muslims had to be tried by the courts of the Kadis, where the status of Jews was inferior. In 1912, when Morocco became a French protectorate, the government permitted the establishment of special Rabbinical courts, to function alongside the Muslim and civil courts. According to the regulations enacted by the French, seven Courts of the First Instance, composed of three rabbis each, were established in the major cities. Communities without a rabbi were visited occasionally by a delegate of one of the courts who would settle disputes. The Supreme Rabbinical Tribunal, a high court composed of three *Dayyanim*, was established in Rabat. Since 1940, a special court, the Tribunal of *Serara* (Notables), has existed to handle cases of inheritance. In addition, Moroccan Jews of French citizenship had the right to apply to the French courts, and Jews of other nationality could turn to the consular courts of their countries of origin.

After the establishment of the State of Israel, violent anti-Jewish disturbances took place in Morocco. Nevertheless, in 1956, Jews became full citizens of the country for the first time. The official Rabbinical courts were then abolished and some of their judges became members of the state law courts. In 1965, the Rabbinical Tribunal of Rabat was abolished and its members were subsequently appointed judges in the state courts.

India

Cochin Jews

The earliest evidence of Jewish settlement in Cochin, southwestern India, is found on two copper plates recording the privileges which the kings of Cranganore (later Malabar) granted Joseph Rabban, headman of the Jews. According to certain Indian and European sources,[1] these plates, which authorized Rabban to exercise plenary jurisdiction in his community, date back to the fifth century, although accepted scholarly opinion dates them between 974 and 1020.[2]

According to one source, these privileges were handed down in Rabban's family until the destruction of Cranganore by the Portuguese in 1524 and the subsequent flight of the Jews to Cochin (now Kerala). In Cochin, the Jews were separated into three differing groups which, according to the Indian caste system, could not intermarry. These were the White Jews, known as *Paradesi* (foreigners), who were composed of exiles from Cranganore and Jews from Spain, Holland, and Germany; the Black Jews, who were mentioned by Benjamin of Tudela in the twelfth century; and the *Meshuḥrarim* (freedmen), ex-slaves and "out-casts" who were not permitted to sit in the synagogues of the two other groups.

Soon after their arrival in Cochin, the Rajah of Cochin appointed a *Mudaliar* (chieftain) over the Cranganore Jews. Once the Portuguese menace had been averted in 1663, the Jews of Cochin enjoyed complete religious freedom and cultural autonomy under the Dutch, who governed the area until 1795. In an apparent revival of the privileges granted earlier in their history to Joseph Rabban, the *Mudaliar* was permitted to exercise civil and criminal jurisdiction over the members of his community. These privileges were renewed periodically until the *Mudaliars* ceased to exercise the right of punishment in the early nineteenth century.[3]

After the seventeenth century, many Cochin Jews moved to the northern parts of India, where, under the British, they became prominent traders. Although they established communities in Calcutta and Bombay, the majority continued to live in Kerala, where they had five *Kehillot* and eight synagogues. By 1968, most of the Cochin Jews had emigrated to Israel. Until that time, they had maintained their own *Batei Din*, composed of the community elders, which handled religious affairs only. Civil disputes could be adjudicated solely by the common courts.[4]

Bene Israel

The Bene Israel have a very old tradition, but only established contact with other Jews after they moved to Bombay at the end of the eighteenth century. Their communities were led both by lay leaders, who handled questions of caste and family disputes, and by religious leaders, who served as arbitrators between members of the community and also as "priests," the Bene Israel having no *Kohanim* of Aaronide descent.[5] According to some sources, when the lay leaders were unable to settle a dispute amicably, a meeting of the adult members of the community would be convened, and the case was then decided by four or five "councillors" who also had other communal functions. Many disputes of the Bene Israel were settled by the general courts, however, and one of their religious leaders would sometimes serve as a member of such a court.[6] By 1970, with the emigration of most of the Bene Israel to Israel, their Jewish courts in India ceased to function.

Iraqi Jews

Many influential foreign merchants settled in Bombay in the second half of the eighteenth century, and these were followed by a large number of Jewish immigrants from Baghdad, Basra, and Aleppo. They settled in other cities as well, including Calcutta, and many became leading members of the Jewish communities. Although these Iraqi Jews established important congregations, they did not have their own rabbis or *Batei Din*. Some disputes were adjudicated by lay members of the community, and others by emissaries from Eretz Yisrael. Most of the disputes, however, were brought to the common law courts, especially after World War II.[7]

South Africa and Australia

South Africa

Jewish merchants trading in the Netherlands were connected with the Dutch East India Company, which established the first white settlement at the Cape of Good Hope in 1652. The first permanent Jewish settlement in South Africa was founded in the early nineteenth century, however, and in 1841 a Jewish congregation was established in Cape Town. Additional *Kehillot* were set up during the nineteenth century, their members hailing from Britain and Germany, and later mostly from Lithuania. Despite movements in some of the provinces to extend full rights to Protestant settlers only, the Jews of South Africa soon enjoyed complete equality in the country's national, political, civic, economic, and cultural life.[1]

The early Jewish congregations provided only the most essential services for their members, and accepted the authority of Britain's Chief Rabbi in "ecclesiastical" matters. Only the two most important communities, Cape Town and Johannesburg, had their own rabbis during the late nineteenth century, recruited at first from England and later also from Eastern Europe. Rabbi Joseph H. Hertz, an outspoken opponent of Boer discrimination, served Johannesburg's Hebrew Congregation (1896–1911) before his election to the British Chief Rabbinate in 1913.

During the early decades of the twentieth century, the Jews of South Africa (mainly Orthodox in affiliation) organized two separate religious bodies, the dominant Federation of Synagogues of South Africa, with headquarters in Johannesburg, and the United Council of Orthodox Hebrew Congregations, based in Cape Town. Although good relations and close cooperation are maintained between the two, each has its own *Beth Din*. Latterly, the Chief Rabbi of the Federation of Synagogues has enjoyed nationwide authority in South Africa.

The Johannesburg *Beth Din,* which also exercised a certain degree of authority over the Ashkenazi community of Rhodesia (now Zimbabwe), meets almost every weekday. Cape Town's *Beth Din* meets only when the necessity arises. Both *Batei Din* deal mainly with religious matters, such as conversion to Judaism, divorce, guardianship of widows and orphans, and *Kashrut.* In accordance with the South African Arbitration Acts, the *Batei Din* function as courts of arbitration in civil and monetary disputes between members of the community. Their verdicts are executable by the common law courts when the litigants have signed a *Shetar Borerut,* declaring in advance their readiness to accept the decision of the *Beth Din.*

No other community in South Africa maintains its own *Beth Din.* Hence, Jewish litigants often bring their disputes before the common courts, sometimes with the consent of the nearest *Beth Din.* Most of the civil cases adjudicated by the *Batei Din* are those which, for special reasons, cannot be dealt with by the common courts.

Australia

The earliest Jewish settlers reached Australia in 1788, and the first *minyan* and burial society were established in 1817. From the 1830s, more Jews arrived and small congregations were founded in scattered localities. Religious observance was lax, and the few strictly Orthodox Jews had to travel hundreds of miles in order to participate in religious services or to have a son circumcised. The danger of assimilation was a constant threat.

The authority of Britain's Chief Rabbi was respected, and in 1831 a member of the London *Beth Din* visited Australia to arrange a *Get* (Jewish divorce). It was, however, only in the latter half of the nineteenth century—when new waves of Jewish immigration began to swell the community—that some *Kehillot* in the larger cities appointed their own rabbis. During the 1920s, assimilation and growing intermarriage again threatened the smaller *Kehillot.* Refugees from Nazi-occupied Europe doubled the size of Australian Jewry from 1933. In response to their stronger religious and cultural demands, a new organizational framework was established with Boards of Deputies in the various states of Australia. Rabbi Israel Brodie, who served as senior minister in Melbourne from 1922 until 1937, later became Chief Rabbi of the British Commonwealth.

There are today *Batei Din* in both Melbourne and Sydney. Each of these Rabbinical courts handles religious affairs only, but is entitled to deal with civil cases as a court of arbitration, by consent of the litigants. When the parties have signed a *Shetar Borerut* in advance, the court's decisions can be executed in accordance with common law. Occasionally, a single rabbi will act as arbitrator, without the authority of the government.[2]

The Western Hemisphere

Brazil

The earliest organized Jewish settlements in Latin America were established in Brazil during the 1630s.[1] A century earlier, however, *Marranos* and "Judaizers" (non-Jews who adopted Jewish precepts) had arrived with the immigrants from Portugal. Crypto-Judaism survived for a time in Brazil, but persecution led to its eventual disappearance among the New Christians.

Jewish soldiers and traders joined the expedition sent by the Dutch West India Company, which occupied Pernambuco (Recife) and other parts of northeastern Brazil in 1630. Many Jewish families subsequently arrived with the company's traders from Holland and established *Kehillot* in Recife and Paraíba. In 1642, Rabbi Isaac Aboab da Fonseca (1605–1693) arrived from Amsterdam together with Moses Rafael d'Aguilar (d. 1679). Aboab became *Hakham* of Zur Israel Congregation in Recife, while d'Aguilar served as rabbi of Magen Abraham Congregation in the adjoining town of Maurícia.

The *Kehillah* of Dutch Brazil was directed by an executive committee of five, called the *Mahamad*. The minutes of this committee were later transferred to Amsterdam, where they have been preserved to this day. Among other functions, the *Mahamad* exercised control over legal issues arising in the community and decided lawsuits between congregation members. No dispute between Jews was permitted to come before a non-Jewish court, the few exceptions requiring the consent of the *Mahamad*. It had jurisdiction in hearings dealing with acts that disturbed the peace of the community, and law enforcement was secured by moral pressure and religious sanctions.

The *Mahamad* functioned until September 1653. A few months later, the Portuguese, who had been fighting the Dutch since 1642, won a decisive victory, as a result of which the Jews were expelled from Brazil. Most of them returned to Holland, but some fled to other regions of the New World that were still under Dutch control, such as Surinam (Dutch Guiana), Curaçao, and New Amsterdam. Thereafter, no Jewish community existed in Brazil until 1822, when the country won its independence from Portugal. North African Sephardim established congregations in Belém, and a few agricultural settlements were founded in southern Brazil by Ashkenazim coming from Europe. The major *Kehillot* of Rio de Janeiro and São Paulo date from the late nineteenth century. After World War I, European refugees greatly increased the size of the Jewish community. Rabbinical courts, which also functioned as courts of arbitration, were established in the principal *Kehillot* of Brazil.

Argentina

After 1580, when Spain and Portugal were temporarily united, Portuguese New Christians began arriving in Argentina. They were subjected to persecution by the Inquisition, which was only abolished in 1813, but crypto-Judaism had no significant effect in the country. In 1825, religious freedom was extended to Protestants, and the Constitution of 1851 granted religious freedom to the Jews as well. It was only the secular liberal legislation of the 1880s, however, which gave legal status to the Jews.[2]

Beginning in the 1840s, Jewish immigrants from Western Europe arrived in Argentina, and a congregation was established in Buenos Aires in 1868. Many Jewish refugees from the Russian pogroms settled in Argentina in the 1880s, but they were frequently harassed by anti-Semitic press campaigns. A number of agricultural settlements, initiated and financed by Baron Maurice de Hirsch (1831–1896), were established in the 1890s.

By 1904, a number of Ashkenazi and Sephardi communal organizations had been founded. There were further anti-Semitic outbursts during the 1920s and 1930s, based on nationalism, fear of Communism, and general xenophobia. Despite the legal restriction of Jewish immigration, a large number of Jews continued to arrive from Central and Eastern Europe. In 1939, all the congregations united and established the *Delegación de Asociaciones Israelitas Argentinas* (DAIA), a defense organization to combat anti-Semitism. The DAIA has since assumed a general representative role in Argentine Jewry.

Although President Juan Perón, who came to power in 1946, enacted a special clause in the Constitution prohibiting racial discrimination, anti-Semitism was not diminished. By and large, however, the situation of Argentine Jewry improved, and there are today a number of flourishing Ashkenazi and Sephardi congregations, largely concentrated in metropolitan Buenos Aires. Many of these *Kehillot* are affiliated with the *Asociación Mutual Israelita Argentina* (AMIA), which in addition to its administrative functions also maintains a three-man Rabbinical court. This *Beth Din* deals with various civil and religious cases and with matters of personal status. It also serves as an

officially recognized court of arbitration, and its decisions are implemented by the authorities. Only rarely has a case adjudicated by
this *Beth Din* been appealed to the official courts.[3] There are no
regular *Batei Din* in the smaller *Kehillot* today, nor does the Sephardi
community maintain such a Rabbinical court. Occasionally, however, a
Sephardi rabbi constitutes an arbitration tribunal, either by himself or
in conjunction with two lay leaders.[4]

Canada

The original Jewish settlement in Canada dates back to 1759, when
the British wrested Quebec from the French.[5] The first synagogue,
She'arith Israel in Montreal, was established in 1768 by Ashkenazim
who adopted the Sephardi ritual of the New York congregation bearing
that name. In 1778, they appointed a Jew from London as rabbi.

During the 1840s, there was some small-scale immigration from
Western and Central Europe, and *Kehillot* were established in To-
ronto, Kingston, and Hamilton. Larger numbers of immigrants, mainly
from Lithuania and Russia, began to settle in Canada during the late
nineteenth century, and many more *Kehillot* were founded by European refugees before and after World War II.

The founders of the Montreal congregation set up a *Beth Din*
composed of their elders. It was empowered to order any member to
appear before it and to impose penalties for misdemeanors.[6] Today,
almost all the larger communities maintain *Batei Din*, and an official
Court of Arbitration was established in Ontario by the Canadian Jewish
Congress, founded in 1919.[7] In some communities of eastern Canada,
leading members of the *Va'ad ha-Ir* (community council) functioned as
a board of arbitration. Their clientele consisted mainly of the new
Jewish immigrants, who were reluctant to bring their problems to the
government courts. Eventually, the use of Jewish courts declined and,
following World War II, few cases were handled by these tribunals.

The Canadian Jewish Congress Court of Arbitration functioned in
accordance with the Government Arbitration Act, and its decisions
were recognized and implemented by the government authorities. As a
rule, it was active in cases which, if brought to government courts,
might constitute *Ḥillul Ha-Shem* (desecration of God's Name), such as
disputes within or between congregations or organizations, or between
these institutions and their functionaries. This tribunal, which seldom
dealt with civil cases, was composed of a representative of the Canadian Jewish Congress and two other judges chosen by the litigants. The
arbitrators were often rabbis, lawyers, or leading laymen. Some of
these tribunals were established with the help and guidance of the

Jewish Court of Arbitration in New York, later known as the Jewish Conciliation Board of America. After World War II, however, they were infrequently utilized.

United States of America

The earliest group of Jewish immigrants arrived in the port of New Amsterdam, now New York City, on September 4, 1654, fleeing from the Portuguese invasion of Brazil.[8] Peter Stuyvesant, Governor-General of the New Netherlands, allowed these twenty-three Jews to settle in New Amsterdam, but only after having been ordered to do so by the Dutch West India Company. Despite the generally tolerant attitude of the Dutch, the Jews suffered from certain disabilities in the New World. Stuyvesant did not allow them to open retail shops, a restriction which was not lifted until the British capture of New Amsterdam in 1664.

A Jewish burial society was founded in 1656, and a Sephardi congregation, She'arith Israel, was established in 1695. The congregation's first building was erected in 1730, with financial assistance from Jews in London, Barbados, Curaçao, and Surinam.[9] Many Ashkenazim from England and the European continent belonged to this synagogue until the first Ashkenazi congregation, B'nai Jeshurun, was established in 1825.[10] Other Jewish communities and congregations were soon formed in Newport, Savannah, Philadelphia, Charleston, and Richmond.

Jews coming to the New World had been accustomed previously to bringing their disputes before Jewish tribunals. Such procedures were less frequent in the colonies.[11] In 1784, Rabbi David Tevele Schiff of the Great Synagogue in London requested that Haym Salomon of Philadelphia, known for his financial role in the American Revolution, adjudicate a claim concerning partnership in an estate. Rabbi Schiff intended to have this dispute settled by arbitration, rather than by a government court.[12] A year later, Congregation She'arith Israel in New York City undertook to arbitrate an account of two estates.[13] In 1787, however, plaintiffs were given permission by another New York congregation to utilize the civil courts because the defendants refused to heed the summons of a Jewish arbitration court.[14] Three years later, in 1790, the leaders of Congregation Mikveh Israel in Philadelphia asked Benjamin Nones, a onetime aid to General George Washington, to obtain a judgment from the London *Beth Din* in regard to the conversion to Judaism of a woman who had married a prominent member of the community. The case was referred to the Chief Rabbi's court in London because "there was no *Ḥakham* or *Beth Din* appointed in any congregation of this continent."[15]

The Jewish population of North America remained predominantly Sephardic until the early eighteenth century, when a fairly large number of Central European Jews began to settle in the British colonies. Unfavorable conditions in Poland during the 1770s induced other Jews to follow them. These Ashkenazi immigrants soon outnumbered the Sephardim, and the complexion of the Jewish communities changed. Many new Ashkenazi congregations were founded in the nineteenth century, and they developed their own religious, educational, and philanthropic activities. Since few ordained rabbis were available, Rabbinical functions were often performed by Jewish teachers who had immigrated from Europe.

Throughout this period, individual Jews and Jewish communities in New York continued to turn to the *Beth Din* in London for settlement of their legal disputes. The records of Congregation B'nai Jeshurun in New York contain a number of ritual questions which, during the 1830s, were referred to the Ashkenazi Chief Rabbi, Solomon Hirschel, in London. Rabbi Hirschel's authority was recognized in the absence of an indigenous Rabbinical authority.[16]

The substantial new immigration from Central Europe was reflected in the rise of the Reform movement.[17] A Reform congregation established in Charleston, South Carolina, in 1824 and consolidated in 1841 was followed by Har Sinai in Baltimore (1842) and by Emanu-El in New York (1845). A number of Reform temples were established in other cities, and several German Reform rabbis of prominence came to the United States to head them. Thus, in 1849, Rabbi Max Lilienthal (1815–1882), a Reform rabbi born in Munich, presided over a short-lived union of German congregations in New York—Anshe Chesed, Shaaray Shomayim, and Rodeph Sholom. Lilienthal, together with two other rabbis, set up a *Beth Din* to serve these congregations, but it held only one meeting.[18] At this same time, Congregation She'arith Israel of New York, which had an existing arbitration council, decided that it was no longer capable of dealing with disputes between its members. In 1857, several congregations joined forces to organize a *Beth Din*, but it was dissolved in the same year.[19]

Some of the hitherto Orthodox congregations now began to introduce certain reforms, such as family pews, organ music, and women in the choir, although in the main they retained the traditional prayer book. Eventually, these congregations formed the first nucleus of the Conservative movement in the United States. In 1875, B'nai Jeshurun, the first Ashkenazi congregation in New York, introduced certain changes, but stopped short of radical Reform, thus becoming the first Conservative congregation in the United States.[20]

The increasingly large number of Jews immigrating from Eastern Europe during the late nineteenth and early twentieth centuries strengthened the forces both of Orthodoxy and of Zionism in the United States. A large number of strictly Orthodox congregations were established, particularly in New York City and along the eastern seaboard. The Yiddish language, Yiddish theater, and Yiddish press found their support among these newcomers. It may be assumed that *Batei Din* were then established which functioned more or less as they had done in the Old World. When, in 1887 and 1888, an attempt was made by Orthodox congregations in New York to unite under a Chief Rabbi, this move did not meet with success. Another such unsuccessful attempt was made in 1909.[21]

The East European Jewish immigrants also founded *Landsman-shaften*, associations of Jews who originated from the same town or region of the Old World. These organizations served as social and philanthropic societies, and usually provided sick benefits, funeral arrangements, and burial plots for their members.

American Jewry was no longer entirely dependent on European sources of learning or religious authority. It had developed its own institutions for the training of rabbis and teachers. In 1875, Rabbi Isaac Mayer Wise had established the (Reform) Hebrew Union College in Cincinnati. In 1887, to counter this radical trend, a group headed by Rabbi Sabato Morais of Philadelphia founded the (Conservative) Jewish Theological Seminary in New York, which was reorganized in 1902 by Professor Solomon Schechter, who had been Reader in Rabbinics at Cambridge University in England. The (Orthodox) Yeshiva University in New York, which evolved from the Rabbi Isaac Elhanan Theological Seminary founded in 1897, developed into a ramified institute of higher secular, as well as religious, education.

By 1914, there were approximately three million Jews in the United States. The period of World War I (1914–1918) was an era of consolidation for the American Jewish community. Prominent Jews such as Justice Louis D. Brandeis, Louis Marshall, and Rabbi Stephen S. Wise were influential in American life generally. The American Jewish Joint Distribution Committee (JDC) administered a huge program of postwar relief and reconstruction for Jews in the stricken countries of Europe. In 1919, a delegation of American Jews attended the Peace Conference in Versailles to plead for the rights of East European Jews and to urge the implementation of the Balfour Declaration.[22] American Jewry had become the acknowledged leader of World Jewry.

As a result of Congressional legislation which restricted general immigration from Eastern and Southern Europe, Jewish immigration into the United States diminished considerably after the 1920s. The immigrant Jews of an earlier generation had become increasingly Americanized, and they and their offspring had risen to positions of prominence. The menace of assimilation and intermarriage increased accordingly.

Following the rise of Nazism in the 1930s, there was a new influx of Jews from Europe. After World War II, the American Jewish community, in addition to maintaining support for its own philanthropic, educational, and religious institutions, faced the challenge of helping to reconstruct the remnants of European Jewry and of mobilizing political and financial support for the *Yishuv* in Eretz Yisrael. The Joint Distribution Committee had a major share in rehabilitating survivors of the European Holocaust, and the Zionist movement in the United States, under the aegis of the World Zionist Organization, played a leading role in furthering the establishment of a Jewish state in Palestine, fulfilling the age-old dream of the Jewish people.

While engaged in these new and extraordinary tasks, the American Jewish community continued to develop and strengthen its own communal institutions. Some of these, whose constituencies included, in part, immigrant elements, bore the stamp of Old World patterns.

Batei Din and courts of arbitration have functioned in the United States throughout the twentieth century. The rabbis of larger Orthodox congregations established their own *Batei Din*. Some also formed committees of arbitration and conciliation, composed of rabbis and lay leaders. These committees usually functioned in accordance with American Arbitration Society procedures and state arbitration laws. According to the latter, an arbitration agreement must be signed in advance by the litigants in order to make the decision binding. Some local nonreligious bodies, such as the Jewish Education Committee of New York,[23] maintained non-Rabbinical arbitration boards.

Tribunals also exist within the various religious bodies. The (Orthodox) Rabbinical Council of America maintains a court of arbitration. The Conservative congregations, organized in the United Synagogue of America, have a similar tribunal.[24] Both organizations have to deal with *Kashrut*, marriage, divorce, and other issues of personal status. Occasionally, they are also called upon to handle other matters.

The Reform movement in the United States has no organized Rabbinical courts, although both the Union of American Hebrew Congregations and the Central Conference of American Rabbis nominate arbitration committees to handle disputes. There have been cases, however, where even a rabbi has preferred to bring personal grievances against his congregation to the civil courts.[25]

In addition, a number of cities in the United States have either *Batei Din* or Jewish courts of arbitration, or both. A Jewish Court of Arbitration was established by the Federated Jewish Charities in Baltimore to handle cases involving domestic relations.[26] Two official *Batei Din* function in Chicago, one affiliated with the (Orthodox) Rabbinical Council of America, and the other with the National *Beth Din* of the Conservative movement.[27] Similar *Batei Din* also exist in Los Angeles.[28] The extent to which these institutions have been utilized is not readily ascertainable.

In 1949, the Associated Synagogues of Massachusetts established a *Beth Din Tzedek*, or Rabbinical Court of Justice, which also supervises a court of arbitration composed of rabbis and laymen.[29] This *Beth Din* has endeavored to apply *Halakhah* to contemporary social problems. Thus, at the height of the Vietnam War, Rabbi Samuel I. Korff, the court administrator, issued a Responsum on selective conscientious objection which became the basis for draft appeals by many Jewish draftees. Following the death of Rabbi Korff in 1973, the tribunal reverted to its previous role as a Rabbinical court dealing with conversion and *Kashrut* supervision, and with problems of marriage and divorce.

The best known of the non-Rabbinical courts of arbitration has been the Jewish Conciliation Board of America, founded during the 1920s in New York as the Jewish Court of Arbitration. Since 1930, under new leadership, it has played an increasingly important role in the life of New York Jewry. The thousands of cases which it has handled have covered a wide gamut of Jewish life in the world's largest Jewish community. For thirty-eight years, from 1930 until 1968, it was the writer's privilege to have headed it. In recent years, the Board's work has come under the aegis of the Jewish Family Service of the New York Federation of Jewish Philanthropies, while its official entity continues, with the sponsorship of a devoted group of men and women.

The Jewish Conciliation Board's history and development, and the extent of its program during the nearly four decades of the writer's presidency, form the major content of this volume.

Notes

CHAPTER ONE: Introduction (pp. 3–8)

1. Gedalya Alon, *Toledot ha-Yehudim be-Eretz Yisra'el bi-Tekufat ha-Mishnah ve-ha-Talmud*, I (Tel Aviv, 1952), pp. 53 f.
2. H. H. Ben-Sasson, *Perakim be-Toledot ha-Yehudim bi-Ymei ha-Beinayim* (Tel Aviv, 1969), pp. 90 f.
3. *Talmud Bavli, Gittin* 88b.
4. I Corinthians 6:1.
5. H. S. Hirschberg, "Erka'ot shel Goyim bi-Ymei ha-Ge'onim," in *Memorial Volume for Chief Rabbi J. H. Herzog* (Jerusalem, 5722/1962), p. 494.
6. Ibid., pp. 492–506.
7. *Responsa* (Pittsburgh, 5717/1957), No. 221.
8. Cf. his commentary on Ex. 21:1.
9. *Takkanot Shum*, ed. Abraham Epstein (Berlin, 5670/1910), pp. 70–71.
10. Cf. B. M. Levin, *Otzar ha-Ge'onim, Bava Kamma* (Jerusalem, 5703/1943), Responsa, No. 227.
11. *Mishneh Torah, Hil. Sanhedrin* XXVI, 7.
12. Louis Finkelstein, *Jewish Self-Government in the Middle Ages* (New York, 1924), p. 156, n. 1.
13. Ibid., p. 42; full text, pp. 152 f., translation, pp. 155 f.
14. For example, Naḥmanides (cf. S. Assaf, *Sifran shel Rishonim* [Jerusalem, 5695/1935], p. 98); the Council of Ferrara, Italy, in 1554 (cf. Finkelstein, op. cit., pp. 301 f.); Rabbi Joseph Caro (*Shulḥan Arukh, Ḥoshen Mishpat* 26, 1, 2); the Rabbinical Conference of Frankfurt-on-Main, 1603 (cf. Marcus Horovitz, *Die Frankfurter Rabbinerversammlung v. Jahre 1603* [Frankfurt-on-Main, 1897], pp. 20 f.; Finkelstein, op. cit., pp. 79 f. and 257 f.); Rabbi Ezekiel Landau of Prague (*Derushei ha-Tzelah* 8, 14; 22, 24).
15. *Codex Theodoseanus* II, ii, 10 (published in 438 C.E., and tanslated by Clyde Pharr, Princeton, 1952).
16. S. Assaf, *Batei ha-Din ve-Sidreihem Aharei Ḥatimat ha-Talmud* (Jerusalem, 5684/1924), pp. 57 f.
17. E.g., "Bishop of the Jews" in medieval England, *Judenrichter* in German-speaking countries, etc.
18. S. W. Baron, *A Social and Religious History of the Jews*, 2d ed. (New York, 1952–69), Vol. XI, pp. 64 f. and notes.
19. Assaf, *Batei ha-Din*, pp. 38 f.
20. Ibid., p. 38.
21. *Talmud Yerushalmi, Mo'ed Katan* 82a.
22. Menahem Elon, *Ha-Mishpat ha-Ivri* (Jerusalem, 5733/1973), pp. 87 and 645 f.; full text of the *Takkanah* is given by Finkelstein, op. cit., p. 356; cf. also Ben-Sasson, op. cit., pp. 84 f.
23. Assaf, *Batei ha-Din*, pp. 51 f.; idem, "Le-Korot ha-Rabbanut," in *Reshumot*, ed. Druyanov, II (5687/1927), pp. 259 f.

24. *Mishnah, Bekhorot* 4.6; and Rabbi Obadiah of Bertinoro's commentary on same.

25. Assaf, op. cit., pp. 93 f.

26. *Sh. Ar., Hoshen Mishpat* 123–124; Assaf, op. cit., pp. 95 f., also quotes many sources from other times; cf. also Baron, op. cit., IV, pp. 215 f., and a short article by Rav Tza'ir (Haim Tchernovitz), "Ha-Sanegoriyah be-Vatei Dinim shel Yisra'el," *Hashiloah*, III (1898), pp. 418 f.

27. The question was often discussed in Rabbinic literature: cf. Rashi, *Responsa*, ed. Elfenbein (New York, 5703/1943), No. 224; Maharam of Rothenburg, *Responsa*, Prague No. 357, Cremona No. 246; and Rashba, *Responsa*, I, No. 743; III, No. 141.

28. *Talmud Bavli, Sanhedrin* 31b.

29. Quoted by Ben-Zion Dinur, *Yisra'el ba-Golah* (Tel Aviv, 1961–71), Vol. III, p. 98 and n. 47.

30. *Responsa*, Prague No. 917; Cremona No. 280.

31. *Mishneh Torah, Sanhedrin* VI, 6.

32. *Responsa* (Jerusalem, 5720/1960), No. 13.

33. According to Abraham Neuman, *The Jews in Spain: Their Social, Political, and Cultural Life during the Middle Ages* (Philadelphia, 1942), Vol. I, p. 168.

34. Israel Heilprin (ed.), *Takkanot Medinat Mähren* (Jerusalem, 5713/1953), No. 379, p. 125.

35. On penalties, cf. S. Assaf's special book, *Ha-Onshin Aharei Hatimat ha-Talmud* (Jerusalem, 5682/1922).

36. *Sh. Ar., Hoshen Mishpat* 2; Asheri, *Responsa* XVII, 1.

37. Yitzhak Baer, *A History of the Jews in Christian Spain*, Vol. I (Philadelphia, 1961), pp. 232, 315, 323, etc.

38. For details, see M. Elon, "Ha-Ma'asar ba-Mishpat ha-Ivri," in *Sefer Yovel* [Jubilee Volume] *le-Pinhas Rosen* (Jerusalem, 1962).

39. Cf. Selma Stern, *Der Preussische Staat und die Juden*, Vol. II (1962), index, s.v. "Bann."

40. Assaf, *Batei ha-Din*, pp. 25 f.; Dinur, op. cit., Vol. I, 3, p. 332.

41. *Talmud Yerushalmi, Pe'ah* 15d, where it is said that if someone refuses to feed his father, "the synagogue may be locked before him."

42. F. Rosenthal, "Einiges über die Tekanoth des R. Gerschom b. Jehuda, der 'Leuchte des Exils,'" in: *Jubelschrift zum 70. Geburtstag des Dr. Israel Hildesheimer* (Berlin, 1890), pp. 49 f. The custom was mentioned in *Jüdische Merkwürdigkeiten*, a notorious work by J. J. Schudt (1714–18, IV, 2, p. 351), under the designation of "Klamer." This word has been explained by some as deriving from the English "claim" or "clamor," and by others as stemming from the Hebrew *ani kela'o*, "I lock him out."

43. Cf. Elon, op. cit., p. 11.

CHAPTER TWO: *Jewish Courts in Individual Countries* (pp. 9–72)

Eretz Yisrael, pp. 9–15.

1. See Jacob Mann, *The Jews in Egypt and in Palestine under the Fatimid Caliphs* (New York reprint, 1970), Vols. I, pp. 65–66, and II, pp. 49, 53.

2. There is, however, no proof that this title refers to the head of a *Beth Din* or academy as such.

3. S. Assaf, *Mekorot u-Mehkarim be-Toledot Yisra'el* (Jerusalem, 5706/1946), p. 24.

4. Ibid., p. 31.

5. Ibid., pp. 10, 44.

6. Ibid., p. 11; *Sefer ha-Yishuv*, ed. S. Assaf and L. A. Mayer (Jerusalem, 5704/1944), Vol. II, p. 9.

7. Mann, op. cit., Vols. I, p. 179, and II, p. 216; *Sefer ha-Yishuv*, Vol. II, pp. 32 f.

8. This fact, among others, demonstrates the existence of a Palestinian Gaonate,

similar to that of Babylonia; for details see S. D. Goitein, *A Mediterranean Society: The Jewish Community of the Arab World as Portrayed in the Documents of the Cairo Geniza* (Berkeley, 1971), Vol. II, pp. 33 f., 311–327, and notes on pp. 594 f.

9. Sh. H. Kook, *Iyyunim u-Mehkarim*, Vol. II (Jerusalem, 5723/1963) p. 137.

10. Avraham Yaari, *Iggerot Eretz Yisra'el* (Ramat Gan, 1971), pp. 155 f.

11. See A. L. Frumkin, *Sefer Toledot Hakhmei Yerushalayim* (during the years 5250–5630, i.e., 1490–1870), ed. E. Rivlin, 3 pts. (Jerusalem, 5688–5690/1928–30), passim.

12. For details, see H. Graetz, *Geschichte der Juden*, Vol. IX (Leipzig, 1866), pp. 301 f.; and H. H. Ben-Sasson, *Toledot Am Yisra'el bi-Ymei ha-Beinayim* (Tel Aviv, 1969), pp. 264 f.

13. H. S. Dimitrovsky, "Vikku'ah she-avar bein Maran R. Yosef Karo ve-Hamabit," in *Sefer Tzefat*, ed. I. Ben-Zvi and M. Benayahu, I (Jerusalem, 5722/1962), pp. 73 f.

14. Norman Bentwich, "The Application of Jewish Law in Palestine," *Journal of Comparative Legislation and International Law*, 3d series, IX (1927), pp. 59 f.; and A. H. Freimann, "Dinei Yisra'el be-Eretz Yisra'el," in Ya'akov Bazak, *Ha-Mishpat ha-Ivri bi-Medinat Yisra'el* (Jerusalem, 1969), pp. 36 f.

15. *Ha-Mishpat ha-Ivri* (periodical) (Tel Aviv, 5686–96/1926–36); Y. Adler, *Mishpat ha-Shalom ha-Ivri be-Eretz Yisra'el* (Jerusalem, 5697/1937), passim; Paltiel Daykan (Dikstein), *Toledot ha-Mishpat ha-Shalom ha-Ivri* (Tel Aviv, 1964).

16. Mordecai ben Hillel ha-Cohen, "Le-Toledot Mishpat ha-Shalom ha-Ivri," in *Mishpat ha-Shalom ha-Ivri*, I (5686/1926), pp. 3 f; M. Elon, "Mishpat ha-Shalom ha-Ivri," *Israel Law Review*, III (July 1968), No. 3, p. 427.

17. Daykan, op. cit., pp. 14 f.

18. Proclamation, *Ordinances and Notices by Occupied Enemy Territory Administration (O.E.T.A.)*, South, Courts, p. 9, No. 42.

19. For a detailed report of the meetings of this Assembly, see *Hator* (5681/1921), Nos. 18, 21, 22.

20. Ibid.

21. Drayton, *Laws of Palestine*, Vol. III, pp. 2581 f.

22. Elon, op. cit. The regulations were published in a special booklet by the Chief Rabbinate.

23. Elon, in *Ha-Mishpat ha-Ivri*, pp. 74 f.

24. Daykan, op. cit., p. 28; Elon, "*Mishpat ha-Shalom ha-Ivri*," p. 422.

25. Full text in *Ha-Mishpat, Yarhon la-Mishpat ha-Iyyuni ve-ha-Shimmushi*, ed. S. Eisenstadt, II (1927), pp. 256 ff., 299 f.

26. Full text, cf. Adler, op. cit., pp. 10 f.

27. Elon, "Mishpat ha-Shalom ha-Ivri," ibid.

28. Such as cases of the institutions of the Jewish community; cf. Daykan, op. cit., pp. 31 f., and his (and other authors') articles in the aforementioned periodicals.

29. See also Elon, "Mishpat ha-Shalom ha-Ivri," pp. 423 f.

30. For details of these courts, see Y. Bar-Shira, in *Ha-Mishpat*, I (1927), pp. 49 f.

31. Haim Harubi, *Ha-Shipput ha-Tenu'ati be-Moshevei ha-Ovedim* (Tel Aviv, 1962).

Babylonia (Iraq), pp 15–17.

1. E.g., *Talmud Bavli, Megillah* 16b.

2. *Talmud Yerushalmi, Megillah* 75a; *Talmud Bavli, Bava Kamma* 82a.

3. For a detailed historical survey, see Jacob Neusner, *History of the Jews in Babylonia*, 5 vols. (1965–70).

4. Moshe Beer, *Al ha-Yehudim be-Bavel bi-Tekufat ha-Mishnah ve-ha-Talmud* (Tel Aviv, 1970), pp. 57 f.

5. Louis Ginzberg, *Geonica*, I (New York, 1909), pp. 1–71.

6. E.g., Baron, *Social and Religious History of the Jews*, 2d ed., Vol. V, pp. 14 f., 20 f.; Leo Landman, *Jewish Law in the Diaspora: Confrontation and Accommodation* (Philadelphia, 1968), pp. 28 f.

7. Quoted by Assaf, *Batei ha-Din*, pp. 47 f.

8. For the following section, see Abraham Ben-Jacob, *Yehudei Bavel mi-Sof Tekufat ha-Ge'onim ad Yameinu, 1038–1960* (Jerusalem, 5725/1965).
9. M. Benayahu, *Marbitz Torah* (Jerusalem, 5713/1953), pp. 119 f.
10. Ibid., p. 103.
11. Ibid., pp. 119 f.
12. Ben-Jacob, op. cit., pp. 275 f.
13. Assaf, op. cit., p. 54, n. 4.
14. Ben-Jacob, op. cit., p. 273.
15. Ibid., p. 277

Italy, pp. 17–23.

1. For details, see Cecil Roth, *A History of the Jews in Italy* (Philadelphia, 1946), passim.
2. Josephus, *Antiquities* XIV, 7.2, 10.1–3; *Contra Apionem* II, 4.
3. *Antiquities* XVI, 6.1.
4. Ibid., XIX, 5.2. For more details, see Emil Schürer, *A History of the Jewish People in the Time of Jesus* (Edinburgh, 1924), Div. II, Vol. II, pp. 259 f., 276 f.; Jean Juster, *Les Juifs dans l'Empire Romain* (Paris, 1914), Vol. II, pp. 110 f.; Dora Askowitch, *The Toleration of the Jews under Julius Caesar and Augustus* (New York, 1915), pp. 192 f.
5. *Antiquities* XII, 3.1.
6. Abraham Berliner, *Geschichte der Juden in Rom* (Frankfurt-on-Main, 1893), pp. 67 f., 95 f.
7. *Talmud Bavli, Sanhedrin* 32b; Hermann Vogelstein and Paul Rieger, *Geschichte der Juden in Rom,* I (Berlin, 1895–96), pp. 31, 49.
8. Vogelstein and Rieger, op. cit., p. 129; Solomon Katz, *The Jews in the Visigothic and Frankish Kingdoms of Spain and Gaul* (Cambridge, Mass., 1937), pp. 106 f.
9. Assaf, *Batei ha-Din,* p. 54; Roth, op. cit., pp. 76, 124, 297; M. A. Shulvass, *Hayyei ha-Yehudim be-Italyah bi-Tekufat ha-Renaissance* (New York, 5715/1955), p. 177.
10. Vogelstein and Rieger, op. cit., p. 263.
11. Ibid., p. 342.
12. Ibid., p. 347; J. E. Scherer, *Die Rechtsverhältnisse der Juden in den Deutsch-Oesterreichischen Ländern* (Leipzig, 1901), Vol. I, p. 280.
13. Vogelstein and Rieger, op. cit., p. 416.
14. Berliner, op. cit., p. 99.
15. Vogelstein and Rieger, op. cit., pp. 330, 360.
16. Scherer, op. cit.
17. Finkelstein, op. cit., p. 92; for full text of the decision, see p. 301.
18. Ibid.; Assaf, op. cit., pp. 22–23.
19. Roth, op. cit., pp. 333, 368 f.
20. M. D. Cassuto, *Ha-Yehudim be-Firenze bi-Tekufat ha-Renaissance,* trans. from the Italian by M. Artom (Jerusalem, 1962), pp. 151 f.
21. Ibid., p. 156.
22. Baron, *The Jewish Community* (Philadelphia, 1942), Vol. I, pp. 275–276.
23. *Israelitische Annalen,* ed. I. M. Jost (1840), No. 13.
24. Roth, op. cit., pp. 348, 368 f.
25. For details concerning the Jews in the Duchy of Mantua, see Shlomo Simonsohn, *Toledot ha-Yehudim be-Dukkasut Mantovah* (Jerusalem, 2 vols., 1962–64); and, for the later period, idem, "Hitargenut ha-Shilton ha-Otonomi ha-Yehudi be-Mantovah, 1511–1630," in *Zion,* XXI (5716/1956), pp. 143–182.
26. *Responsa,* Part I, No. 745.
27. Simonsohn, *Toledot,* pp. 3, 233.
28. Ibid., pp. 256 f.
29. Jewish National and University Library, Jerusalem, Ms. Heb. 8°1995, quoted by Simonsohn, ibid., p. 237.
30. Published originally by Moses Zacuto himself (Mantua, 5438/1678); reprinted by A. Cahane in *Hagoren,* III, pp. 180 f., and partly by Assaf, *Batei ha-Din,* pp. 130 f.

31. Simonsohn, "Ha-Ghetto be-Italyah u-Mishtaro," in *Isaac Baer Jubilee Volume* (Jerusalem, 5721/1961), pp. 270 f.
32. Published and edited by Benjamin Klaar (Jerusalem, 5704/1944).
33. Ibid., p. 17, and passim.
34. See Klaar's notes, ibid., p. 161.
35. See also Joshua Starr, "The Jews in the Byzantine Empire," *Texte für Forschung zur Byzantisch-Neugriechischen Philologie*, No. 30 (Athens, 1939); Baron, *The Jewish Community*, Vol. I, p. 231.
36. Scherer, op. cit., pp. 280 f.
37. Baron, op. cit., Vol. I, p. 292.
38. Shulvass, op. cit., p. 95.
39. Assaf, op. cit., p. 90.
40. Ibid., p. 61.
41. Baron, op. cit., Vol. I, p. 275; Roth, op. cit., pp. 368 f.; Shulvass, in his introduction to Simhah Luzzatto's *Ma'amar al Yehudei Venetziyah* (Jerusalem, 5711/1951), pp. 14–15, n. 7.

The Iberian Peninsula, pp. 24–33.

1. Y. Baer, "Ha-Hathalot ve-ha-Yesodot shel Irgun ha-Kehillot ha-Yehudiyot bi-Ymei ha-Beinayim," in *Zion*, XV (5710/1950), pp. 1 f.; Haim Beinart, "Hispano-Jewish Society," in *Journal of World History*, XI (1968), p. 227.
2. Solomon Katz, *The Jews in the Visigothic and Frankish Kingdoms*, p. 106.
3. For details, cf. ibid.
4. Assaf, *Batei ha-Din*, p. 48.
5. Eliahu Ashtor, *Korot ha-Yehudim bi-Sefarad ha-Muslemit*, Vol. II (Jerusalem, 1966), p. 236.
6. Ibid., Vol. I (1960), p. 185.
7. Ibid., Vol. II, p. 239.
8. Landman (*Jewish Law in the Diaspora*, p. 91) sees in the many Spanish *Takkanot* against Gentile courts a proof that such courts were often used by Jews for litigations against their fellow Jews.
9. Baer, *Christian Spain*, Vol. I, pp. 86 f.; Neuman, *The Jews in Spain*, Vol. I, pp. 19 f.
10. Baer, op. cit., pp. 159, 175, etc.
11. E.g., Adret, *Responsa*, V, No. 284; Rosh, *Responsa*, VI, 11; Baer, op. cit., pp. 233 f.; Beinart, op. cit., pp. 231 f.
12. Assaf, op. cit., pp. 86, 75–76; Baer, op. cit., I, pp. 212 f.; Neuman, op. cit., Vol. II, pp. 86 f. The latter two generally rely on Responsa literature of the time.
13. Neuman, op. cit., Vol. I, pp. 153 f.
14. Ibid., pp. 147–148.
15. Baer, op. cit., pp. 212 f.
16. Assaf, op. cit., p. 55; Zerah Wahrhaftig, "Dinei Borerut ba-Mishpat ha-Ivri," in *Memorial Volume for Rabbi I. H. Herzog* (Jerusalem, 5722/1962), p. 513, n. 60.
17. *Responsa*, I, No. 743.
18. Neuman, op. cit., Vol. I, pp. 117 f.
19. Scherer, *Rechtsverhältnisse*, Vol. I, p. 267.
20. Baer, op. cit., Vol. I, pp. 315 f.; Beinart, op. cit., pp. 235 f.
21. Baer, op. cit., pp. 51, 131, 173.
22. Ibid., p. 224.
23. Ibid., pp. 115 f., 118 f., 214.
24. Scherer, op. cit., Vol. I, p. 267.
25. Baer, op. cit., p. 310.
26. Rosh, *Responsa*, CVII, 6, reports a trial held by order of the queen.
27. *Responsa*, xviii, 8.
28. *Sefer Zikhron Yehudah*, No. 63.
29. Baer, op. cit., Vol. II, p. 118; Neuman, op. cit., Vol. I, p. 113, note.

30. Scherer, op. cit., Vol. I, pp. 267 f.; Baron, *Social and Religious History,* 2d ed., Vol. XI, p. 69.
31. Graetz, *Geschichte,* Vol. VIII, n. 4, 1; Baer, op. cit., Vol. II, pp. 260 f.
32. Baer, op. cit., p. 269.
33. Assaf, op. cit., p. 75; Baer, op. cit., pp. 167 f. For full text of the *Takkanot,* see Finkelstein, op. cit., pp. 356 f.
34. Baer, op. cit., pp. 314 f.; Neuman, op. cit., Vol. II, p. 272.
35. Baer, op. cit., Vol. I, p. 86.
36. Ibid., p. 143; idem, *Urkunden und Regesten zur Geschichte der Juden im Christlichen Spanien* (Berlin, 1929), Vol. I, pp. 92, 96, 113.
37. Baer, *Christian Spain,* Vol. I, pp. 215 f.; Neumann, op. cit., Vol. I, pp. 15 f., 145 f.
38. Baer, *Christian Spain,* pp. 223, 231 f.; *Urkunden,* Vol. I, pp. 133 f., 154 f., etc.
39. Baer, *Christian Spain,* Vol. II, pp. 21 f.; Beinart, op. cit., p. 228.
40. Baer, *Urkunden,* Vol. I, p. 847.
41. Baer, *Christian Spain,* Vol. II, p. 51; Baron, *The Jewish Community,* Vol. I, pp. 238 f.
42. M. Kayserling, *Geschichte der Juden in Portugal* (Leipzig, 1867).
43. Scherer, op. cit., Vol. I, pp. 233 f.
44. Graetz, op. cit., Vol. VIII, pp. 487 f.

Central and Western Europe, pp. 33–46.

1. Moshe Frank, *Kehillot Ashkenaz u-Vatei Dineihen* (Tel Aviv, 5698/1938), pp. vi, 20 f.
2. Ibid., and Assaf, op. cit., pp. 52 f.
3. Julius Aronius, *Regesten zur Geschichte der Juden im Fränkischen und Deutschen Reich bis zum Jahre 1273* (Berlin, 1902), No. 78.
4. Otto Stobbe, *Die Juden in Deutschland während des Mittelalters* (Brunswick, 1886; reprinted Amsterdam, 1969), p. 6.
5. Assaf, op. cit., p. 18.
6. Aronius, op. cit., Nos. 168, 170, 171; Stobbe, op. cit., p. 142; Scherer, op. cit., pp. 170 f., 254–256; Guido Kisch, *The Jews in Medieval Germany* (Chicago, 1949), pp. 101 f.; idem, in *Forschungen zur Rechts und Sozialgeschichte der Juden* (Stuttgart, 1955), pp. 104 f., 134 f.
7. Frank, op. cit., p. 62.
8. Aronius, op. cit., Nos. 282, 459, 488, 496; Stobbe, op. cit., p. 81; Herbert Fischer, *Die Verfassungsrechtliche Stellung der Juden in den Deutschen Städten* (reprint Aalen, 1969), pp. 13 f., 125, 130, 170.
9. Berthold Bretholz, *Quellen zur Geschichte der Juden in Mähren* (Prague, 1935), Nos. 56, 77, 85, etc.
10. M. Wiener, *Regesten zur Geschichte der Juden in Deutschland während des Mittelalters* (Hanover, 1863), pp. 63 f.
11. Ibid., pp. 95, 99.
12. Irving A. Agus, *Rabbi Meir of Rothenburg* (Philadelphia, 1947), Vol. I, pp. 14 f.; J. Kahan, "Or Sarua als Geschichtsquelle," in *Jahrbuch der Gesellschaft für Geschichte der Juden in der CSR,* IX (1938), pp. 56 f.
13. Finkelstein, *Self-Government,* p. 228.
14. Kisch, *Jews,* pp. 62 f., 172 f., etc.
15. G. Wolf, "Zur Geschichte der Juden in Oesterreich," in *Zeitschrift zur Geschichte der Juden in Deutschland,* ed. Geiger, I (1887).
16. Alfred F. Pribram, *Urkunden und Akten zur Geschichte der Juden in Wien,* Allg. Teil (Vienna, 1918), Vol. I, pp. 115 f.; Assaf, op. cit., p. 81.
17. Israel Heilprin (ed.), *Takkanot Medinat Mähren, 5410–5548* (Jerusalem, 5712/1952).
18. Published in part by Simon Adler in *Jahrbuch der Gesellschaft für Geschichte der Juden in der CSR,* III (1931), pp. 217 f.

19. Kook, *Iyyunim u-Mehkarim*, Vol. I (5721/1961), pp. 179 f.

20. Pribram, op. cit., Vols. I, pp. 522 f, and II, pp. 561 f.

21. Marcus Horovitz, *Die Frankfurter Rabbinerversammlung*.

22. I. Kracauer, in *Zeitschrift zur Geschichte der Juden in Deutschland*, ed. Geiger, III (1889), pp. 348 f.; Rabbi Ya'ir Haim Bacharach, *Responsa Havvot Ya'ir*, No. 2, etc.

23. Assaf, op. cit., p. 83.

24. Heilprin, op. cit., Nos. 547, 584, etc.

25. I. M. Jost, *Geschichte der Israeliten*, Vol. XI (Berlin, 1846), p. 368.

26. C. E. Koch, *Die Juden in Preussen* (Marienwerder, 1833), pp. 129 f.; Joseph Meisl, *Pinkas Kehillat Berlin*, ed. Shaul Esh (Jerusalem, 5722/1962), pars. 8, 84, 106–107.

27. Yehezkel Kaufmann, *Golah ve-Nekhar*, Vol. II (Tel Aviv, 5690/1930), pp. 36 f.; Azriel Shohet, *Im Hillufei Tekufot* (Jerusalem, 1960), passim.

28. See Mendelssohn's introduction to the translation by Marcus Herz of Menasseh ben Israel's *Vindiciae Judaeorum*, in *Gesammelte Schriften* (Leipzig, 1843), Vol. III, p. 299.

29. Wilhelm Freund, *Zur Judenfrage in Deutschland* (Berlin, 1843), Vol. I, p. 118.

30. Scherer, op. cit., p. 638.

31. Alfred Wienre, "Al Yissud Bet Din shel Borerut," in *Hamishpat*, II (1927), p. 141 (from the *Gemeindeblatt der Berliner Jüdischen Gemeinde*).

32. According to written information received (in December 1973) from Rabbi H. I. Grünewald of Munich.

33. For details concerning Jews in Switzerland, see Augusta (Welder) Steinberg, *Studien zur Geschichte der Juden in der Schweiz während des Mittelalters* (Zurich, 1902), and *Geschichte der Juden in der Schweiz vom 16. Jahrhundert bis nach der Emanzipation*, ed. Florence Guggenheim-Grünberg, 2 vols. (Zurich, 1966, 1970), passim.

34. S. Katz, op. cit., p. 157.

35. Scherer, op. cit., pp. 252 f.

36. Assaf, op. cit., p. 48.

37. Frank, op. cit., p. 62.

38. Finkelstein, op. cit., p. 92; for text of the *Takkanot*, see pp. 301 f.

39. Scherer, op. cit., pp. 260 f.

40. Graetz, *Geschichte*, Vol. VIII, p. 10.

41. L. Bardinet, "Antiquité et Organisation des Juiveries du Comtat Venaissin," in *Revue des Etudes Juives*, I (1880), pp. 262 f.

42. Bernhard Blumenkranz, *Histoire des Juifs de France* (Toulouse, 1972), pp. 96 f.

43. Ibid., pp. 120 f.

44. The text of these privileges was published by M. de Boug in a rare work, *Recueil des Edits, Déclarations, etc.* (Colmar, 1775), Vol. II, pp. 365–366, 419, 693, 765–766; see also Zosa Szajkowski, *Franco-Judaica* (New York, 1962).

45. Blumenkranz, op. cit., p. 275.

46. Ibid., p. 278.

47. Baron, *The Jewish Community*, 2d ed., XV (1973), p. 39.

48. Salomon Ullman, "Geschichte der Spanisch-Portugiesischen Juden in Amsterdam im 17. Jahrhundert," in *Jahrbuch für Jüdische Literatur und Geschichte*, V (1907), pp. 1 f.

49. Baron, op. cit., p. 34.

50. Scherer, op. cit., pp. 92, 277; Charles Egan, *The Status of the Jews in England* (London, 1848), pp. 8 f.

51. Hermann Adler, *Papers*, Anglo-Jewish History Exhibition (London, 1887); Joseph Jacobs, *The Jews of Angevin England: Documents and Records* (London, 1893), pp. 45, 89, 184 f.; Michael Adler, "Aaron of York," in *Transactions*, Jewish Historical Society of England, XIII (1936), pp. 113 f.

52. H. P. Stokes, *Studies in Anglo-Jewish History* (Edinburgh, 1918), pp. 4 f., 37 f., 48 f.; Cecil Roth, *A History of the Jews in England* (Oxford, 1941), pp. 29 f.; idem "Elijah of London," in *Transactions*, Jewish Historical Society of England, XV (1946).

53. Vivian D. Lipman, *The Jews of Medieval Norwich* (London, 1967), p. 150.

54. Stokes, op. cit., p. 50.
55. H. G. Richardson, *The English Jewry under Angevin Kings* (London, 1960), p. 150.
56. Roth, *England*, pp. 89, 104.
57. Egan, op. cit., p. 26; Roth, *England*, p. 188.
58. Egan, op. cit., p. 35.
59. L. Dushinsky, "The Rabbinate of the Great Synagogue in London from 1756 to 1842," in *Jewish Quarterly Review*, N.S. IX (1918–19), pp. 37 f., and X (1919–20), pp. 445 f.
60. Dayan A. Feldman, "The London Beth Din," in *Juridical Review*, XLI (London, 1929), pp. 1 f.
61. *T.A.C. Constitution and Rules* (revised edition, 1945), and other publications, proceedings, etc., of the T.A.C.

Eastern Europe, pp. 46–51.

1. S. M. Dubnow, *History of the Jews in Russia and Poland*, trans. I. Friedlaender (Philadelphia, 1916–20), Vol. I, pp. 45 f. On the *Voivoda* and his functions as Judge of the Jews, see Benjamin Cohen, in *Galed, Me'assef be-Toledot Yahadut Polin*, Tel Aviv University, Vol. I (1973), pp. 1 f.
2. Dubnow, op. cit., pp. 51 f.
3. Ibid., pp. 61 f.
4. H. H. Ben-Sasson, "Toledot Yisra'el bi-Ymei ha-Beinayim," in *Toledot Am Yisra'el*, II (Tel Aviv, 1969), p. 270.
5. Dubnow, op. cit., p. 72.
6. Ibid., p. 103.
7. Ibid., p. 73.
8. Ibid., pp. 83 f., 105 f.; Raphael Mahler, *Toledot ha-Yehudim be-Polin* (Merhavia, 1946), pp. 139, 153.
9. For this period, see Dubnow, op. cit., pp. 108 f., 188 f.; Ben-Sasson, op. cit., pp. 270 f.; Jacob Katz, *Masoret u-Mashber* (Jerusalem, 5718/1958), pp. 157 f.
10. Assaf, *Batei ha-Din*, pp. 57 f.; Elon, op. cit., p. 10, n. 20. For Posen, see Dov Avron, *Pinkas ha-Kesherim shel Kehillat Pozna ("Acta Electorum Communitatis Judaeorum Posnansiensium") 1621–1835* (Jerusalem, 5727/1966), passim.
11. Elon, op. cit., ibid.
12. Edited by Israel Heilprin (Jerusalem, 5705/1945); cf. the editor's introduction. On the courts of this council, see also N. N. Hannover, *Yeven Metzulah*, an account of the persecutions of 1648–49 (Tel Aviv, 5726/1966), p. 90.
13. Ben-Sasson, op. cit., p. 277
14. S. Dubnow, ed., *Pinkas ha-Medinah, o Pinkas Va'ad ha-Kehillot ha-Rashiyyot bi-Medinat Lita* (Berlin, 1925).
15. Ibid., No. 48 (from 1623), No. 171 (from 1628).
16. Ibid., No. 12 (from 1623), No. 113 (from 1627), and No. 328 (from 1639); Heilprin, op. cit., No. 911 (from before 1756).
17. Dubnow, *Pinkas ha-Medinah*, No. 683 (from 1673), No. 788 (from 1684).
18. Ibid., No. 819 (from 1687); No. 851 (from 1691).
19. Katz, op. cit., p. 159.
20. Assaf, op. cit., pp. 16, 49, 55; Ben-Sasson, op. cit., pp. 273 f.; Heilprin and Dubnow, many items. According to Baron (*The Jewish Community*, 1st ed., Vol. II, p. 63), the lower court of Cracow acted as a Minor *Sanhedrin* and was composed of twenty-three members.
21. See, for example, Heilprin, op. cit., No. 308 (from 1672) and No. 437 (from 1688); Dubnow, *Pinkas ha-Medinah*, No. 364 (from 1639) and No. 888 (from 1695).
22. Dubnow, *Pinkas ha-Medinah*, No. 817 (from 1687); Heilprin, op. cit., No. 841 (from 1766).
23. Martin Philippson, *Neueste Geschichte des Jüdischen Volkes*, I (1907), p. 52.
24. Mahler, op. cit., p. 448.

25. Dubnow, *History*, Vol. I, pp. 309 f.; Isaac Levitats, *The Jewish Community in Russia 1772–1844* (New York, 1943), p. 200.

26. Dubnow, *History*, pp. 274 f.

27. Ibid., pp. 344, 366 f.

28. This item and those following are based on information supplied by former leaders of Soviet Jewry who emigrated to Israel.

29. Cf. above, Section on Eretz Yisrael.

30. Daykan, *Toledot ha-Mishpat ha-Ivri*, p. 19.

31. Benjamin Pinkus, "Batei ha-Mishpat be-Idish bi-Verit ha-Mo'etzot," in *Haever*, XVIII (Iyyar, 5731), pp. 124 f.

32. E. Singer, "Die Juden in Bulgarien Einst and Jetzt," in *Menorah*, V (Vienna, 1927), pp. 543 f.

33. Haim Kashales, *Korot Yehudei Bulgariyah* (Tel Aviv, 1971–73), Vol I, pp. 249 f.

34. Ibid., Vol. II, pp. 208 f.; Assaf, op. cit., p. 85 (on the high court).

The Ottoman Empire and Yemen, pp. 51–55.

1. Graetz, *Geschichte*, VIII (1864), p. 215.

2. Leah Bornstein, "Mivneh ha-Hanhagah ha-Ruhanit u-Vatei ha-Din ha-Yehudim ba-Imperiyah ha-Ottomanit" (M.A. thesis, Bar Ilan University, 1972), p. 79.

3. Assaf, op. cit., pp. 19 f., 111.

4. Morris S. Goodblatt, *Jewish Life in Turkey in the 16th Century* (New York, 1952), pp. 86 f.

5. Bornstein, op. cit., pp. 121 f.

6. Ibid., passim.

7. Ibid., pp. 158 f., where detailed information about the composition and functions of these various courts is supplied.

8. Ibid., p. 26.

9. Barukh Uziel (ed.), *Ginzakh Saloniki*, Vol. I (Tel Aviv, 5721/1961), p. 14.

10. Cf. various works by Abraham Galanté: *Histoire des Juifs de Rhodes* (Istanbul, 1935), p. 32; *Histoire des Juifs d'Anatolie* (Istanbul, 1937–39), Vol. I, p. 47; and different quotations in his *Documents officiels turcs concernant les Juifs de Turquie* (Istanbul, 1931–).

11. A. Ben-Jacob, *Kehillot Yehudei Kurdistan* (Jerusalem, 5721/1961), pp. 46, 48, 141.

12. David Benvenisti, *Yehudei Saloniki ba-Dorot ha-Aharonim* (Jerusalem, 5733/1973), p. 162.

13. Bornstein, op. cit., p. 138; Assaf, op. cit., p. 77.

14. As known from a letter of 1153; cf. E. Strauss (Ashtor), in *Zion*, IV (1939), pp. 226 f.

15. For this and the following section, cf. S. D. Goitein, "Al ha-Hayyim ha-Tzibburiyyim shel ha-Yehudim be-Eretz Teiman," in *Mordecai M. Kaplan Jubilee Volume* (New York, 1953), Hebrew section, pp. 50 f.; and Yosef Kapah, *Halikhot Teiman* (Jerusalem, 5721/1961), pp. 69 f.

North Africa, pp. 55–61.

1. For a general survey of Jewish history in these countries, see H. S. Hirschberg, *Toledot ha-Yehudim be-Afrikah ha-Tzefonit*, 2 vols. (Jerusalem, 1965), and S. D. Goitein, *A Mediterranean Society* (1971).

2. Hirschberg, op. cit., Vol. I, pp. 161 f.

3. S. Assaf, *Mekorot u-Mehkarim*, p. 137; Jacob Mann, *The Jews . . . under the Fatimid Caliphs*, p. 266; Goitein, op. cit. Vol. II, pp. 22 f., 266.

4. Goitein, op. cit., pp. 38, 54.

5. Assaf, op. cit., p. 160.

6. Ibid., pp. 137, 171; Hirschberg, op. cit., pp. 163 f., 246 f.

7. Assaf, *Batei ha-Din*, p. 48; Goitein, op. cit., p. 315.

8. Mann, op. cit., pp. 337 f.

9. See Maimonides, *Kovetz Teshuvot* (Leipzig, 5619/1859), No. 140; A. Cahen, *Les Juifs de l'Afrique Septentrionale* (Constantinople, 1867), quoted by Abraham Hershman, R. *Yitzhak bar Sheshet* (Jerusalem, 5716/1956), p. 25; Assaf, op. cit., p. 17; J. Mann, in *Jewish Quarterly Review*, N.S. X, pp. 137 f.

10. Julius Fürst, *Geschichte des Karäerthums* (Leipzig, 1862–69), Vol. II, pp. 252, 283.

11. On the *Nagid*, his functions and authority, see Mann, op. cit., Vol. I, pp. 215 f.; E. Ashtor (Strauss), *Toledot ha-Yehudim be-Mitzrayim ve-Suryah* (Jerusalem, 1944, 1951), Vol. II, pp. 237 f.

12. *Megillat Ahima'az*, ed. B. Klar (1944), pp. 43 f.

13. Hirschberg, op. cit., Vol. II, pp. 19, 97; Isidore Epstein, *The Responsa of Rabbi Simeon b. Zemah Duran as a Source of the History of the Jews in North Africa* (London, 1930), pp. 65 f.

14. Ashtor, op. cit., Vol. II, pp. 458 f.

15. Ibid., pp. 237 f. (for Egypt); and Edouard Mouillefarine, *Etude Historique sur la Condition Juridique des Juifs au Maroc*, dissertation, (Paris, 1941), pp. 111, 122 (for Morocco).

16. Ashtor, op. cit., pp. 195 f.

17. *Vilna* (5639/1879), Nos. 393, 506.

18. Epstein, op. cit.

19. Ashtor, op. cit.

20. *Yahadut Luv*, published by the Committee for Libyan Jewish Communities in Israel (Tel Aviv, 1960), pp. 21 f.

21. *Djerba*, no date (probably 5650/1890); this very rare publication includes reports about *Batei Din* between 1815 and 1827, and decisions of different courts until 1865.

22. Raoul Darmon, *La Situation des Cultes en Tunisie* (Paris, 1930), pp. 85 f.; Jacques Chalom, *Les Israélites de Tunisie* (Paris, 1908), pp. 60 f.; R. Arditi, *Recueil des Textes Législatifs et Juridiques Concernant les Israélites de Tunisie de 1857 à 1913* (Tunis, 1915), pp. 144 f.; and Salomon Tibi, *Le Statut Personnel des Israélites et Spécialement des Israélites Tunisiens* (Tunis, 1923), pp. 108 f. (The latter three publications should be studied together.)

23. P. Marty, "Les Institutions Israélites au Maroc," in *Revue des Etudes Islamiques*, IV (1930), pp. 308 f.; Mouillefarine, op cit., pp. 80 f., 126 f.; André Chouraqui, *La Condition Juridique de l'Israélite Marocain* (Paris, 1950), pp. 115 f.

India, pp. 61–63.

1. Padmanabha Menon, *History of Kerala* (Ernakulam, Cochin State, 1924–37), Vol. II, pp. 506 f.; Edward Balfour, *The Cyclopedia of India*, 3d ed. (London, 1885), Vol. II, p. 434.

2. Walter J. Fischel, an authority on Indian Jewry, in *Encyclopaedia Judaica*, V, cols. 621 ff.

3. Menon, op. cit., pp. 521 f.

4. Information supplied by a former member of the Cochin community, Mr. Eliya Ben-Eliahu, who now lives in Israel.

5. Salomon Reimann (ca. 1815–1880), Galician traveler, in his *Massa'ot Shelomoh* (1884): excerpts published in Chief Rabbi Itzhak Nissim's *Benei Yisrael: Pirkei Halakhah* (Jerusalem, 5722/1962), pp. 180 f.; Shifra Stritzower, *Exotic Jewish Communities* (London–New York, 1962), pp. 61 f.

6. Hayim Samuel Kehimkar, *The History of the Bene-Israel of India* (Tel Aviv, 1937), pp. 252 f.

7. Information received directly from Rabbi S. D. Sassoon, a member of one of the most prominent ex-Baghdadi families of Bombay, now resident in Jerusalem.

South Africa and Australia, pp. 63–65.

1. Details concerning *Batei Din* in South Africa have been supplied directly by the

former Chief Rabbi, Dr. L. I. Rabinowitz, and (in writing) by Rabbi A. J. Duschinsky, *Av Beth Din* in Cape Town.

2. Information supplied by Dr. Israel Porush, former Chief Rabbi of Sydney, Australia.

The Western Hemisphere, pp. 65–72.

1. For the earliest period of Jewish settlement in Brazil, see Arnold Wiznitzer, *Jews in Colonial Brazil* (New York, 1960).

2. Fred Bronner and Haim Avni, in *Encyclopaedia Judaica*, III, cols. 408 ff.

3. Information supplied by Rabbi J. Fink (Haifa), a former member of the *Beth Din* in Buenos Aires, and by Rabbi J. Oppenheimer, one of its current members.

4. Information supplied by Rabbi J. M. Shehebar, Sephardi Chief Rabbi of Buenos Aires.

5. Ben G. Kayfetz, in *Encyclopaedia Judaica*, V, cols. 102 ff.

6. Benjamin G. Sack, *History of the Jews in Canada* (Montreal, 1945), Vol. I, p. 61.

7. Details here and in the following section have been supplied by Ben Kayfetz and Saul Hayes of the Canadian Jewish Congress.

8. Israel Goldstein, *A Century of Judaism in New York* (New York, 1930), pp. 30 f.

9. Ibid., p. 31.

10. Ibid., pp. 51 f.

11. Hyman B. Grinstein, *The Rise of the Jewish Community of New York, 1654–1860* (Philadelphia, 1945), p. 15.

12. Edwin Wolf and Maxwell Whiteman, *The History of the Jews of Philadelphia from Colonial Times to the Age of Jackson* (Philadelphia, 1957), p. 133.

13. Grinstein, op. cit., p. 310.

14. Ibid., p. 404.

15. Wolf and Whiteman, op. cit., p. 127.

16. Goldstein, op. cit., pp. 323–339.

17. Ibid., p. 105.

18. Grinstein, op. cit., p. 397; see also Sefton D. Temkin, "A Beth Din for America," in *Perspectives on Jews and Judaism: Essays in Honor of Wolfe Kelman*, ed. Arthur A. Chiel (New York, 1978), pp. 413–420.

19. Grinstein, op. cit., pp. 76, 80.

20. Goldstein, op. cit., pp. 158 f.

21. Arthur A. Goren, *New York Jews and the Quest for Community: The Kehillah Experiment, 1908–1922* (New York, 1970), passim.

22. Goldstein, op. cit., p. 249.

23. Daniel J. Elazar and Stephen A. Goldstein, "The Rabbinical Courts" (part of "The Legal Status of the American Jewish Community"), in *American Jewish Year Book* (1972), pp. 82 f.

24. Ibid.; Goren, op. cit., pp. 198 f.

25. *CCAR Yearbook*, 1897 and following years.

26. Isaac M. Fein, *The Making of a Jewish Community: The History of Baltimore Jews from 1730 to 1920.* (Philadelphia, 1971), pp. 216 f.

27. Elazar and Goldstein, op. cit.

28. Ibid.; Max Vorspan and Lloyd P. Gartner, *History of the Jews of Los Angeles* (San Marino, Calif., 1970), p. 164.

29. Information received from the late Rabbi S. I. Korff, Rabbinical administrator of the court; material published by the tribunal has also been consulted.

Part Two
THE JEWISH
CONCILIATION
BOARD OF AMERICA

Jewish Conciliation Board in session at Madison Street Courthouse, New York City. Right, two litigants at dais are heard by the judges: from left to right, *Hon. Bernard S. Deutsch, Dr. Israel Goldstein, and General David Sarnoff. Far left, JCB Executive Secretary Louis Richman;* right foreground, *three Yiddish press reporters. (Photo: courtesy of The Daily News, New York.)*

III
History of the
Jewish Conciliation
Board of America,
1930–1968

Founding Principles and Organizational Structure

During the past two millennia, autonomous court systems and legal codes have been widely characteristic of Jewish life in diaspora communities. Throughout the generations, and in different lands, the motivating factors were similar: mistrust of the civil court systems, exclusion of the Jews from the normal life of the country, the traditional Jewish ban on the use of Gentile courts, and the synonymity of religious and civil law, as, for example, in Muslim lands.

The immigrant Jews of New York City's Lower East Side, in the 1920s, had their own special needs. These needs led to the setting up of tribunals capable of handling cases in which the complainants were disinclined to have recourse to the ordinary courts of law. In the New World, too, Jews felt uneasy in the regular courts: the English language was unfamiliar to them and the legal procedures were often both cumbersome and costly, involving delays as well as expense. Moreover, the newcomers were reluctant to air internal Jewish disputes publicly, and they had a deep-rooted mistrust of civil courts, following generations of alienation in the countries of Eastern Europe. Many of these immigrants were overawed by a courtroom, and regarded appearances

87

there as an ordeal. Indeed, Gentile judges were often unable to comprehend the uniquely Jewish character of certain cases. Besides, there were the delays and the costs involved in hiring legal representation.

In an attempt to meet the needs of this segment of the New York population, Mr. Louis Richman and Rabbi Samuel Buchler, both lawyers, established the Jewish Arbitration Court in 1919. Their aims were strengthened by the passage of the New York State Arbitration Law in 1920, which upheld the legality of an agreement between two litigants to abide by the decision of a third party. Not only were such arbitration agreements legally valid, but the judgments of such tribunals were enforceable in the same manner as those of the civil courts.

The Jewish Court of Arbitration held its first session on February 18, 1920, in the Grand Jury Room of the New York Criminal Court Building on Madison Street. Operating under a charter granted by the State of New York, it was the first organized institution in the United States devoted exclusively to the settlement of disputes of a specifically Jewish character, in accordance with Jewish law and principles. During the first decade of its existence, it was unfortunately plagued by a variety of internal problems, which culminated in Rabbi Buchler disassociating himself and establishing a rival court. Mr. Louis Richman remained with the Jewish Court of Arbitration, however, as Executive Secretary.

Fourteen years after its first establishment, Rabbi Buchler published an account of the tribunal embodying a number of typical cases.[1] Almost four decades later, another, more popular, work came off the press, written by James Jaffe, who received access to some of the Jewish Conciliation Board's files.[2] Neither book was an authoritative study of the Board's origin, development, and significance. As mentioned in my Foreword, the JCB has itself published a *festschrift* in honor of Rabbi Julius Mark, who succeeded me as President of the Board.[3]

It was out of a deep concern for social justice and for Jewish dignity that, in January 1929, I accepted an invitation by Mr. Richman to participate in the work of this tribunal. In the following year I was elected its President and, shortly thereafter, we arranged for its name to be changed to "The Jewish Conciliation Court," in order to indicate two fundamental characteristics: first, that this tribunal had no

1. Samuel Buchler, *"Cohen Comes First" and Other Cases* (New York: Vanguard Press, 1933).

2. James Jaffe, *So Sue Me! The Story of a Community Court* (New York: Saturday Review Press, 1972).

3. Rabbi Ronald B. Sobel and Sidney Wallach (eds.), *Justice, Justice Shalt Thou Pursue*, (New York: KTAV, 1975).

pretensions to being a court of law; and second, that its purpose was conciliation even more than adjudication. It was incorporated under this name in 1930. The emphasis of the tribunal was thus shifted from the adjustment of differences by an arbitrator, a third party who determines the outcome, to conciliation—the attempt not merely to adjudicate, but to restore peaceful relations. The final alteration in name to "The Jewish Conciliation Board of America" took place in 1939. The elimination of the word "court" served to emphasize our role primarily as voluntary conciliators.

The Jewish Conciliation Board functioned throughout in such a manner as to win the confidence of those Jews, mostly immigrants, who turned to it for assistance. One must bear in mind the atmosphere on the Lower East Side of Manhattan during the 1920s. Many Jews of that area and generation shied away from what they considered to be the uncongenial atmosphere of American courts. Uncomfortable before a Gentile judge, they felt more at home in what they called "the Jewish court." Besides, there was no expense or delay, such as one found in government courts. The Board's services were free of charge and continued to be so throughout the years.

Frequently, litigants were impelled by the consideration to avoid *Hillul Ha-Shem*, the dishonoring of the Jewish good name by dragging unseemly situations into a non-Jewish court. Many would talk their hearts out in their own *Mamme-loshen*, Yiddish. The listening ears on the "bench" were those of a rabbi (Orthodox, Conservative, or Reform), a lawyer or a Jewish judge from one of the civil courts, and a layman—all drawn from a panel of volunteers.[4] We had no ecclesiastical jurisdiction, but the rabbi's presence was helpful in applying the spirit of Jewish law. Although the use of Yiddish diminished in later years, when the previous generation's Americanized children began to utilize the Board's facilities, it was the primary language heard during sessions in the early period. General David Sarnoff, head of the Radio Corporation of America and a patron of the Jewish Conciliation Board, enjoyed sitting as a judge on this tribunal, where he had the rare opportunity to practice his fluent Yiddish.

Everything was done to make the applicants feel completely at ease. In keeping with Jewish tradition, no lawyers were permitted to represent the litigants,[5] thereby sparing the latter both expense and undue formality. No oaths were administered. Everyone was allowed his say. No evidence was ruled out of order and no testimony was stricken from the record. When the verdict rendered by the volunteer judges was

4. See Appendix VI-B for the names of the volunteer judges.
5. See above, p. 6.

unacceptable to one of the parties involved, the judges often took the time and trouble to speak to this party, attempting to persuade him or her of the justice of their decision. The judges were, for the most part, not trained lawyers or judges, but men and women who nevertheless exercised moral authority at the hearings; seasoned experience, social concern, communal leadership, and *sekhel ha-yashar* (common sense) were their chief credentials Such qualifications went far in leading to sensible decisions and in winning the confidence of the litigants. Not the least in importance was a listening ear.

Some litigants requested private hearings because of the special nature of their cases. The Board always went out of its way to grant this request, whenever possible. Although the New York City Small Claims Court initiated evening sessions only in 1956, the Jewish Conciliation Board, from the outset, frequently held evening sessions for the convenience of persons who could not afford to lose a day's pay. Ordinarily, its sessions were held in the late afternoon and ran into the evening.

The tribunal soon acquired the reputation of being "the court without a gavel." Having become the most effective medium for achieving peaceful solutions, it was influential in Jewish life on the Lower East Side from the 1920s onward.

Cases were heard with a minimum of delay. After a complaint had been filed, the principals were notified to appear before the Board, often within a few days of the filing. No one was ever coerced to appear before the Board; people did so out of respect for the principles of fairness for which the JCB had become known.

"This confidence," wrote Louis Richman in his article, "The Court without a Gavel,"[6] "is due, in great measure, to the fact that the Board does not represent any one point of view; it has always sought to represent every segment of Jewish society."

The only condition to which clients had to adhere was their prior agreement to abide by the decisions of the Board, in accordance with the New York State Arbitration Law and the Civil Practice Act.[7] Very few cases heard by the JCB were ever appealed to the civil courts, and in those instances where they were appealed the Board's decisions were consistently upheld by the New York Supreme Court.

Often, after receiving an invitation to appear before the Board, the principals would settle their differences between themselves, without a hearing. On occasion, problems were resolved during a talk with the Executive Secretary or the social worker at the Board's offices. The

6. In *Two Generations in Perspective*, ed. Harry Schneiderman (New York: Monde Publishers, 1957), pp. 317–322.
7. For the various arbitration agreements, see Appendix I.

Social Service Department, initiated by volunteers from the Sister-hood of Congregation B'nai Jeshurun, was established in 1931 to follow up cases which involved social welfare problems. In 1938, this depart-ment began to receive financial support from the Friedsam Founda-tion, through the courtesy of John S. Burke, head of the B. Altman Company and President of the Friedsam Foundation. This support was continued by his son, John Burke, Jr., who, upon his father's demise, succeeded to the presidency of these two bodies.

In 1936, a trained social worker was hired to supplement the work of the volunteer committee. During the early 1950s, psychiatric services were occasionally engaged. Problems began to be discerned as com-plex; the aftermath of the Second World War, the Holocaust, and the increased stress and tension of metropolitan life were all contributing factors. Shortly afterward, the valuable psychiatric services of Dr. Howard E. Berk were made available on a volunteer basis, and he served as consultant to the judges during most of the hearings.[8]

Louis Richman served as Executive Secretary until his untimely death in 1956. Thereafter, his widow, Ruth, was designated Acting Secretary and later elected Executive Director, thereby assuming her late husband's responsibilities.

The JCB budget grew from approximately $1,200 annually in 1931 to $20,000 a year during the 1960s. In 1933, at the height of the Depression, the Board asked Jewish religious schools and congrega-tional sisterhoods to include it among the causes to which their charity funds made annual contributions.

After the Madison Street courthouse was closed down, the sessions were held at the Jewish Educational Alliance, 197 East Broadway. In later years, sessions were held occasionally at the Municipal Court, the State Office Building, and the American Arbitration Services offices, as well as at the Synagogue Council of America and at the headquarters of the New York Federation of Jewish Philanthropies. Scores of in-terested onlookers would often pack the courtroom. Among the visitors to these sessions, who sometimes also served as judges, were Jewish community leaders from distant lands such as Australia, England, France, Israel, and South Africa.

For many years, the JCB office was at 225 Broadway. The annual meetings of the Board were held on the second Wednesday of every January. In 1932, the first annual dinner was held to honor those who had volunteered their time and effort as officers and as judges.[9] The Hon. Charles H. Tuttle, United States Attorney, was chairman of the dinner.

8. Cf. Chapter VI.
9. See Appendix VI.

Several important anniversaries were also marked in a festive manner. At the thirty-fifth anniversary celebration of the Jewish Conciliation Board, in January 1954, General David Sarnoff presided. He introduced himself in Yiddish and brought the house down when he began, "My name is David Sarnoff, and I am a Jew from Minsk." Supreme Court Justice William O. Douglas was the keynote speaker. This occasion also marked the twenty-fifth anniversary of my presidency. Justice Douglas spoke on "The Problems of the Little People."[10] Among the congratulatory messages received on this occasion were those of Eleanor Roosevelt, Chief Rabbi Kurt Wilhelm of Sweden, the New York Board of Rabbis, and the Philadelphia Council of the American Jewish Congress.

General Sarnoff was again chairman in 1959 at the Board's fortieth anniversary, and Justice Douglas was once more the principal speaker. Among those sending congratulations were Governor Nelson A. Rockefeller of New York, New York City's Mayor Robert F. Wagner, Senator Jacob Javits, the Zionist Organization of America, and Mrs. Caroline K. Simon, Secretary of the State of New York. The guests included New York State Attorney General Louis J. Lefkowitz, Judge Bernard Botein, Presiding Justice of the Appelate Division, and Judge Jonah Goldstein.

The Board's forty-fifth anniversary was celebrated in 1965, with Harry Golden, an East Side boy who became widely known as an author and as editor of the *Carolina Israelite*, serving as chairman, and with Judge Simon E. Sobeloff, of the United States Court of Appeals, as principal speaker. Others participating were Representative Theodore R. Kupferman and two Vice-Presidents of the Board, Rabbi Dr. Leo Jung and Rabbi Dr. Julius Mark. Congressman John V. Lindsay, later Mayor of New York City, was among the guests. A congratulatory letter was received from Hubert H. Humphrey, Vice-President of the United States, who observed:

> In a world of discord where tempers are so often heated by irresponsibles, rather than cooled by thinking people, in an age which has been scarred by so much violence, in a time when man possesses ever deadlier means to annihilate the human race, how we do need the type of spirit—with compassion, justice and wisdom—which your noble organization represents.[11]

Justice William O. Douglas, Arthur Goldberg, United States Ambassador to the United Nations, Senator Jacob Javits, U.S. Attorney

10. See Appendix II for the text of his speech.
11. For the full text, see Appendix IV-C.

Presentation of scroll to Dr. Israel Goldstein on the twenty-fifth anniversary of his presidency, January 1954. From left to right, JCB Executive Secretary Louis Richman, Dr. Israel Goldstein, General David Sarnoff, and U.S. Supreme Court Justice William O. Douglas. (Photo: courtesy of The New York Times.)

U.S. Supreme Court Justice William O. Douglas speaking at the twenty-fifth anniversary celebration of Dr. Israel Goldstein's presidency of the JCB. In the audience (from left to right), front row: two clients, Louis Richman, General David Sarnoff, and Dr. Israel Goldstein; second and third rows (straight through): client, Shad Polier, Dr. David W. Petegorsky, Judge Justine Wise-Polier, Judge I. Montefiore Levy. (Photo: court-

Fortieth anniversary celebration of the JCB (and thirtieth of Dr. Israel Goldstein's presidency), at Grand Street Boys' Association, New York City, December 1959. Seated (from left to right): Dr. Israel Goldstein, General David Sarnoff, U.S. Supreme Court Justice William O. Douglas; standing: JCB Executive Secretary Ruth Richman and Judge Jacob Panken. (Photo: courtesy of Herbert S. Sonnenfeld, New York.)

Token naming of JCB ("Conciliation") Square by New York City Council resolution of September 16, 1965, on the occasion of the Board's forty-fifth anniversary. Pictured standing in foreground (from left to right): Jacob Goodman, Rabbi Leo Jung, Harry Golden, Judge Simon E. Sobeloff, Dr. Israel Goldstein, and Rabbi Julius Mark.
(Photo: courtesy of Herbert S. Sonnenfeld, New York.)

General Robert F. Kennedy, and New York State Attorney General Louis J. Lefkowitz also cabled felicitations.[12]

Mayor Wagner renamed the corner of East Broadway and Jefferson Street "Conciliation Square" for this occasion, and a New York City Council resolution declared September 13–19, 1965, "Conciliation Week."[13]

Although, by that time, I had retired from the American scene, to make my home in Israel, the presidency of the Jewish Conciliation Board was the one active public responsibility which I retained, at the urging of the Board. I had felt that it might be possible to manage at long distance, with an annual visit to New York, but I was finding this increasingly difficult. Fortunately, Rabbi Julius Mark, Vice-President of the Board, agreed to bear a considerable amount of the responsibility. I pleaded with him to take the presidency, but until 1968 he declined. At that time, when we met in Jerusalem, he acceded to my request, and thus, at the annual meeting of the Jewish Conciliation Board in 1968, he was unanimously elected President of this important tribunal. The Board elected me Honorary President for life.

Therewith ended my leadership of this tribunal, after a period of thirty-eight years. In the midst of a busy career in the rabbinate and in other areas of Jewish and civic public service, it came to hold a special place in my life.[14]

The Jewish Conciliation Board, in recent years, has undergone important changes. It is presently part of the Jewish Family Service in the New York Federation of Jewish Philanthropic Societies.

Change and Continuity

Perusal of the annual reports of the President and the Executive Secretary, as well as of the speeches delivered at anniversary celebrations and annual dinners, indicates that the general pattern of the Board's activities may have undergone superficial changes, but in essence remained much the same. Hundreds of cases were dealt with by "the court without a gavel," and hundreds of others were adjusted in the offices of the JCB. Thousands of litigants were served. Throughout the years, certain aspects were the constants amid the variables: the undeviating concern shown by the Jewish Conciliation Board for the rights and dignity of all people, the number of cases adjudicated

12. Some of these messages appear in Appendix IV-C.

13. For the texts of the Council's resolution and the Mayor's proclamation, see Appendix IV-A and IV-B.

14. See my address to the Board on its forty-fifth anniversary, Appendix V-E.

successfully, the growing respect shown for our Board by individuals, institutions, and organizations, and the periodical requests from other communities for assistance in setting up similar tribunals.

Although, as the years went by, clients came from all parts of the city—especially from Brooklyn and the Bronx—and were no longer concentrated on the Lower East Side, which had lost its predominantly Jewish character, the Board sessions continued to be held mainly at the Jewish Educational Alliance. Among the clients, less and less Yiddish was heard. Their economic situation had visibly improved. Beginning in the late 1930s, many clients approaching the Board for assistance had been refugees from Germany and Austria, fleeing Hitler's reign of terror. More second- and third-generation American Jews also began to seek out the Board's facilities. While the type of litigant which the Board had originally been established to serve had largely disappeared from Jewish life, as was natural to the process of Americanization, the organization's usefulness had extended to include the second generation as well as the elderly. Through all the changes, however, the traditional Jewish *mitzvah* of "bringing peace between man and his fellow man," practiced by the Jewish Conciliation Board, remained the constant amidst the variables.

Another unchanging element has been the Board's commitment to conciliation more than to arbitration. At the first annual dinner, held on January 27, 1932, I told those assembled: "More and more, we stress the element of conciliation . . . to help the children of the ghetto understand their parents, who still remain the 'walls' of that ghetto."[15]

The President's Annual Report of January 1935 included a letter written by Max D. Steuer, New York's leading trial lawyer (who had served on several occasions as a JCB judge), to New York's Mayor Fiorello La Guardia:

. . . The litigants, starting with the utmost antagonism, have walked out not only seeming satisfied, but expressing themselves as being so. . . . If one may envision the future development of judicial procedure in this country, one may look forward to a step beyond adjudication, namely conciliation. The ideal court of justice should seek to go beyond justice—to the curing of antagonisms, wherever possible, and to the substitution of good will for ill will, wherever feasible.

At the 1954 anniversary celebrations,[16] I took occasion to say that "I have found relatively few cases of malevolent designs or basic dishonesty. Mostly, disputes arise between parties, each of whom honestly

15. For an additional extract from this address, see Appendix V-A.
16. See Appendix V-D.

believes that the right is on his side." This was my summary impression of the many suits which had come before us.

Numerous Jewish communities and organizations requested material and assistance from the Board in setting up similar courts in other localities. There is no information available to indicate what became of most of these tribunals or, indeed, whether all of them were established. Thus, among the groups requesting material in 1931 were Congregation Beth El, Chelsea, Massachusetts; Brotherhood Temple Ohabei Shalom, Boston, Massachusetts; the Ogantz Shul, Philadelphia, Pennsylvania; the Training School for Jewish Social Service Work, New York; Dayton B'nai B'rith, Dayton, Ohio; Jewish Charities of Chicago, Illinois; and Temple Emanuel, Paterson, New Jersey.

The following year, the communities of Detroit and Rochester also requested information. During this same period, Louis Richman was invited to address a convention of Jewish organizations in New Haven, Connecticut, on the subject of the Jewish Conciliation Court and its work. As a result of his address, a committee was set up to investigate the possibility of establishing a similar institution in New Haven. This committee, composed of the leaders of the community, including Rabbi Louis Greenberg, was favorable in its findings, and the court was established in 1935.

That same year, many other inquiries were received from individuals, newspapers, institutions, and communities throughout the United States and Canada. The Board's reputation had grown, and many other communities were interested in establishing similar courts to try distinctively Jewish cases. In 1936, Dr. Stephen S. Wise conveyed an inquiry from Rabbi Solomon Frank of Winnipeg, Canada, who asked for information regarding the JCB. As a member of the Canadian Jewish Congress, Rabbi Frank was interested in establishing a Jewish Court of Arbitration in his community.

In 1937, a tribunal similar to the Jewish Conciliation Court was established in Cleveland, Ohio. The communities of Detroit, Michigan, Buffalo, New York, and Boston, Massachusetts, were in the process of establishing courts and sought advice from the JCB. Earlier, a Jewish Court of Arbitration had been founded in Baltimore by Judge Simon E. Sobeloff. In later years, such assistance and advice were extended to communities in Cincinnati, Ohio, Newark and Jersey City, New Jersey, and in Kingston, New York.

The Board's reputation was disseminated not only by word of mouth, but also by the wide coverage received in the press throughout the years. The Yiddish newspapers—the *Forward*, the *Morning Journal*, and the *Day*—were our staunchest allies. They sent their reporters to cover the hearings and write up many of the cases, maintaining the anonymity of the individuals concerned. The Yiddish press became an integral part of the work of the Board. Sometimes its columnists served the immigrant community as advisors on many personal problems, and they would often direct people to the JCB for guidance and assistance.

In 1938, the Yiddish Writers' Group of the Federal Writers' Project published a volume (*Jewish Landsmanshaften of New York*) which included a chapter about the Board.

The various anniversary celebrations of the JCB received wide coverage. In 1954, the Board's thirty-five anniversary was the subject of an article by Eleanor Roosevelt in the *New York World-Telegraph and Sun*. Other articles and news items appeared in the *New York Times*, the *Herald Tribune*, the *East Side News*, and the *Jewish Standard*.

In 1959, the anniversary celebrations were reported by the *New York Times*, the *Herald Tribune*, the *New York Post*, the *New York Mirror*, the *Montreal Star*, the *San Francisco Chronicle*, and the *Reconstructionist* magazine. One article was syndicated by the North American Newspaper Alliance.

On August 24, 1962, Martin Tolchin wrote an excellent article about the Board's activities in the *New York Times*. It was a comprehensive and sympathetic report, which brought recognition and support to the Board from many Jews who had previously been unaware of its existence.

Press reports of the forty-fifth anniversary of the JCB in 1965 appeared in three Israeli newspapers, *Davar*, *Haboker*, and *Herut*, as well as in the Seven Arts Feature Syndicate, the Boston *Jewish Advocate*, and the New York *Villager*.

Noteworthy among the coverage received on radio and television was the broadcast entitled "Court Without a Gavel," on the *Eternal Light* program of June 20, 1954. This dramatization of the Jewish Conciliation Board's work was presented by the Jewish Theological Seminary of America in conjunction with the National Broadcasting Company. It was rebroadcast in October 1965 to mark the Board's forty-fifth anniversary.[17]

In February 1962, the New York Board of Rabbis presented two panel discussions concerning the JCB in the framework of its television program, *The Jewish Heritage Hour*. Dr. Julius Mark, Rabbi of Temple Emanu-El, moderated the second telecast. Ruth Richman prepared these programs with the assistance of Rabbi Harold H. Gordon and Rabbi L. Fred Hollander. The program was screened throughout New York State, Pennsylvania, Connecticut, and New Jersey.

During the Board's earlier years, "radio courts" dealing with family

17. The script of this broadcast will be found in Appendix III.

problems and disputes often provided popular entertainment. The directors of the JCB, however, adopted a resolution in 1936, affirming their opposition to public airings of our own sessions. Several offers from commercial sponsors regarding the transmission of JCB hearings were rejected. It was our unalterable policy to avoid use of our cases as a form of public entertainment. Nevertheless, our use of the communications media to explain the purposes of our tribunal continued.

Thus, a radio talk broadcast in 1948 was utilized to explain our "angle" as one of sympathetic human service and Jewish dignity. I laid special emphasis on the fact that, "by the application of common sense, human understanding and feeling for the right, the Jewish Conciliation Board not only dispenses justice, but humanizes justice and exercises conciliation in the good old Jewish tradition of *tzedek ve-yosher*, justice and fairness."[18]

At the first annual dinner of the JCB, held on January 27, 1932, I had occasion to express our overriding concern for the "common man":

> Although, theoretically, the poor man has the same rights before the law as the rich, actually he is at a disadvantage because he is unable to set in motion the legal machinery for the protection of his rights. . . . Until the time arises when governments will establish agencies to make it possible for the poor to receive justice without cost and without delay, it will be the duty of private citizens, of socially minded men and women, to provide those agencies and instrumentalities whereby the poor man may secure his justice.[19]

More than two decades later, at the 1954 anniversary celebration, Supreme Court Justice William O. Douglas paid an incomparably more significant tribute to the JCB, one that reflected his understanding of its *raison d'être:*

> The thing that has interested me particularly about the Board is that it has been more interested in justice than in law. Law and justice are not necessarily the same, as you know. Throughout the centuries, law has been trying to catch up with justice. It has not always succeeded. That is one of the great, eternal struggles of man.
>
> The work of the Conciliation Board, seeking to find what is the truth, trying to apply justice, is a great experiment in a busy community where there are many problems, local and international. It is important to take time out to make adjustments in the little problems of people. That, in the end, marks the difference between a society which administers to the needs of people and a society where sores and troubles fester, where the needs and aspirations of the ordinary man are neglected.[20]

18. For the text, see Appendix V-C.
19. See Appendix V-A.
20. For the full text, see Appendix II.

In his congratulatory telegram of December 3, 1959, Nelson A. Rockefeller, Governor of New York State, said, in part: "The benevolent motive of the JCB's activities is manifested in the fact that, in more than forty years, it has settled thousands of disputes without charge or fee. So doing, it has been a great help to people who cannot afford the cost of litigation."

To summarize, the reluctance of Jews to air internal disputes in public was, throughout, a prime motivation in the New York Jewish community. Many people presented their cases to us instead of to the civil courts, in order to avoid *Hillul Ha-Shem,* the desecration of God's Name, and to safeguard the good name of the Jewish people.

Although it was a secular court, without any claim to ecclesiastical authority, the Board did exert considerable moral authority. In January 1936, in the context of the President's report, I said: "We find that the appeal to the Jewish sense of honor still exercises some moral compulsion upon the men and women who come before us." After two decades as President, I reiterated the same theme: "It enhances the morale and the well-being of a community when tensions are resolved without being brought to courts of law." And in 1965, at the forty-fifth-anniversary observance, I returned once again to this motivation of the JCB—"The human need for a listening ear and an understanding heart and, most of all, the uniquely Jewish need . . . which is not only a matter of language. It is a matter of understanding the 'mores' of Jewish living, the patterns of Jewish organizations and congregations, and the gap between Jewish generations which often leads to tensions, and of being able to appeal in the name of Jewish honor and Jewish tradition."[21]

In measuring the value of the Board's work, this aspect must not be overlooked. An examination of the cases which have come before the Jewish Conciliation Board since its inception, and a study of the decisions which have been rendered, provides, it is hoped, an instructive basis for understanding some of the ideals and traditions which are incorporated in the Jewish sense of justice.

21. For another extract from this address, see Appendix V-E.

IV
Cases

Clients came to the Board from many sources. Some had read reports of the Board's proceedings in the Yiddish press. Others were recommended by friends who had themselves been assisted by the JCB. The civil courts and the various social service agencies recommended our services to those who, they considered, would best be served by the JCB. We, in turn, often recommended to these agencies cases which, strictly speaking, were not within our jurisdiction. Occasionally, we also sent litigants to Rabbinical courts, the Jewish Family Service, psychiatric and psychological counseling agencies, vocational training centers, and services for marriage counseling and for geriatric advice. In each individual case, the welfare of the parties involved was always the primary consideration. In later years, there were clients who had originally learned about the Board's work from TV programs. Some people turned to us after finding the listing in the telephone directory, while others heard about the JCB in synagogue or at fraternal-lodge meetings.

The cases themselves were as varied as the individuals involved. Certain broad categories, however, can be sketched. Thus, on October 7, 1953, the cases scheduled for the Board session included three demands for support, five marital disputes, three family tensions, two demands for loan repayment, five burial plot disputes, two tenant complaints against landlords, one small-business claim, and two cases dealing with claims for sick benefits from fraternal organizations.

The schedule of twenty-five cases set for the hearing at the following session covered similar categories, but also included one case concerning an intermarriage, one dealing with a paternity suit, two involving the children of a first marriage following a parent's remarriage, and one seeking advice in regard to the naming of a child.

Support cases were brought to the Board continuously, but as might be expected, these were especially prevalent during the Depression years. An estranged wife asked the Board to compel her husband to contribute to their child's welfare. A daughter, no longer able to bear either the economic or the psychological burden unaided, begged for a decision that would oblige her siblings to participate in the maintenance of an aged or ailing parent. Destitute parents asked the Board to remind their children of the obligation to support them.

Landsmanshaften, organizations composed of immigrants originating in the same East European region, often granted their paying members sick benefits and burial privileges. Many disputes came before the Board concerning the sale of burial plots, nonpayment of death benefits, or the erection of memorial stones. Members expelled for nonpayment of dues, especially during the Depression, would turn to the Board to plead their cases for reinstatement.

Civil and commercial disputes also came before the Board. One partner would charge the other with having reneged on a loan. Business competitors accused each other of slander. A customer claimed that a butcher was neglecting to observe *Kashrut* strictly. A merchant was accused of failing to mark "Kosher for Passover" clearly on a product.

Another category of disputes which occupied the attention of our tribunal in 1940-41 involved Jewish labor unions. Such cases were internal conflicts within the unions and strife within workers' cooperatives, as well as disputes between organized labor and employers which might have resulted in strikes or lockouts. Non-Jews also invoked the aid of the JCB when lodging claims against Jews and Jewish institutions. Every effort was made in these cases to promote goodwill and understanding between the parties concerned.

A large proportion of the Board's time was taken up with domestic problems: interfering mothers-in-law, parents disagreeing about the kind of Jewish education to give their children, couples arguing about the degree of Jewish religious observance to be maintained in their homes, children resenting parental interference in their lives. Money was often at the root of the difficulties—a wife demanding a larger household budget or accusing her husband of "drinking away" the paycheck, a husband not trusting his wife to pay the bills or alleging that she gambled with the household allowance.

Occasionally, congregations were brought before the Board, sometimes by a teacher or *Shammash* (sexton) or rabbi who had been dismissed or not paid on time; sometimes, also, a case was brought by a member complaining about the way financial or other matters were handled by congregational officials.

As from the mid-1940s, many of the suits concerned the State of

Israel, either peripherally or directly—a couple, only one of whom wished to return to Israel, a child wanting to immigrate to Israel against the parents' wishes, Israelis who had recently emigrated to the United States with the assistance of loans which they were unable to repay. In one case, a synagogue about to dissolve wished to sell a *Sefer Torah*, whereas the original donor preferred to send his Torah scroll to a synagogue in Israel.

The Board also adjudicated a number of cases relating to the Holocaust. Among these were claims for the repayment of loans utilized for transporting refugees to the United States, signatures needed for German reparations payments, properties lost when escaping the Nazis, a former inmate of a Nazi concentration camp now abusing his wife and children, or even individuals accused of having been Nazi collaborators.

No case was ever disregarded or dealt with lightly. Every dispute or problem received the same serious consideration by the judges. Each action was handled with tact and concern for the dignity of the individuals involved. Every claim was heard on the basis of its own merits and was not prejudged by similar cases which, in a court of law, might have been used to establish a precedent.

Guiding Principles

Despite the informality of its sessions, the Jewish Conciliation Board operated according to the guiding principles which had motivated its founding and its subsequent development. These were, in the main, the emphasis on conciliation, the provision of a congenial alternative to the civil courts, an informal atmosphere which permitted the use of Yiddish by clients when they so wished, avoidance of *Ḥillul Ha-Shem*, and the ongoing services of a social worker in cases where this was necessary. Although, in effect, the JCB helped ease the case loads of the civil courts by hearing suits which could be settled by informal arbitration, the primary purpose of the Board was to assist the litigants themselves. Not only were they spared the long delays caused by an overburdened legal system, but they also avoided the considerable expense of legal advice and representation.

During its nearly four decades, the Jewish Conciliation Board adjudicated and restored harmony in many thousands of cases. Thousands more were settled informally through the professional assistance of the Executive Secretary and of the Board's social worker.

The stress was always on solving the disputed matter rather than on bringing every case to a formal session. On a rough estimate, it may be said that the JCB was instrumental in hearing, adjudicating, and settling well over 15,000 cases in the course of its history.

One of the unwritten tenets of this tribunal was that the judges go out of their way in assisting litigants to comply with the Board's decisions. Thus, men and women who had volunteered their time and effort to sit as judges would often spend extra hours, after the proceedings had officially concluded, trying to be helpful to some of those persons whose cases they had already heard in the formal sessions.

As for the avoidance of *Ḥillul Ha-Shem* and concern for the good name of the Jewish community, the court often heard cases which, had they been aired publicly in the civil courts, might have caused embarrassment to the Jewish community.

The basic aim of the Board was to reconcile the parties appearing before it. The healing of a family rift, the renewal of a broken friendship, or the righting of a wrong was as important to the judges as the determination of guilt or innocence.

Citation of many cases which illustrate the translation of such guidelines into action will be presented in the following pages. Such examples have been selected from the many cases handled by the Jewish Conciliation Board. They reflect a cross-section of problems which touched on the lives of a considerable segment of the New York Jewish population, especially immigrants of the early twentieth century, in the process of Americanization. Although New York Jewry was the specific point of reference, this background may be regarded as typical of similar Jewish communities in other American cities, especially those on the Atlantic seaboard.

One note of caution should be sounded, however, in regard to the cases described below.

If one were to write a social history of any community based only on the records of its civil and criminal courts, this would of course convey the impression of a derelict, crime-ridden population. In the case of Jewish communities throughout the world, it is an established and repeatedly confirmed fact that there is less delinquency, immorality, and crime than among any other religious, ethnic, or social group in the general population.

The Jewish community of New York has undoubtedly had such an enviable record in comparison with other religious, ethnic, and social constituencies within the body politic.

Among the situations which came before the Jewish Conciliation Board were broken homes, and broken undertakings and obligations of many kinds and in many areas of human relations. These, however, were rare exceptions in the ongoing and variegated life of what constitutes the largest Jewish community to be found in any one city in the world.

Taking this huge Jewish population into account, the number of altercations which came before this tribunal and other courts, whether governmental or voluntary, was minuscule. What gave significance to this voluntary tribunal was the way in which the problems were handled.

Uniquely Jewish Cases

The majority of the disputes which came before the Board had an obviously Jewish aspect. Certain proceedings, however, were more obvious examples than others, being specifically suited to a Jewish tribunal. Such were situations involving *Kashrut* (Jewish dietary laws), *Shadkhanut* (marriage brokerage), intermarriage, the naming of a child, or *Halitzah*—the releasing of a childless widow from her obligation to marry her husband's nearest surviving male relative.

At times, cases were brought before the Board which involved internal squabbling within the Jewish community. Keeping such disputes out of the glare of publicity served to maintain the good name of the Jewish community.

The cases cited hereinafter under various categories, selected from thousands which came before this tribunal, may help to convey the specifically "ethnic" nature of certain problems which were brought to the Jewish Conciliation Board and the manner in which they were handled.

One example, concerning *Leshon ha-Ra* (mischievous gossip), will serve as an appropriate introduction.

In April 1943, two women came before the Board, each accusing the other of slander and of spreading malicious rumors. The plaintiff first alleged that the defendant had accused her of having an illegitimate son. The defendant then countered that, in an argument between the two in synagogue, her daughter had been termed a "cripple." This offensive remark had caused her to become ill and led to her being hospitalized.

The judges' decision was: "We feel that such a quarrel between two Jewish neighbors like yourselves does neither of you honor. Isn't the world filled with enough trouble without your adding to it? Surely, as Jews, we must protect our good name in every possible way. Evidently, someone started this rumor, and we sincerely believe it to be false. As sensible people and as Jews, you must ignore it and try to live in peace and harmony."

Professional Matchmaking

Marriage brokerage and professional matchmaking, while not exclusively Jewish phenomena, had been practiced widely in East European Jewish communities. Because of the religious and social prohibitions against the mingling of the sexes, there were few opportunities for boys and girls to meet socially. The American custom of "dating" was unknown. It sometimes even happened that the bride and groom did not meet until their betrothal. The arrangements for the match would often be made by the fathers of the prospective couple, frequently with the aid of an intermediary *Shadkhan* (matchmaker), who usually collected a fee after the wedding ceremony.

The services of a *Shadkhan* are still utilized today, especially among the more Orthodox Jewish communities. There are even newspaper ads offering suitable matches. The JCB heard many cases dealing with *Shadkhanut*, where a matchmaker claiming a fee would bring to the Board either the couple or the parents involved.

In 1937, a *Shadkhan* approached the Board, claiming that she had arranged a marriage between a young couple, but that the parents had not paid her fee. The parents denied that their respective children were engaged or even dating each other. The daughter said that she had only seen the young man once, when she had brought her watch into his shop for repair. Although the judges dismissed this case for lack of sufficient evidence, advising the matchmaker to wait until the marriage had actually taken place, the latter was apprehensive lest the defendants conceal their marriage from her in order to avoid paying her fee.

A man, not claiming to be a professional *Shadkhan*, nevertheless demanded a fee for having introduced the defendant's daughter to her future husband. The judges understood from the plaintiff's testimony that a good deal of his resentment stemmed from the feeling that he had been insulted by the defendant's failure to invite him to the wedding. The plaintiff stated that he was a poor man and demanded $1,000 from the well-to-do defendant.. The father of the bride declared that, although he had not been impressed with his new son-in-law, he had sent the plaintiff a $25 payment.

The judges decided that the defendant should pay an additional $125 to the plaintiff within ten days. While he did not refuse to comply with the judges' decision, the defendant remarked, "I would rather donate it to charity."

A woman replied to an advertisement in the Yiddish *Forward* for a wife. She suggested to the gentleman concerned that, for a fee, she would introduce him to several women, and that, if he married one of these candidates, both parties should pay her $100 each. In addition, the matchmaker asked for a $12 fee for the introduction itself. She introduced him to a woman whom he subsequently married. They had each paid a fee of $12 for the introduction, but claimed that the matchmaker had never stated that there would be an additional fee if they married.

The judgment was in favor of the *Shadkhan*, and the couple were ordered to pay her the full amount.

Intermarriages

Although the Jewish community was a closely knit one, with emphasis being placed on marrying within the Jewish faith, intermarriages did take place. When these resulted in friction, they often came before our Board.

The following case indicates how deep were the feelings which sometimes developed. In 1940, a Mr. A. came to the Board complaining that his sister-in-law had married a non-Jew. Both he and his wife were the offspring of rabbis, and Mr. A. took this intermarriage as a personal insult. The fact was that the marriage had taken place a decade earlier, but had not been revealed to him previously. His reaction was one of furious anger, and he threatened to commit suicide if the intermarried couple would refuse to be divorced.

The sister-in-law affirmed that it had been her suggestion to bring this case to the Board. She had known her husband for twenty years, and she loved him. Though a Catholic by birth, he was not an observant Christian. He had no desire, however, to convert to Judaism. There were no children. Divorce, she said, was out of the question.

The judges, realizing that there was little they could do, told Mr. A. that their decision would be held in abeyance until they had perused the thick folder of documents which he had mailed to the Board's office. This provided an interval during which Mr. A. might be mollified. The judges spoke to him of the happy years which he, his wife, and their two children had shared. They also tried to help him understand that his wife must not be punished, nor his marriage suffer, because of the actions of a sister-in-law. They also proposed that she and her husband move to another state. This approach succeeded. Mr. A. promised finally that he would not do anything to hurt his own family.

The formal complaint in the following case was that of a mother against her son. She claimed support and also his help in the erection of a tombstone for her late husband. As the hearing developed and the judges spoke to the son, it became clear that he was already fulfilling his obligations and that his mother's real complaint was something else. After her vague derogatory references concerning the son's wife, the true facts were revealed. The son had married a Catholic woman of Syrian descent, seven years his senior, who had a daughter by a previous marriage, and he himself had been converted to Catholicism. He was a sergeant in the U.S. Army, stationed in Massachusetts, and he considered the Army to be his career. Despite his mother's animosity, he had written several friendly letters to her and to his younger sister. These were produced in court as evidence of his willingness to remain in contact with his family.

The mother finally made plain her real demand—that her son divorce his wife. She stated that her younger daughter had become ill because of the son's marriage. The evidence indicated that this sister was still very fond of her brother. The judges tried to help the mother understand that she was in no way to blame for the path her son had chosen in life, and that she must try to reconcile herself to the situation. They rendered the decision that the son was to continue supporting his mother, should assist the family to erect the monument on his father's grave, and should keep in close communication with his sister and mother. The mother would be informed of this in writing by the Board. She was admonished not to make more trouble for her son. He and his wife were advised to familiarize themselves more closely with Judaism, and to try to establish a better understanding with the mother.

The attitude of the judges in cases of this kind was usually that, although intermarriage itself was to be deplored, such a union should not be interfered with once it had taken place.

The third case in this category was of a different kind. An elderly couple approached the Board requesting advice about the drawing-up of their will. Their daughter had died, leaving a husband and an infant son. Several years thereafter, the husband had married a non-Jewess and had become converted to Catholicism. In addition, he had changed his Jewish-sounding name. The grandson, who had also been converted, was now ten years old and attended a Catholic parochial school with his three stepbrothers and stepsisters. When visiting with his grandparents, he was curious about the lighting of Sabbath candles on Friday night and about the two sets of dishes, meat and dairy, which they used in conformity with the laws of *Kashrut*. Nevertheless, the grandson kept a New Testament and could not grasp the fact that he and his father had been born Jewish.

The grandparents disagreed regarding the terms of the will. The grandfather wished to leave an equal share to all his grandchildren. The grandmother felt that the Catholic grandson should not be included in the will.

The judges decided on a compromise: this grandson should receive a sum in the will, but not an equal share with his Jewish cousins.

Folkways

The following case involves the tradition prevalent among East European (Ashkenazi) Jews of naming a newborn child in honor of a departed relative, so as to preserve the memory of the deceased. This custom is so ingrained, except among Oriental (Sephardi) Jews, that there is a widespread superstition against naming a child after a person who is still living.

A distraught father brought his son before the Board, stating that they had always been on good terms, but that now a dispute had arisen regarding the name to be given to his son's child, who would soon be born. The man's son and daughter-in-law had chosen the name "Joseph," in memory of the daughter-in-law's deceased father. "Joseph," however, was also the name of the plaintiff, who was still very much alive.

The judges asked what Hebrew name had been chosen for the newborn child. "Ḥaim Yosef," was the reply. "And is that your Hebrew name?" they asked the grandfather-to-be. "No," he said, "just Yosef." "In that case," the judges replied, "when the boy is called to the Torah, he will be called Ḥaim Yosef, which everyone knows is not your name."

This did not satisfy Yosef the elder. "I only know what my father told me, and I can't help feeling as I do about this matter."

Responsive to the client's sensibilities, the rabbi on the judges' panel suggested that this family consult an Orthodox rabbi, since he himself was Reform. The father and son then explained that they had both consulted Orthodox rabbis separately, each receiving a different reply. They were then advised by the judges to consult together a third Orthodox rabbi. They did so immediately and returned to inform the judges that his advice had been that there was no basis in Jewish law for the grandfather's belief, but that, taking into account the psychological issues involved, the child should be named Ḥaim Yehosef rather than Ḥaim Yosef. This was adopted as the judges' formal decision.

Where, but in the "Jewish Court," could such a case have been comprehended, as well as mediated successfully?

Religious Observance

Jewish education has always been a prime duty of Jewish parents. Yet, after establishing communities in the United States, Jews were torn between this need to preserve Jewish tradition and learning and the new desire to be accepted by their neighbors, to become "Americanized." This tension between being a "good Jew" and becoming a "good American" eventually found a synthesis. In the intermediate stages, however, there were Jews who found the two goals to be incompatible. This was at the core of many family conflicts, and sometimes it even led to family disruptions.

A father turned to the Board for help in regard to the following conflict. His son refused to adhere to the father's Orthodox religious practices. The father had consulted with two Orthodox rabbis, who advised him to approach the Jewish Court.

It transpired that when he and his wife were first married, they had shared the same "liberal" views concerning religious observance. The father's brother had passed away some years previously, and since that time the father had become increasingly observant. His wife, however, retained her original attitude. She said that her husband was now demanding too much of the children, and she insisted that they and she were entitled to their own way of life.

The plaintiff complained that his wife cooked, watched television, and smoked on the Sabbath, and influenced the children to do the same. They therefore did not keep *Shabbat* in the Orthodox manner. Although their younger son attended a *Yeshivah* where he excelled in his studies, the older boy, who was sixteen at the time, refused to wear a *Yarmulka* (skullcap) or to pray with *Tefillin* (phylacteries). Moreover, he turned on the TV and electric lights and even smoked on *Shabbat*.

In trying to reconcile this family, the judges appealed to the father's understanding of his son. One judge said: "I, too, am a father. I usually try to adjust myself to their way of thinking. You cannot force your boy at this age to be religiously observant."

The father could not accept this reasoning and expressed envy of other parents in the neighborhood whose sons were observant and participated in the activities of the Orthodox synagogues.

The sixteen-year-old boy replied that he took part in the activities of the Jewish Center. "I have been accused of not going along with religion, but my feeling is that religion comes from the heart. I participate in the Center's activities with a great deal of enthusiasm."

The judges urged the wife not to offend her husband by smoking on *Shabbat*. At the same time, one judge said to the father, "You feel hurt because your children don't follow your ways, but they do need a home where quiet reigns, where a mother and father get along. When a man's attitude drives his children away, there is nothing left for him. Try and see the good side of your son's attitude and conduct."

According to *Halakhah* (Rabbinic law), a childless widow is obliged to marry her deceased husband's single brother so as to bear a child who will perpetuate her husband's name. This practice, known as levirate marriage *(Yibbum)*, is of Biblical origin, and one form of it is described in the Book of Ruth. According to Orthodox custom, the widow, in order to be released from this obligation, must receive *Halitzah* from the brother of her late husband. The ritual, described in Deuteronomy 25:9, is practiced by Orthodox Jews to this day.

A complaint came before the Board regarding a mother who, because of a financial dispute, refused to permit any of her sons to give *Halitzah* to her widowed daughter-in-law. It became obvious to the judges that the mother-in-law was utilizing this situation in order to blackmail the widow into paying her a substantial sum of money.

The rabbi on the panel explained to the mother that she had no right to interfere with the performance of a religious obligation. "*Halitzah* is not only for the benefit of the living, but also for your deceased son's peace of soul. As a mother who prays for the soul of her child, you must consider this matter seriously. I implore you to allow your sons to give *Halitzah*. Money should not be demanded, and in no case should a parent prevent a child from giving or taking *Halitzah*."

These strong words of appeal had no effect on the mother, who persisted in displaying the power she exercised over her sons.

After much discussion, the mother's real complaint finally surfaced. She believed that the daughter-in-law's mother had been cruel to her deceased son during his last illness. Since it was the widow's mother who was very religious and who wanted *Halitzah* to be given, the woman felt that, by withholding it, she was hurting her and thus achieving satisfaction.

The judges, by gentle probing, had brought the real issue to the fore. After repeating their admonition to the woman for utilizing a religious ceremony as a weapon for revenge, and having stated that any separate grievances or claims could be taken up at a separate hearing, the judges gave their final decision: "*Halitzah*, being a religious rite, must not in any way be connected with financial complaints. This Court respects religious customs, laws, and traditions, and therefore must uphold the demand of the daughter-in-law for *Ḥalitzah*. It is the religious duty of the older brother. If he refuses, the younger brother must give *Ḥalitzah* without any prior conditions. The Court appeals to the mother to use her influence positively in this matter. Regarding a monetary dispute, the Court is ready at any time to be of service in bringing about an amicable settlement."

Turning to the mother, they said, "We want to make a personal appeal to you. You impress us as being a religious woman. We plead with you, as a mother and daughter in Israel, to cooperate with the Board. Since *Ḥalitzah* is performed at a Rabbinical court, whenever you are ready, we shall be happy to recommend you to a religious authority. We are here to serve both of you."

The woman was moved by this appeal, and she agreed to abide by it.

There was one case in which superstition motivated an appeal for the granting of *Ḥalitzah*. A woman who appeared before the Board stated that her brother-in-law refused to give her *Ḥalitzah*. Strangely enough, although the woman declared herself to be a Christian Scientist, she was anxious for the ceremony to be performed. Her own mother had apparently urged her to receive *Ḥalitzah* from the brother-in-law on the ground that her late husband's soul would otherwise find no peace.

After some further negotiation between the parties, the woman eventually obtained her release from the brother-in-law.

Dietary Laws

Strict observance of Jewish law involves regulations specifying what foods may and may not be eaten, as well as how they may be prepared and when consumed. These food regulations constitute the laws of *Kashrut*. Thus, Jews observing *Kashrut* will not eat dairy products until a number of hours have passed after a meat meal. Dishes for dairy and meat products must always be kept separate. Cooking is forbidden on the Sabbath. Foods prepared on Friday, therefore, are kept warm on a hotplate. In addition to the normally forbidden foods (such as pork products and shellfish), there are foods considered to be *Kasher* all year, except on the Passover festival, when yeast products or foods prepared by a fermentation process are not *Kasher* for Passover.

The following are cases involving problems related to *Kashrut* which came before the Jewish Conciliation Board.

A seventy-six-year-old man appealed to the Board regarding his daughters, with whom he lived. He said that they did not keep a clean home, and for this reason he was forced to eat in restaurants. The

Board's social worker visited their home and discovered it to be immaculate. The father's real complaint was then revealed: although the food itself was *Kasher,* the daughters preferred to cook their vegetables fresh on Saturday. For the father, this meant that the food cooked on the Sabbath was not *Kasher.*

The judges decided that the father should cook his own food, in accordance with his own religious beliefs.

Kasher meat must come from a permitted animal, it must be slaughtered in a specific manner, and the internal organs must be examined to make certain that the animal was not diseased. Jews who observe *Kashrut* buy meat only from an authorized *Kasher* butcher.

One such butcher brought suit against his competitor, a block away, who was spreading the rumor that he sold non-*Kasher* meat and poultry. When questioned, the defendant claimed that he "knew for a fact" that the plaintiff sold non-*Kasher* meat, since it was cheaper and he could thus undersell the other butchers. The defendant not only denied the charges but threatened to bring a libel suit against the plaintiff.

After hearing all the evidence, the judges decided that the defendant's charge that his competitor sold non-*Kasher* meat was not supported by convincing proof, and he therefore must cease his charges. They also asked the plaintiff to drop any slander suit which he might have planned against the defendant.

Products which are permitted for consumption during Passover are labeled "Kosher for Passover." This labeling is particularly important with respect to those products which are usually eaten or used in cooking during the entire year, such as *matzah* meal.

A woman complained to the Board that a box of *matzah* meal which she had purchased especially to prepare the Passover dishes had not been labeled "Kosher for Passover." The problem was that she had not become aware of this oversight until four days of the holiday had gone by, when she had already prepared all her special holiday cakes and other foods. A religious woman who had never contravened the laws of *Kashrut,* she was also upset at the possibility of having to discard all her good cooking.

The *Mashgiah* (religious overseer) who supervised the *Kashrut* of this particular manufacturer testified that all the *matzah* meal which it produced during the year was fit for Passover use. The company did not label all its boxes "Kosher for Passover," since that would date them in the eyes of the consumer. Those boxes sold immediately before and during the festival received a special marking. This particular unmarked box had been shipped in error, said the *Mashgiah*, but since all the firm's *matzah* meal was "Kosher for Passover," the plaintiff had no reason for concern.

The judges incorporated the *Mashgiah's* testimony into their decision, assuring the woman that she had not eaten non-Passover food and that she need not throw away any of the items cooked with this *matzah* meal.

Landsmanshaften and Lodges

The *Landsmanshaften*, an integral part of the social structure of the immigrant Jewish communities, were fraternal organizations composed generally of people originating from the same localities in the "old country." Although the *Landsmanshaften* continued to function during the entire period under review, the majority of the cases involving these organizations which came before the Board were heard during the 1930s and 1940s.

The *Landsmanshaften* served two seemingly contradictory purposes. On the one hand, they reinforced ties with the countries of origin in Europe by keeping alive memories, customs, and names of the many towns and villages from which their members had come. On the other hand, through their detailed constitutions and by-laws and the orderly conduct of meetings and discussions which often related to current events and developments, the *Landsmanshaften* contributed to the Americanization process of these Jewish immigrants, some of whom had originated in parts of Eastern Europe where laws were often arbitrary and law enforcement capricious. These organizations thus provided a training ground in democratic procedure.

The informal atmosphere of the *Landsmanshaft* gatherings also provided a sounding board for members who were having difficulty in understanding the mores of their "American" children. *Landsleit* who had arrived years earlier, and who were now well on the way to acculturation, were often able to impart advice to the more recent arrivals and to assure childhood acquaintances and friends that they were no longer alone and strangers in the *Goldene Medine*.

In addition to their social advantages, these societies provided members with many other services. Sick benefits, payments to those "sitting *Shivah*" after a death in the family (to compensate them for loss of earnings), also burial plots and funeral expenses, were made available to paid-up members in good standing. The payment of these benefits, as well as disputes regarding who was and was not qualified to become a member or to remain a member, were often the subject of actions brought before the Board. Other related cases involved the dissolution of these organizations when they became obsolescent, requiring the allocation of any remaining funds in their treasuries. Many cases also involved the use or misuse of the burial grounds owned by these societies. Such situations will be dealt with in a separate section.

The following case typifies the kind of service given in this particular area.

A religious corporation, organized for the purpose of conducting religious services and providing cemetery benefits, had been functioning for forty years alongside a membership society, which had been established for the purpose of furnishing its members with a free loan service. After many years of active existence, the membership society ceased functioning and passed a resolution dissolving the body. It was resolved that its assets be turned over to the original religious corporation, to form part of a larger contribution to the United Jewish Appeal.

When, later on, the society changed its mind about transferring the balance of its money and insisted on distributing it among its members, an action in the State Supreme Court was undertaken by the religious corporation so as to compel the society to carry out its original plan. Many proceedings were instituted, including an application for a temporary injunction. Finally, the contending parties and their lawyers decided to submit the matter to the Jewish Conciliation Board. The case came up for hearing within ten days.

After due deliberation, the judges resolved that members of the society who were in need should have a distributive share in the available funds, with a limitation of $100 for each member. The balance was ordered distributed to three organizations, in the following proportions: sixty percent to the United Jewish Appeal, twenty percent to the Federation of Jewish Philanthropies of New York, and twenty percent to the American Red Cross.

The members of both organizations were unanimous in their praise of the wisdom of this decision and warmly thanked the judges for the sympathetic attention which they had given to this problem. The Board supervised the carrying out of its decision. Thus, worthy agencies in the community benefited, and the decision put an end to much acrimony engendered in the organization by the bitterly contested proceedings in the State Supreme Court.

Payment of Benefits

Sometimes a *Landsmanshaft* proved reluctant to pay sick or death benefits, if there was doubt as to the member's eligibility. Mr. K. had belonged to his *Landsmanshaft* for over forty years. At the time of the litigation, he was eighty years old and had contracted a cold which developed into pneumonia. After four months of illness, he still had not received the sick benefits to which he believed he was entitled.

The president of the society stated that Mr. K. suffered from chronic bronchitis and was ineligible for sick benefits, since the *Landsmanshaft* had a regulation that chronic illness did not entitle a member to receive such payments.

The judges ruled that a cold did not constitute a chronic illness, and that Mr. K. was therefore entitled to the sick benefits.

These organizations usually had rules concerning the benefits payable to a member who had been delinquent in paying his dues.

Mr. M. approached the Board with a claim for sick benefits. The president of the *Landsmanshaft* testified that this member had not paid his dues for the last quarter of the year. The president had given his personal guarantee that Mr. M. would pay when he was able and, on this basis, the society had reinstated him. The *Landsmanshaft* was now concerned that this might have set an improper precedent and requested a ruling before paying Mr. M. the sick benefits.

The judges ruled that the president's guarantee was valid until the delinquent dues would be paid, and that Mr. M. should be given his sick benefits. They proposed that, in the future, similar matters should be put to a formal vote, and that the decision be entered in the minutes of the society.

In order to be eligible for an endowment payment following the death of a spouse, proof of legal marriage had to be established. During a time when immigrant couples were sometimes married in a religious ceremony, without the necessary civil license from the state authorities, this was not always a simple matter to adjudicate.

Mrs. L. appeared before the Board, claiming that she was being denied the endowment due her after her husband's death. Her husband's son by a previous marriage had told the society involved that she had been his father's housekeeper and not his legal wife. She had a Jewish marriage certificate *(Ketubbah)*, which the son claimed was a forgery, but no civil document. Since she could not prove that she was the legal widow according to American law, the son had sold his father's house as executor of his estate, and had settled a certain amount of money on Mrs. L. He did not consider her eligible for the *Landsmanshaft* death benefits.

A representative of the *Landsmanshaft* stated that Mr. L. had informed the society of his marriage, and had paid dues as a married man. The president considered Mrs. L. to be entitled to the death endowment which she claimed.

The judges ruled that the *Ketubbah* was authentic. They indicated that the fact that Mr. L. had informed the society of his marriage was further proof of the validity of the marriage. In addition, they said, Mr. L., as an observant Jew, would not have cohabited with a woman to whom he was not legally married. The society was instructed to pay the death endowment to Mrs. L.

Mr. S.'s problem was not only to furnish proof of marriage, but also to produce a death certificate.

He had come to the United States in 1927, leaving a wife and two children in Europe. He had sent them money throughout the years and, in 1948, learned that his wife had died. He now made application to his society for the death endowment which was due to widowed members.

The *Landsmanshaft* claimed that it had no documentary proof of either the marriage of Mr. S. or the death of his wife. The society's representative admitted, however, that Mr. S. had been paying dues as a married man.

On the strength of this evidence, the judges decided in favor of Mr. S.: "Why would a man pay dues for a married couple, if he were not really married? We don't believe that anyone would do such a thing in order to receive a death endowment at some questionable future date."

In many instances, financial stringency compelled a *Landsmanshaft* to reduce the sums granted as endowments and benefits.

Mrs. R. filed a complaint with the Board regarding the society to which her deceased husband had belonged. She claimed that it owed her a $300 endowment, plus funeral expenses. In addition, she felt that she should be reimbursed for the burial costs, since her husband had not been buried in the society's cemetery.

The president of the *Landsmanshaft* explained that two years earlier, in 1937, it had voted to reduce the sum of a death endowment from $300 to $200, and a letter explaining this had been mailed to every member. Moreover, the society's constitution included a provision stating that the family of a member who was not buried in the *Landsmanshaft*'s cemetery was not entitled to payment of the funeral expenses.

The judges took all the facts into consideration. The deceased had been a member in good standing of this society for thirty-eight years, during which time he had paid almost $500 in dues. The judges ruled that, taking this into consideration, the society ought to be lenient. In addition to a $200 endowment for the widow, the society was asked to pay the funeral expenses. The *Landsmanshaft* accepted the decision in good faith and informed Mrs. R. that, at the next meeting, she would receive a check for these amounts.

Occasionally, there were hearings where the *Landsmanshaften* did not dispute the amount owed, but turned to the Board for a ruling as to the proper method of procedure.

In two such cases, the societies involved had become so insolvent, owing to the Depression and to the deaths of many members, that they were unable to pay endowments which had fallen due. In both these cases, the judges ruled that members be taxed small amounts in order to fulfill the endowment payments.

The third case involved a man who had lost both his daughter and his son-in-law, a childless couple, within a short period of time. He claimed the death endowment from his son-in-law's *Landsmanshaft*. The society was willing to pay, but requested a judgment from the Board declaring that it would not be liable to additional claims by other members of the families of the deceased. The family members involved were willing to make the sum over to the father, and the endowment was awarded to him.

The judges did not always decide in favor of the plaintiff. Mrs. F. complained to the Board that the *Landsmanshaft* to which her deceased husband had belonged had paid her only $200, instead of the $300 which (she said) was the proper amount of an endowment. The society's secretary quoted from the constitution, stating that a widow was to receive $200. Mrs. F. admitted that she knew of no one who had received $300. The judges decided in favor of the society.

A son appeared before the Board, claiming $50 from the society to which his late father had belonged. He had already received $150 from the society, but the usual endowment was $200.

The president testified that the deceased had not paid his dues for many years, yet the *Landsmanshaft* had not expelled him. As a matter of fact, every year before the Passover holiday, it would give him funds to help buy food. When the son was requested to pay his father's dues, he refused. This society had a rule that if a member was delinquent in the payment of dues for more than three years, the sum of $52.80 would be deducted from the death endowment.

The judge ruled not only that the *Landsmanshaft* did not owe the son money, but also that the son owed the society $2.80.

A man came to the Board, claiming the endowment, funeral expenses, and *Shivah* mourning benefits due to him, following his wife's demise. The society's secretary read out the minutes of the meeting at which the member, who had been expelled for nonpayment of dues, was reinstated on the understanding that he would not receive any benefits connected with his wife, from whom he was separated. The judges decided that the *Landsmanschaft* was justified in its refusal to submit to the demands of this member.

Conditions of Membership

Most *Landsmanshaften* had strict rules as to who was eligible for membership. One condition was a physical checkup, to insure that the prospective member was in good health.

Mrs. W.'s membership in a certain society was in question. When she and her husband had originally applied for membership, and had undergone medical examinations, her husband was found to be in good health and was accepted. She was denied membership, however, because of high blood pressure. This proved to be a temporary problem, and when she returned three months later for a medical examination, her blood pressure was normal. She received the necessary medical certificate and was subsequently voted in as a member.

Unhappily, on the very evening that Mrs. W. had become a member, her husband passed away. The society allocated a grave site only to Mr. W., because he had been a member for a very short time, and it subsequently refused to recognize Mrs. W.'s membership, claiming that she had never been accepted.

Contrary to assertions made by the secretary of the *Landsmanshaft*, the doctor's certificate did not mention the need for additional treatment. As a matter of fact, he had recommended that she be accepted by the society. Several witnesses also testified that they had been present on the night when Mrs. W. had been voted into the *Landsmanshaft*.

In view of this, and of the fact that Mrs. W.'s father was a charter member of the society, the judges ruled that Mrs. W. be accepted as a full member.

Some *Landsmanshaften* had regulations concerning the maximum age of applicants for membership. The society in this case included a clause in its constitution to the effect that forty-five was the age limit for a new member. There was no provision, however, with regard to the age limit of a new member's wife.

Mr. G. contracted a second marriage with a forty-eight-year-old woman, and the society refused to accept her as a member. The president testified that no provision had been made for such a situation, as it had never before arisen. The society also had different provisions for a member's second wife. Mr. G. stated that he accepted the fact of only partial privileges in this case, but insisted on recognition of his wife as a member.

The judges decided for Mr. G., and furthermore advised the society to incorporate into its by-laws a provision covering such situations.

Most *Landsmanshaften* were eager to have the children of members join, but they were rarely successful. This was a basic reason for the failure of these institutions to survive the test of time. Not enough new young members were attracted to ensure their continuance. The following case, however, involved a son who wished to join his father's *Landsmanshaft* but was denied membership.

Mr. S., a pious Jew, complained to the Board that the society of which he had been a member for forty-three years refused to accept his son as a member. The society's objections were based on the fact that the son had married a proselyte. The daughter-in-law had been converted by an Orthodox rabbi and was religiously observant.

The president of the society was vehemently against accepting the son. When confronted by the judges with the fact that "according to Jewish law, this woman is a Jewess," he rudely replied, "Then take him into *your* society!"

The judges admonished this *Landsmanshaft* official for questioning the authority of the Orthodox rabbi who had presided over the woman's conversion, and ruled that the society must accept Mr. S.'s son and daughter-in-law as full members.

Members of some *Landsmanshaften* were subjected to rigid sanctions, even after years of membership. The societies often had strict regulations concerning remarriage, payment of dues and taxes, and conduct at meetings. There were rules according to which the rights of wives were dependent on the membership of their husbands. If a woman became widowed and later remarried, she would generally lose her membership rights. Rulings often discriminated against divorced persons, especially women.

Mrs. E.'s complaint was that she had been expelled from her *Landsmanshaft* after her remarriage following the death of her first husband, with whom she had a joint membership for thirty-eight years.

The society's representative testified that a widow could continue as a society member, but that following remarriage she must reapply for membership in her own right and pay an initiation fee. When one judge stated that, after thirty-eight years of membership together with her husband and her own continued membership after she was widowed, Mrs. E. should be given some consideration, the *Landsmanshaft* secretary said he felt sure they "could work something out." He expressed regret that she had referred the matter to the Board instead of first coming directly to the society.

A compromise was reached, and the judges decided that Mrs. E. was to pay an initiation fee in small monthly installments and that she be reinstated.

The case of Mrs. D. was more complicated. She had originally joined the *Landsmanshaft* without her husband. During thirty-one years of membership, she had been separated from her husband for twenty years, after which she obtained a divorce. The *Landsmanshaft* had made an exception in this case, allowing her to remain a member, although she was not widowed but no longer married. When she remarried, however, they terminated her membership.

The judges ruled that, since the society had made an exception for Mrs. D. when she had been divorced, it was to allow her to retain membership.

It was not unusual for a *Landsmanshaft* to have a clause in its constitution specifying that high moral and ethical conduct was expected from members.

Mr. W. was expelled from his *Landsmanshaft* after being found guilty of conspiracy to commit fraud and receiving a one-year jail sentence. His wife approached the Board to claim reinstatement in the society and the relief assistance to which she was entitled.

The judges agreed with the society that Mr. W.'s offense had been a serious one, but they requested that reinstatement be reconsidered after his release from prison. They also ruled that the society should assist Mrs. W.

The failure to pay dues or fines was one of the most frequent causes for expelling a member. Especially during the Depression, it was not easy to keep up membership payments. The fact that most members did manage to pay their dues can be regarded as a tribute to the *Landsmanshaften* and as an indication of their importance in the lives of immigrant Jews. There were, of course, many who could not continue their payments and who, after being expelled for this reason, sought the Board's help in obtaining reinstatement.

Mr. N. was expelled from his society after failing to pay a fine imposed for not attending a meeting. He had not had the benefit of a hearing and therefore felt that he should be reinstated.

The society's secretary presented evidence from the *Landsmanshaft* by-laws regarding the fine imposed for nonattendance at a meeting, without prior notice from the member. This fine was designated for charity, and failure to pay it resulted in expulsion. Mr. N. stated that, after eleven years of membership, he had been unaware of this by-law. He expressed willingness to pay the fine in order to be reinstated.

The judges ruled that, although the society's position was justified, the plaintiff had not acted in an arbitrary or spiteful manner and that he should therefore be reinstated, upon payment of the fine. They further stated that, in the future, all members should be informed of such by-laws, so as to avoid misunderstandings.

Mr. P. was a member of his society for thirty-five years. His claim was that when he became ill and applied for sick benefits, the society expelled him.

The president testified that the *Landsmanshaft* had informed Mr. P. in writing that, since he was chronically ill, he would have to pay an additional sum for membership in order to be eligible for assistance. He added that the society had in fact given Mr. P. his sick benefits.

At this point, the more personal emotions of the parties involved were revealed. Mr. P. admitted to having received the sick benefits, but had taken offense over the thoughtlessness displayed by other members, in that no one had bothered to visit him when he was ill. The president, for his part, was disturbed that Mr. P. had taken the matter to the Board instead of replying directly to the *Landsmanshaft*'s letters. He then modified the society's stand, saying that if the plaintiff could not afford to pay the extra dues, the society would be willing to make an adjustment.

After thus bringing the parties to a state of willingness for compromise, the judges ruled that Mr. P. be reinstated, upon payment of the sums overdue. Thereupon, the plaintiff gave the president a check and was immediately reinstated.

Mr. K. had been expelled from his society for nonpayment of a relief tax which was to be donated to a fund assisting European refugees. He explained to the Board that he was employed by the Work Projects Administration and earned barely enough to support his family.

The *Landsmanshaft* representative stated that this tax had been discussed at an open meeting, and the membership vote had been in favor of it. They would not agree to waive the tax, but were willing to reinstate Mr. K. if he paid it in small installments.

While the judges commended the society for its charitable efforts, they recommended that it also consider the needs of its own members. The judges ruled that Mr. K. be reinstated as a member in good standing, and that he pay the relief tax over an extended period of time.

Mr. B. had been expelled from a *Landsmanshaft* after a membership of nineteen years. He had recently lost his job and could not afford to pay his dues.

The president stated that Mr. B. had more than once been suspended for nonpayment over the years, in addition to which he had also refused to pay the initiation fee for his second wife.

The judges observed that the plaintiff was no longer a young man and that, for this reason, no other society would accept him. Accordingly, he was to be reinstated and his dues should be paid in installments, but he would forfeit sick benefits for six months and the membership of his present wife.

Although, in the majority of cases, the Board took the part of members claiming reinstatement in their society, they sometimes ruled in favor of the *Landsmanshaft.*

In one such case, a plaintiff claimed that he had been insulted and threatened by the president of the society. He therefore wished to leave the organization, and demanded that his initiation fee be refunded. It was obvious to the judges that a serious personal conflict was involved. They ruled, however, that they could find no basis for refund of the fee, and that the choice of whether or not to remain a member of the society rested with the plaintiff.

In another case, the society was the plaintiff. It had ousted a member who had become a follower of Father Divine, a Christian preacher claiming to have healing powers. The *Landsmanshaft's* constitution had laid down the rule that membership was limited to believing Jews.

The woman involved insisted on her right to membership. She complained that the members of the society were prejudiced against her. Though proud of her association with Father Divine, considering herself one of his "angels," she nevertheless wished to retain her membership in order to be assured of a burial site. However, she had been informed that, according to the by-laws of the society, a convert to Christianity could not be interred in the society's burial ground.

When one judge suggested that, instead of expelling her, the *Landsmanshaft* suspend her temporarily, also recommending that she study "Jewish Science" in the hope that she might be drawn back into the Jewish fold, the woman declined. She preferred to leave the society and forfeit her benefits. The judges therefore ruled that she submit a written statement relinquishing her membership and the associated privileges.

Society Finances

Landsmanshaft members often complained about various financial irregularities, from the levying of extra taxes to mismanagement of funds.

One member approached the Board, complaining that his society was levying taxes indiscriminately. He had requested a copy of the constitution and by-laws, in order to ascertain his rights, and was told by the *Landsmanshaft* officers that only the original copy of the constitution, written seventy-five years earlier, now existed.

The officers explained to the Board that printing copies of the constitution would involve the imposition of a $6 tax on each member.

They preferred to send any surplus funds to Israel, and observed that it was the levying of a $4 tax intended for Israel that had brought the plaintiff before the Board. The president stated that "the society does not want a member who refuses to contribute $4 to help the Jewish homeland," and declared that the plaintiff would therefore be expelled at the next meeting.

The judges ruled that the society was not required to print copies of the constitution, but that the plaintiff was entitled to have all his questions regarding the constitution and its by-laws answered by the society's officers. The plaintiff was ordered to pay the tax.

Mr. C.'s complaint was that his *Landsmanshaft* assessed its members for an annual tax in favor of the United Jewish Appeal, but that he had never received a receipt from the UJA. Besides, he preferred to contribute to a charity of his own choice.

The secretary explained that each year members voted at an open meeting with regard to the levying of this tax, and that, although there was a clause in the by-laws authorizing the expulsion of a member for nonpayment of the tax, it was rarely enforced. In cases where a member was unable to pay this tax in any one year, he was permitted to do so the following year, and although a fixed amount was set, everyone was permitted to give according to his ability.

Mr. C. had written to the society, declaring that he could not pay the tax and asking to be released from the obligation to do so. This matter was considered by the entire membership, which had voted to deny Mr. C's request.

The judges ruled that they could not order a *Landsmanshaft* to make an exception for a single member. They advised Mr. C., however, to ask the society to reconsider his letter and grant him special consideration.

A member of one *Landsmanshaft* complained to the Board about the financial management of the society. He claimed that the president endorsed checks before the members had voted whether or not to spend the money involved. He also complained that no financial statement was issued to members and that the books were not accurate. The president stated that this was the first time that the society's bookkeeping had been questioned, but that it would be willing to submit to an audit "even tomorrow."

The judges ruled that in order to satisfy the plaintiff, who had been a

member for fifty years, an independent accountant would be selected
by the Jewish Conciliation Board to audit the society's books.

As the members of the *Landsmanshaften* aged, the resources of
these societies were increasingly drained for sick benefits, death
endowments, and funeral costs. Moreover, fewer new members joined
to replace those who had passed away. Thus, many of these organizations found themselves obliged to disband. Disputes often arose among
the remaining members as to how their residual funds should be disbursed.

A man came before the Board to plead that his wife be reinstated as a
member of a *Landsmanshaft* which was about to be dissolved. This
woman had devoted thirty-five years of work to the society, but had
been expelled two years earlier for failure to pay dues, and illness had
prevented her from protesting the expulsion.

Now that the society was on the point of dissolution, she wished to
be reinstated so that she might participate in discussions regarding the
disbursement of any remaining funds to various charities. Upon the
urging of the judges, the society agreed to reinstate her if she would
pay her arrears. The judges ruled, in addition, that she was to have a
voice in deciding how the society's funds were to be distributed.

A final case in this category was that of two members who came
before the Board to settle their dispute regarding the disposal of a
society's funds. One man wished to establish a congregation in Israel so
as to perpetuate the name of the *Landsmanshaft*. The other insisted
that a fund be established to provide for the maintenance of their
cemetery.

The judges ruled that a meeting of the remaining members be
called, and that the entire membership decide how the funds should be
disbursed. In order to prevent suspicion and arguments, the Jewish
Conciliation Board's executive secretary was asked to supervise the
calling of the meeting and the mailing of proxies.

The judges expressed the hope that such a procedure might set a
precedent for other *Landsmanshaften* in New York which were
similarly approaching dissolution.

Congregations

In the wake of the mass migration from Eastern Europe, the synagogue
continued to be an integral part of Jewish life on the Lower East Side of

New York. Considering the great number of congregations which had been formed, notably few disputes came before the Jewish Conciliation Board from this source. Congregational disagreements were generally resolved internally. The following are a sampling of the rare instances where an aggrieved party felt the need to turn to an outside arbitrator and where the Jewish Conciliation Board was in a position to become helpfully involved.

A plaintiff maintained that, as a charter member who had contributed toward the establishment of the synagogue, he was entitled to have his name engraved on a plaque in the building.

The president of the congregation testified that this was correct and that, indeed, the plaintiff's name did appear on two panels in the synagogue. The secretary stated further that one plaque bearing the complainant's name was in the entrance lobby, along with the names of all other charter members. The plaintiff admitted this, but complained: "It's in an obscure place."

The judges' decision was succinct: "We are dismissing the complaint."

The next case is on a more serious note. A widow approached the Board, claiming that the synagogue where her deceased husband had been employed as *Shammash* (sexton) had promised her a monthly allowance of $150 for life. After five years, the payments ceased, hence her complaint.

The president of the congregation exhibited a copy of a letter to the widow, written at the time of her husband's demise, promising her $150 monthly for a period of five years, in appreciation of the work which her husband had performed for this synagogue. In addition, he showed the judges the widow's reply to this letter, accepting their offer and thanking them.

The widow testified that she had been confused when she sent the congregation her letter of acceptance and had, in fact, assumed that the payments were to be for life. She also stated that she had been promised an additional $250. The president claimed that he knew nothing of this latter sum, but affirmed that he was willing to examine the synagogue records and that, if the minutes showed that she was entitled to the $250, she would receive it. Regarding the continuation of her monthly grant, he refused to accept an obligation to authorize such a payment.

Although the widow insisted that "legally, they may owe me nothing, but morally they owe me a great deal," the judges ruled that this congregation had demonstrated its good faith and that she was not entitled to any further payments.

It was not always easy to determine whether a ritual object which had been donated to a synagogue was the permanent and complete property of the synagogue or, in some degree, continued to be the property of the donor. This sometimes became an issue, especially if a synagogue was about to dissolve and to sell its possessions.

A woman came to the Board, claiming a Torah scroll which her father had donated to his synagogue many years earlier. The congregation was about to disband, and had sold the Torah scroll without notifying her or any other member of her family.

The former synagogue president admitted that this was so. The scroll had already been bought by someone who wished to donate it to another synagogue, and the purchaser had promised that the original memorial inscription would not be removed. The proceeds of the sale had been contributed by the synagogue to the United Jewish Appeal.

The judges ruled that under no circumstances might the congregation sell this *Sefer Torah* to anyone, that the scroll must be repurchased from the buyer, and that the family of the deceased donor was then to be consulted as to which congregation should receive the Torah scroll.

In a similar case, a man asked the Board for a ruling with regard to the *Sefer Torah* which his late uncle had donated to a synagogue. This synagogue was about to disband, and the family of the deceased wished to donate the scroll to a synagogue in Israel in honor of the congregation's rabbi, whom the uncle had greatly revered.

The synagogue president testified that there had been a misunderstanding and that the synagogue was planning to relocate, but not to disband. The officers had made a pledge to donate the scroll to Israel if the congregation should ever dissolve, but the rumors that the congregation was about to close down were unfounded.

The judges ruled that, as long as this synagogue continued to function, the Torah scroll remained its property. In the event that the synagogue would disband sometime in the future, the scroll was to be returned to the family of the donor, to be given to an Israeli congregation.

Although congregations, like *Landsmanshaften*, required payment of dues and adherence to certain rules and standards of conduct, few cases of that nature were brought before the Board.

There was, however, one case involving an eighty-year-old man who complained to the Board that he had been expelled for nonpayment of dues. He wished to pay the arrears and be reinstated, but the congregation had requested an additional sum.

The judges decided that, in the light of the plaintiff's age and forty years of affiliation with the congregation, he was to be reinstated as a full member upon payment of his dues.

A man complained that there had been no cause for his expulsion from a congregation. The congregation's president testified that the plaintiff was a troublemaker, that he constantly insulted and annoyed the rabbi, and that he had refused to attend a meeting called specifically to discuss his conduct.

The judges ruled that the congregation had the right, under its constitution, to run its own affairs and to suspend a member. This right must be upheld, and the plaintiff had no claim against the synagogue.

Contractual Obligations

Most of the complaints against congregations involved breach of contract.

A Hebrew school teacher complained that the congregation where she had been employed had not paid all of the salary due her. The amount in dispute was $75 for two weeks of teaching.

The rabbi testified that the teacher was unable to control her classes and, for this reason, he had been forced to dismiss her two months before the completion of the school year. When she had appealed the dismissal, he allowed her to remain until the end of the year, since he would have had to compensate her for the two months in any case. The two weeks in dispute were vacation time. The rabbi added that, early in the school year, she had been informed that there would be no classes during those weeks.

The teacher said that she had assumed she would be paid, regardless of the fact that the two weeks were vacation time.

The judges reached a compromise decision of $60 as a fair amount in settlement of the teacher's claim. The rabbi agreed to pay her immediately.

A cantor told the Board that the vice-president of a congregation had promised to hire him. After he had officiated only once, he was not retained. His compensation claim was based on the fact that, because of this congregation's promise, he had not taken another position which had been offered him.

The secretary testified that the congregation had been obliged to correct the cantor's errors when he conducted the services. The cantor had admitted that he had not conducted services for twenty years and was out of practice. The congregation had decided to pay the cantor $15, but this he refused to accept, demanding a payment of $25. Now the congregation refused to pay anything.

The judges ruled that the cantor had no basis for his claim, since there was no contract involved. The secretary again offered to pay the cantor $15, although the judges had not obliged him to do so.

A man was suing a congregation for breach of contract. He stated that he had been hired as assistant sexton, on the understanding that his position would be a temporary one until his work could be evaluated.

After a period of service, during which he received no complaints, the man had assumed that his position was now permanent. Following a disagreement with the sexton, however, he had been dismissed. He asked to be rehired, or compensated for breach of contract.

The sexton testified that he had final authority for the hiring and dismissal of assistants and that the plaintiff had been dismissed because his work had proved unsatisfactory.

The judges ruled that the plaintiff was to be retained in his position for another four months, after which time his contract could be renewed or terminated.

The following case illustrates a common practice during the 1930s and 1940s. A sexton, upon being hired by a congregation, would pay them a certain sum of money, usually about $2,000. On leaving his post, he would receive a similar amount from his successor.

A sexton approached the Board with the complaint that his congregation refused to return the $2,000 which he had paid when he was first engaged. He was now seventy-one years old and unable to continue working.

The president explained that the sexton was obliged to find a replacement who could then pay him the $2,000. The congregation would not assume the responsibility.

The sexton testified that it was specifically the well-known attitude of the congregation which prevented him from finding a successor. No other sexton would agree to work for them.

The rabbi on the panel, announcing the decision of the judges, said that he was aware that this was not the only congregation which resorted to such dubious practices. "Every decent person feels a sense of shame that disputes of this kind must be brought here. The good name and honor of the Jewish people would suffer, were this type of case to come before the municipal courts. We should be grateful that we have a Jewish court to handle such cases."

The judges ruled that a successor should be found within four weeks, either by the defendant congregation or by the plaintiff. If this effort proved unsuccessful, the congregation would become liable for the repayment of $2,000 to the plaintiff.

Burials

Proper ritual burial has always been an important obligation in Judaism. One of the first acts of a Jewish community, upon settling in a new location, was the buying of land for a cemetery.

It is not surprising, therefore, that many disputes over burials, involving *Landsmanshaften* and lodges, came to the Jewish Conciliation Board. These cases included disputes regarding the sale or ownership of graves, the erection of memorial stones, provisions for the saying of *Kaddish,* and other issues relating to Orthodox burial practices.

The refusal of *Landsmanshaften* to grant a member burial rights led to a number of referrals to the Board.

Mrs. K. complained that her late husband's fraternal lodge refused to grant her a deed for a burial plot in the cemetery. The president of the lodge explained that she had remarried, thereby forfeiting her right to a burial plot, according to the lodge's constitution.

The judges upheld the position of the lodge, stating that "every society has a constitution and by-laws which must be adhered to. According to the by-laws of this lodge's constitution, Mrs. K. has no right to a grave in the cemetery where her first husband is buried. Such rights terminated upon her remarriage."

Another woman, who had been a member of her congregation for forty-three years, filed a similar complaint. The congregation, upon the death of her husband, from whom she had been separated for thirty-five years, declared that she was not entitled to a burial plot in its cemetery.

The treasurer of the congregation, who had been a close friend of her late husband, testified that the deceased had often told him that he did not want to be buried near his wife. Furthermore, he had paid dues as a single man.

The woman stated that she had paid her own dues as a separate member, and that the congregation had offered to sell her a burial plot for $50. As a dues-paying member, however, she considered herself entitled to the plot without charge.

The judges upheld her claim and ruled that, as long as she continued to pay dues, she was entitled to a plot in the congregation's cemetery.

Mistakes were sometimes made in regard to the location of burial plots. In one such case, the congregation had mistakenly buried a woman in a plot which had been reserved for a widow next to her deceased husband. The congregation had admitted its error and had offered the widow another burial plot, but she insisted on having the site on the other side of her husband's grave. She also demanded a refund of the $60 which she had paid to reserve the original plot. The congregation insisted on an additional fee for reserving an alternative site.

The judges ruled that the widow was entitled to the site she had specified, and that the congregation had no right to any additional sum, since it was the party at fault.

In the following case, a blunder was committed on the very day of the funeral. After Mrs. L. had expressed the wish to be buried near her husband and son, the surviving children reserved a site for her in accordance with her request. At the funeral, however, they were too upset to notice that their mother was being interred in a grave which was not in the location which they had reserved and paid for in advance.

The financial secretary of the society admitted that there had been a mistake, but maintained that this site was more expensive than the one paid for. Moreover, he said, although Mrs. L. had not paid dues for many years, her membership was not suspended, so that now her time had come to "go the way of all flesh," the children would be recompensed for the funeral expenses, in accordance with the standard procedure of the society.

The judges decided that some compensation should be made by the society. They ruled that, for a period of five years, the society should take upon itself the cost of maintaining the grave.

Some cases involved requests for refunds, for a variety of reasons.

A woman had paid $250 to her society for a burial plot. She stated that when the society refused to give her a deed to the plot and to tell her the location of the cemetery, she became suspicious, and subsequently she demanded the refund of her payment.

The judges ruled that, since the woman had lost confidence in the society, the sum of $225 should be returned to her. The remaining $25 of the original payment should be retained by the society to reimburse it for any expenses which it had incurred. Both the plaintiff and the president, who represented the society, willingly accepted the judges' decision.

The litigants in the following case had been unable to settle their dispute privately, and therefore decided to approach the Board for mediation.

Mr. R. had reserved a grave in the society's burial ground. However, when he died, the family buried him in another cemetery. They now wished the cost of the first burial plot to be refunded them. The secretary of the society affirmed that the sum in question had also included funeral expenses, as well as the costs incurred for the shroud, casket, and hearse. Accordingly, the society was of the opinion that no money was owed to the family.

After commending the disputants for applying to the Board for an amicable settlement, the judges ruled that half the sum paid for the grave site be refunded. This amount was to be utilized by the family for the erection of a tombstone over the grave of the deceased.

Many cases which came before the Board were concerned with the setting of memorial stones. A congregation or a *Landsmanshaft* would often hold a certain amount of money in trust for a member, as eventual payment for a stone to be erected over his or her grave. The payment of such amounts was a frequent cause of disputes.

Mr. K. had agreed to forfeit the endowment payable to his family after his death, on the understanding that this amount would go to pay for his grave. This arrangement had been made without his children's knowledge. When their father died, they asked for the sum of $100, now owed to them, for the purpose of erecting a stone over their father's grave. The society refused, claiming that this amount had been applied toward the cost of the grave.

Upon examining the society's by-laws, the judges discovered that $50 of the amount was supposed to be used for a headstone. By allowing the total sum to be used for the purchase of the grave, the society had violated its own by-laws. The judges ruled, therefore, that the society should pay $50 to the children of the deceased, this sum to be used for the erection of a monument.

The estranged family of a deceased member claimed a certain amount from his society, in order to pay for the erection of a stone. The recording secretary, who had been a friend of the deceased, testified that the man had written his family out of his will and had requested that the society make all the funeral and memorial stone arrangements. The secretary added that the family had not even attended the funeral.

The judges decided that $125 of the $200 benefit payment should be given the widow, and that the remaining $75 be paid to her after the cost of the headstone had been defrayed.

According to Jewish law, the mourner's *Kaddish* must be recited daily for eleven months following the death of a parent, and for the week of *Shivah* after the death of a brother, sister, spouse, or child. It is also recited annually on the *Yahrzeit* (Hebrew anniversary) of the death. Orthodox observance prescribes that only men say *Kaddish* and that, when there are no male survivors, an outsider be hired to recite the prayer.

Mr. R. gave his society $75 to hold in trust until after his death, when someone would have to be hired to say *Kaddish* for him. His widow now appealed to the Board to grant payment of this amount to her orphaned grandson, who was saying *Kaddish* daily in memory of his grandfather.

The society's president, though eager to fulfill the wishes of the deceased, claimed that if the latter's intention had been for his grandson to say *Kaddish* for him, he would have so indicated, especially since this grandson was the notary public who had certified the grandfather's original request.

The judges based their decision on the view that it was preferable that a blood relative fulfill this obligation than a stranger. They therefore ruled that the $75 be paid to the grandson. They also commended the society's president, however, for the concern he had shown regarding the fulfillment of the deceased man's wishes.

Although the Jewish Conciliation Board was not a Rabbinical court empowered to deal with problems of *Halakhah* (Jewish law), such issues were occasionally brought before the judges. The tribunal did not undertake to decide on Halakhic questions, and would refer them to Orthodox authorities. In cases where *Halakhah* was not strictly involved, however, the Board would do its best to be helpful to the litigants.

The representative of an Orthodox lodge brought a complaint against the children of several members. He claimed that they had interred their parents in the lodge's cemetery, but that the funerals were conducted in a non-Orthodox manner. He specifically referred to the use of elaborate caskets and vestments, and even the use of rouge, all of which is strictly prohibited by Jewish law.

The representative of the defendants maintained that the way in which the burials were conducted should not be an issue, and that those desiring more elaborate funerals for their loved ones should be allowed to have them.

The children of the deceased members had agreed to abide by the judges' decision.

The judges decided that, since the lodge and its members were Orthodox, the children must adhere to Orthodox Jewish practice. Ritual washing must be performed and the body must be dressed in a shroud, no makeup might be applied, and a simple coffin must be used, with no inside fittings.

The rabbi on the panel spoke for all the judges when he said: "The organization involved is an Orthodox one, and members joined with that understanding. No one may use this society's cemetery to bury their dead, unless they abide by the Orthodox Jewish laws."

Commercial Matters

The fact that many cases of a commercial nature were brought to the Jewish Conciliation Board, rather than to the civil courts, indicates the degree of trust and confidence which the Jewish community, especially on the Lower East Side, placed in this tribunal. It was also indicative of the great need for such a tribunal. Cases of a commercial nature included disputes involving loans, agents' services, wages, dismissal from employment, and various forms of breach of contract. Some of these claims had a specifically religious character.

Mr. M., a Yiddish author of some repute, had been hired by Mr. P. to edit a book in the Yiddish language. The fee agreed upon had been $300, to be paid upon completion of the work. After working on the manuscript for six months, Mr. M. was approached by Mr. P., who claimed that he had no funds to publish the manuscript. He asked for its return and offered Mr. M. $25 for the work done by him up to that time. After some argument over the fee, the two men agreed upon $60 as the final payment, half of which Mr. P. handed over immediately. The balance was to be paid within a short time. After Mr. M. returned the manuscript, he discovered that another author had been hired to complete the editing job and that, in fact, the book was about to be published.

Mr. M. applied to the court, claiming the balance of the $300 originally agreed upon.

Mr. P. protested that the author had done almost no work on the manuscript. "I hired him on the basis of other works which he had published, especially his Yiddish dictionary, but all he did for me was to change a few punctuation marks. I told him that I had decided not to publish the book because I did not want to hurt his feelings by indicating that he was not capable of doing the job."

Mr. M. stated calmly that he was quite used to criticism and that his feelings would not have been hurt. He believed, however, that Mr. P. had made him return the manuscript under false pretenses. He had been hired to edit, but Mr. P. had really wanted him to rewrite the material.

The judges agreed with the author. The defendant was ordered to pay the plaintiff $125 in addition to the $30 already paid. When Mr. P. vigorously protested that "the man isn't entitled to the money, and I don't have it," the judges asked him, "If Mr. M. *had* done the work for you, how would you have paid him?" "*Then* I would have found the money," was the defendant's vehement reply.

"Then find the money now!" a judge retorted. "You have signed an arbitration agreement and you must now abide by the judges' decision." The defendant was given ten days to do so.

In a more prosaic case, a man employed in the fur trade complained to the Board that he had not received his full wages. His employers had promised to retain him with pay even during the slow season, but they had failed to do so.

The employers claimed that their guarantee to employ the plaintiff during the slow season included a mutual understanding that he would remain with them once the busy season recommenced. He had left their employ, however, when the busy season began, and for this reason they refused to pay his wages.

The judges decided that the plaintiff was entitled to a sum equal to one-third of the agreed wages.

When the employer-employee relationship coincides with family ties, business disputes can be exacerbated. Thus, Mr. D. testified that while his sister had been hospitalized, he had helped in her store. He had not drawn wages and had even paid for merchandise. His sister was now living with him and had not paid rent for three months. His claim to the Board was for the arrears and the current rent due him.

The sister maintained that her brother had been instructed to accept merchandise on credit rather than pay cash. She also said that he had taken money from her store to pay for his rent. She did not keep any records of transactions. When her brother exhibited records which he had kept while working in the store, she claimed that they were falsified accounts and even accused him of stealing from her business.

The judges advised the defendant to take action independently of the present case, if she was convinced that her brother had behaved dishonestly. In this case, however, they decided that she had failed to prove her claims and ruled that she owed her brother back pay and three months' rent.

In a number of cases involving loans, the dispute did not arise out of any dishonest intention, but stemmed rather from a real inability to repay.

Mr. L. testified that in Ecuador, South America, before immigrating to the United States, he had loaned $100 to Mr. S. on the understanding that this sum would be repaid after he arrived in New York. Mr. S. had failed to return the money.

When he spoke before the judges, Mr. S. seemed sincere in his intention to repay the loan, but was at a loss as to how he could manage to do so. After five-and-a-half months in the United States, he was earning $45 a week and his wife had just given birth. He had offered to pay Mr. L. $5 a week, but the latter refused to accept this arrangement. He demanded $20 immediately, and $10 each week thereafter until the loan would be repaid in full.

The judges ruled that Mr. S. must pay $10 a week for two weeks, and $5 a week thereafter until the debt had been discharged.

Business firms which appeared before the Board were often more than glad to settle their disputes amicably. The following case is such an example of goodwill.

Mr. V. complained to the Board that his daughter had bought him a hearing aid for $175, but it had never functioned properly. He asked that Mr. K., the manufacturer of the hearing aid, be ordered to refund the money. In addition, he wanted the money returned to himself rather than to his daughter.

The manufacturer stated that, although the hearing aid guarantee was good for one year, he had offered a two-year guarantee in this case. Since he knew Mr. V. to be poor, he had given him free batteries in addition to adjusting the appliance many times. He failed to understand what the problem was. Although the original cost amounted to $240, he had charged Mr. V. only $175 and had never in fact charged him for the time and labor spent on repairs. The manufacturer suggested that Mr. V. consult a social service organization which could supply him with free batteries and repairs.

The judges commended Mr. K. for the service and attention he had given to Mr. V. They then asked the manufacturer if, as an act of charity, he would be prepared to return $30 to Mr. V. He agreed to do so, and the judges ordered the plaintiff to stay away from Mr. K.'s place of business and to cease abusing him.

Mr. M. complained to the Board that an organizational summer camp owed him two weeks' refund on a three-week stay at the camp from which his daughter had come home after only one week's vacation.

In his testimony, the treasurer of the organization disclosed that the period alluded to in Mr. M.'s complaint had been three years prior to this appearance before the Board. The refund was complicated by the fact that the organization only kept records for two years' duration. Mr. M. had retained his receipt of payment for a three-week stay, but he had no proof that his daughter had indeed come home after only one week.

The judges decided in Mr. M.'s favor, but reprimanded him for having waited three years to apply for the refund. They also commended the organization for its good work and for its willingness to bring the matter to the Jewish Conciliation Board.

Matters of Conscience

There were certain cases in which one party, who had been appointed as an agent by another party, requested advice as to how to discharge his responsibilities in the proper manner. Generally, the agent had not been appointed legally, but had been asked to safeguard a particular sum of money as a friend of the family.

After falling ill and being hospitalized, Mrs. K. had called upon her friend, Mrs. L., to take charge of a $1,000 savings bond. The bond had been intended for Mrs. K.'s niece, then an infant, and was to be given to her on her eighteenth birthday. Mrs. K. had passed away when the niece was still quite young, and Mrs. L. was unsure as to what she should do with the bond. The deceased had specified that the bond was to go to the niece, and not to her mother.

The judge complimented Mrs. L. on the care, discretion, and thoughtfulness which she had given this matter, and on her earnest desire to abide by the wishes of the deceased.

They recommended that the bond be entrusted to the mother, with the stipulation that she should not cash it unless this would prove absolutely necessary.

Mrs. B. had given her friend, Mrs. C., the sum of $900 to hold for her. When Mrs. B. died, her husband brought Mrs. C. before the Board and demanded this sum which had belonged to his late wife. Pointing out that all his three sons were mentally retarded and lived in an institution, he declared that he needed the money in order to reserve burial plots and memorial stones for himself and the three boys, adjoining the grave of his deceased wife.

Mrs. C.'s testimony revealed that she had promised Mrs. B., "on her deathbed," that the money would not be relinquished to Mr. B., since Mrs. B. had intended that it be utilized only for her three sons. Mrs. C. therefore refused to hand over the money unless she had Rabbinical authorization to do so. In addition, she stated that the institution where the boys lived had her name on file as the party responsible for them in case of an emergency. She insisted that she be freed of her responsibility for the boys if the money were to be relinquished to Mr. B.

A nephew of Mr. B. appeared on his behalf and suggested that the $900 be turned over to the funeral home, to be kept in trust for the boys, while he himself would provide for Mr. B. He also proposed that his name be entered in the files of the mental institution as the one responsible for the sons.

The judges decided that the money should be deposited in a joint account in the names of Mrs. C. and the nephew of Mr. B. The money was to be utilized only for the boys, in keeping with Mrs. B.'s wishes. They also complimented Mrs. C. on her performance of a *mitzvah* by fulfilling the wishes of a dying friend.

Mrs. F. accused her deceased mother's sister, Mrs. S., of holding money which was to have been inherited by herself and her children.

She had no proof of this accusation, but insisted that the defendant swear on a Bible that she had no such funds.

Mrs. S. testified not only that she did not hold any money of her late sister, but that she had in fact spent $1,000 of her own cash to pay for the funeral of the deceased. Mrs. F. continued to insist that her aunt swear on a Bible, and while the Bible was being brought Mrs. S. changed her testimony. She now told the judges that her sister had indeed given her money, which had been spent on the funeral expenses. This she was prepared to swear on the Bible.

This disclosure satisfied the plaintiff and the case was closed.

Homes for the Aged

Elderly persons who wished to reside in a home for the aged would often sign over their money and possessions to the institution. If, after a period of time, they decided to leave the home, they would ask that such monies be returned to them. The institutions did not always readily comply. Many cases of this type came before the Jewish Conciliation Board.

Mr. and Mrs. D. brought an action against the home in which they resided. They wished to leave because the food and care they were receiving was inferior, but the institution agreed to refund only half of the $8,000 which had been paid in originally.

The director of the home testified that Mr. D. had been a problem for the institution. In fact, this couple had a long history of problems in other homes for the aged, where they had continually been dissatisfied. In this particular institution, Mr. D. was carrying on a feud with another resident. Both Mr. and Mrs. D. were also accusing the staff of attempting to poison them. When the couple declared their wish to leave, the board of directors agreed to refund them the sum of $4,000. Actually, this was contrary to the rules of the home, but the director stated that the board was prepared to make an exception in this case and to authorize such a payment.

The decision of the judges was as follows: "We feel that the entire situation is very unfortunate. On the one hand, you agreed to enter this home and to turn over all your personal belongings to them, to be retained permanently. Now, on the other hand, you wish to leave. As far as this home is concerned, they have been fair even in making an offer of $4,000. We have decided, however, to go beyond the measure of fairness and to ask the home to pay you $6,000."

Mr. T. complained to the Board that the home where he resided refused to give him spending money. The director of the home testified that Mr. T. had always been given whatever sums of money he requested from his account. The real problem, he said, was that Mr. T. refused to abide by the rules and regulations of the institution and was a disruptive influence. In addition, he had assured the director that he would finance his stay at a hospital from the account he held at the home, but had not done so, thereby leaving the home to be billed by the hospital.

Mr. T.'s reaction to the director's testimony was to say, "I can do as I like as long as I have the money there."

The judges ruled that Mr. T. should leave the home within a month, at which time he would receive the balance of his money.

The last case history of this kind involved a couple who had been residing in a home as recipients of municipal welfare funds. When the wife suddenly inherited a large sum of money from her deceased brother, she left her husband and the home. Although she was ordered by the Domestic Relations Court to finance her husband's expenses in the home, in accordance with the rules of this institution, she had not done so. After a short sojourn at the home, following her appeal to be readmitted, she again left. Now she was once more applying for readmission, but the home considered itself entitled to refuse. Hence, the woman brought action against the home.

The representative of the institution declared that the husband was residing with other single men, and that there were no rooms available for couples at that time. The daughter of the couple told the judges that she believed her mother would be happier in the home, but she was concerned that the home would keep any inheritance to which she herself might be entitled upon her parents' death, were her mother to resume living there.

The judges ruled that the home accept the woman again but that, upon the demise of both the man and his wife, their daughter inherit the balance of their funds.

Fees and Contracts

Another group of cases were related to commercial disputes of a religious nature, often involving commission fees.

Mr. A. claimed that he had negotiated a position as *Ḥazzan* (cantor) for the Reverend R. The cantor, however, stated that although Mr. A.

had informed him of this vacancy, he had obtained the position through his own efforts.

After hearing the testimony, the judges ruled that Mr. A. had been instrumental in the appointment of Rev. R. to the position, and that the defendant should therefore pay the commission fee.

When such cases involved breach of contract, the contracts often proved to have been informal and oral.

Mr. L. complained that he had repaired a number of sets of *Tefillin* (phylacteries) for Mr. N., who subsequently refused to pay for his work. Mr. N. testified that he had given the plaintiff twenty-two pairs of *Tefillin* for repair, but that only ten had in fact been repaired. The remainder had been returned without the handwritten parchments inside.

Mr. L. then explained that he had performed this task in accordance with *Halakhah* (Jewish law). The twelve sets of *Tefillin* which were returned unrepaired had contained parchments too worn to be used. According to Jewish law, ritual scrolls which are in any way damaged must not be used. In order to prevent anyone making a mistake, he had cut the faulty parchments with scissors. He refused to reinsert any scroll that was *pasul* (invalid) into a *Tefillin* case.

The judges ruled that Mr. L. had acted properly, and that he was therefore entitled to receive payment from Mr. N.

A father complained to the Board that his son had been hired to sing in a synagogue choir during the High Holy Days, but had not yet received payment. The cantor who had hired the boy testified that although the lad had attended the choir on *Rosh Hashanah*, he had not participated in the singing. Furthermore, although the father had notified him that his son would not attend on *Yom Kippur*, thus obliging the cantor to hire someone in his place, the boy still came. He stood with the choir, but did not sing.

The judges ruled that, since the cantor had allowed the boy to remain, he should pay him. The cantor paid the father, who then signed an undertaking that he would make no further claims against the cantor.

Mrs. S. testified before the Board that she had paid $300 to a *Yeshivah* (religious day school) as tuition for her son. Although she had asked to be allowed to pay in installments, the director told her that the money would have to be paid in one sum. He gave her an address where she could borrow the amount. During the school year, her son had been suspended and she was informed that the tuition fee would be refunded. Thus far, the *Yeshivah* had failed to make any repayment.

The director's brother, who was also the boy's teacher, said that he had been a troublesome student, that he refused to study, used profane language, and had broken a window. The boy had been suspended for a week, after which the parents refused to send him back to school. When the lad was questioned, he denied the accusations and complained that the other boys teased him. His mother added that the conditions at the *Yeshivah* were so bad that she had decided not to send her son back.

The judges ordered the *Yeshivah* to refund the tuition.

After this decision had been announced, another teacher at the school came forward and told the judges that the description given of the boy's behavior had been false. He had found him to be a conscientious, polite student. When the director's brother asked the Board whether the *Yeshivah* might be permitted to refund the tuition in installments, protesting that the school could not afford the entire sum, the judges advised him to borrow the money from the same source that had been recommended to the plaintiff.

Mrs. G. brought action against a firm which inscribed ritual objects. Wishing to present her synagogue with new coverings for the Torah ark and *Bimah* (reading table), in memory of her late husband and son-in-law, she had ordered these to be made up with appropriate inscriptions. When they were completed, she discovered that the inscriptions did not match her specifications.

The owner of the firm stated that the completed inscriptions corresponded exactly to Mrs. G.'s original instructions, but that she had changed her mind and now wanted them to be redone. He protested that the cost of redoing the inscriptions was high, and that he could not afford it. One of the judges asked him: "Wouldn't it pay to lose a few dollars in order to satisfy a customer?"

The judges decided for the plaintiff. If the new inscriptions failed to satisfy Mrs. G., the company was instructed to refund the money in the form of a contribution to the synagogue.

Mr. B. was claiming fees for the *Bar Mitzvah* instruction of Mr. K.'s son. His regular fee was $5 a month for Hebrew lessons, with an additional fee of $30 for special *Bar Mitzvah* training. Mr. K. explained to the Board that he was a poor man and had paid whatever he could to the teacher, who had never informed him of the additional fees. Furthermore, when he tested his son, he discovered that the boy had not been adequately prepared.

The teacher indignantly declared that he would never allow a boy to face a congregation unless he had been carefully trained for the *Bar Mitzvah* ceremony, since he would then be imperiling his own reputation as a teacher. He added that if he could be sure that the family was a needy one, he would be ready to accept a reduced fee.

The judges ruled that Mr. K. pay $15 to Mr. B. for the lessons.

Domestic Problems

The great majority of cases brought for adjudication to the Jewish Conciliation Board involved domestic issues. These can be classified generally as follows: support claims, infidelity, estrangement, children's education, custody and visitation rights, problems of step-parents, dissension between siblings, parental or in-law interference, and financial problems. There were cases in which the official complaint brought by the litigants to the Board was really a pretext for airing a totally separate grievance. It is to the Board's credit that many seemingly irreconcilable differences, often of an intensely emotional character natural to this category of actions, were reconciled and the litigants placated and, sometimes, hopefully reunited.

Claims for support appeared on the calendar of the Board almost every month, but as might have been expected, they increased greatly during the Depression years. Many claims for support were made by wives against their husbands, but our court dealt with many more claims for support brought by parents against their children.

Wife's Maintenance

The plaintiff testified that she and the defendant had been married for twenty-two years, but had not lived together for sixteen of those years. They had arrived from Europe about ten years before the proceedings. The plaintiff stated that in Europe her husband, while married to her, had cohabited with another woman, by whom he had four children. This woman lived in Lithuania, and the defendant had been sending her $25 every two months. The plaintiff testified that previously she had never asked her husband for support, because she had been employed and earning a good salary. Now, however, she had lost her job, and she asked for $10 a week support from her husband.

The husband admitted his wife's story and indicated his willingness to assist her financially. However, he was not working steadily and could not afford to pay her more than $5 a week.

The judges asked whether there was any chance of reconciliation. The defendant replied that he had not been able to stand his wife's nagging, and that she had always made him feel that he could not discharge his responsibilities toward her. The wife asserted that, after so many years of separation, it was too late to try again.

The judges ruled that the defendant must pay his wife $7.50 a week until he would find permanent employment, at which time the payment would have to be increased to $10 a week. In answer to his protest that he could not afford more than $5 a week, the judges said, "If you had gone to the civil courts, you would probably have been ordered to pay more and, had you refused, the punishment would have been a jail sentence." Reluctantly, therefore, the defendant agreed to comply.

In the following case, the wife's claim for support was countered by the husband's demand that her brother move out of their apartment.

The wife claimed that "he spends very little time with me and the children. He probably dates other women. He is lazy. Whenever he is at home, he is very abusive. He buys expensive shoes for himself, but when the baby needs shoes he doesn't have the money." She also stated that her brother had moved into their apartment in order to help with the expenses and that, thereupon, her husband had moved out. Although, under questioning, the wife admitted to having no proof that her husband had been living with another woman, she refused to allow him to move back with her "until he mends his ways."

The husband denied all of the wife's accusations. Although he expressed longing for his children, he refused to consider returning home until his brother-in-law had left. He said that this relative interfered in their lives. Then he turned to his wife, claiming that "for me you could never make a sandwich in the morning, but for your brother you do everything."

Realizing the impossibility of a reconciliation while the wife's brother remained a boarder in the couple's home, the judges ordered the husband to pay support, with the proviso that the case might be reopened if the brother were to move.

A couple, each of whom had been married before, realized that they had made a mistake in marrying each other. On their first appearance before the Board, the judges prescribed a one-month trial separation for the couple, and the husband was ordered to pay the rent and $25 a week support for his wife.

A short while later, they reappeared before the Board with a long list of new complaints. The husband claimed that, on the morning after the hearing, his wife had demanded the $25 support money immediately. When he told her that he did not have the money at that time, she threw all his clothing into the hallway outside the apartment, and he was forced to move after the Sabbath had begun. A few days later she put new locks on the door, and when he tried once again to visit her, the neighbors told him that she had gone on vacation. "I couldn't get over it," he told the judges with dismay, "that she was enjoying herself on a vacation."

The wife testified that although her husband had promised her gifts of money and jewelry before the marriage, not only had he never given her anything, but she was forced to use her own money to furnish their apartment. After their marriage, she added, he gave her very little money for household expenses and he would deduct the cost of his meals from the household allowance whenever he ate away from home. She claimed that, on the morning after the hearing, her husband had packed all his belongings and had moved out without leaving her any money. In addition, she said, he had accused her of stealing his radio.

The judges decided that, under the circumstances, it would be better for the couple to remain apart. They ordered the husband to pay $40 a week to his wife for support. When the husband vehemently protested his inability to pay such a sum, the judges added a proviso that the stipulated amount could be renegotiated after the husband's retirement from his job.

Mrs. F. brought her son-in-law, Mr. K., before the Board for non-support of her daughter, who had suffered a mental breakdown after giving birth to their first child. The daughter was now confined in a private sanitarium, which charged $300 a month. Mrs. F. and her husband, a pushcart peddler, were spending all their savings on their daughter's care, while Mr. K., who was a self-employed trucker, lived with his mother and did not contribute to the cost of his wife's hospitalization.

The young husband testified that his business was not doing well and that he was deeply in debt. His mother was taking care of his seven-month-old baby boy and was not charging him for rent or child-care. Mr. K.'s mother also pointed out that her son had been extravagant when he married and had never saved any money.

Mrs. F. was very concerned lest, for lack of funds, her daughter be transferred to a state institution where the care would not be adequate to assure her eventual recovery. One of the judges on the panel said he would attempt to obtain a reduction in charges from the sanitarium.

The judges ruled that Mr. K. should pay $5 a week toward his wife's medical fees, and they advised him to seek permanent employment which would guarantee him a fixed income, so that he could assume his full responsibilities as head of the family. He promised the judges that he would try to implement their decision.

In 1945, a young woman brought her mother-in-law before the Board, requesting financial assistance in bringing up her infant child. The young woman's husband had been killed in action during World War II and was posthumously awarded the Purple Heart for bravery. The woman and her child received monthly pension allowances from the government, while the soldier's mother had received the proceeds of the insurance money, since he had designated her as beneficiary under his policy. The widow felt that this insurance money, though legally her mother-in-law's, should go toward the upkeep of herself and the child.

The mother-in-law challenged her daughter-in-law's claim to the insurance and, to prove her contention, related facts purporting to show how the young woman had ensnared her son into matrimony and how selfish, grasping, and cruel she had been to her husband following their marriage. The judges hearing this case realized at once that the problem was not one of money but of a bitter relationship between the two women, both of whom had lost the one dearest to them.

For the sake of the infant child, and out of respect for the memory of the fallen soldier, the judges prevailed upon the two women to forget their animosity and concentrate on the child's future welfare.

The social worker contacted both parties and arrangements were made to have the child visit the grandparents. They responded by purchasing warm winter clothing and other necessities for the child. Thus, the two families sharing a common tragedy were assisted toward a more friendly understanding than had previously been possible.

Support for Parents

The *Yom Kippur* prayer, "Cast us not off in old age," is unhappily sometimes directed by aged parents toward their own children. During the Depression years, such claims, brought before the Jewish Conciliation Board, increased substantially. A contributing factor was occasionally the government's refusal to pay a relief allotment. Such payments were only granted if the applicant had no children capable of supporting him or her. If there were children, their refusal to support their needy parents did not alter the government's policy.

The following case was typical. A man's application for relief payments had been turned down because his daughter, with whom he resided, was employed. Her work, however, was not steady, and the father therefore came to the Board with the request that his other children help support him. He admitted that it would be difficult for them to do so, since they were all struggling to earn decent livelihoods.

The judges explained to the children that as long as they were employed, their father would not be eligible for relief payments. After questioning each one as to his or her salary, the judges set an amount for every child to contribute weekly. The amounts were small enough for each to manage, but the total sum would be enough for the father's subsistence.

———————

It can justly be said that the cases of tension between parents and children which came before the Jewish Conciliation Board were the exceptions which proved the rule, namely, the close family ties which have been characteristic of the Jewish family relationship.

There can be little doubt that the Americanization process also carried with it some negative developments. One of these was a weakening of the family bond and of the readiness to honor father and mother. Yet it was significant that the judges appealing to litigants, in more than one case which came before the tribunal, found it helpful to invoke the Fifth Commandment.

In all of these cases, the judges would remind the children of their moral as well as legal responsibility to support a parent. They always awarded some amount of support to the parent, no matter how small. When necessary, the judges would take it upon themselves to write to other children living outside the area, requesting that they contribute to the parent's support. Frequently, they interceded with the Welfare Department to ask for a reinvestigation of the children's financial situation. These cases presented a living panorama of the poor immigrant Jewish community, and shed light upon the emotional as well as the physical toll of poverty.

In the case of Mr. S., the reluctance of his daughters to support their father stemmed from their antagonism toward him rather than from their financial inability.

The application of Mr. S. for an old-age pension had been denied when it was discovered that he had three daughters who could support him. One married daughter invited him to live with her, but he refused to do so. The other two daughters lived with his wife, from whom he had been separated for many years. This separation had led to an estrangement between the daughters and their father, and they refused to assist him.

The Welfare authorities had suggested that Mr. S. take his children to the Domestic Relations Court, where their financial obligations toward him would be assessed. Rather than subject his daughters to the publicity of a trial in a civil court, Mr. S. had turned to the Jewish Conciliation Board.

After listening to the daughters' excuses for not supporting their father, the judges stated that "the primary obligation to support a parent rests upon the children, rather than on the community." The daughters failed to respond, and the judges were forced to order them to support their father. Mr. S. was also advised to reconsider his refusal to live with his third daughter, who had invited him to do so.

Mr. W. had seven children. He lived with one son, who had no means of his own, and received some financial support from a second son. The third son had never offered to assist his father financially, and it was he whom Mr. W. brought before the Board. When questioned by the judges, it became apparent that this son, a sixty-two-year-old man, had been too ill to work and was supported by his own son, who was himself without steady employment, and by various relief agencies. The astonished judges asked Mr. W. why he had brought to the hearing the only one of his children who could not possibly support him.

The plaintiff explained that his other four children were daughters and that he "did not believe in taking money from daughters." The judges affirmed that the man's daughters had the same responsibility to support him as his sons. Mr. W. agreed to let the court contact all his children so as to negotiate a support settlement. This decision was carried out by the Social Service Department.

Mr. B. came all the way from Florida to present his case. He received no support from any of his four sons, all of whom lived in New York. He complained that he had given them everything when they were young, and now they refused even to speak to him.

One son, acting as spokesman for all four brothers, explained that their father had divorced their mother and had cut himself off from his children. He had not even recognized one of his sons when passing him on the street. The father had remarried twice and, through the years, had never given his children any emotional support. The son insisted that his father was living comfortably with a woman in a Florida bungalow.

One of the judges said to the son, "Good, bad, or indifferent, he is your father."

"I don't go along with that," replied the son.

"I am speaking of a natural father," the judge continued, "and, if he *is* your father, you are duty-bound to support him." Turning to Mr. B., the judge observed, "Your children seem to be decent and respectable people. We believe that this is not the kind of case in which we can decide how much your children should give, so we suggest that they decide among themselves."

The sons agreed that they would subsidize their father in the amount of $30 a week and would pay for his return fare to Florida.

Mr. M. approached the Board, claiming support from the children of his first marriage. He was sixty-seven years old and was now married to his third wife, a thirty-six-year-old nurse, who refused to support him.

The testimonies of the children all amounted to case histories in poverty. One son had supported his father for twenty years, but was currently unemployed and unable to continue the assistance. A second son declared that he was a pushcart peddler, had supported his father until his own wife had become ill, and that his married children, who were themselves in financial straits, could not assist him and his wife. The third son had refused even to sign the arbitration agreement. He had been working as a truck driver, but was currently on strike and living on welfare. The only daughter had been giving her father one dollar a week, even though she was the sole support of her blind husband. The latter was about to be hospitalized for an operation, but she would continue the weekly payments to her father.

The judges ruled that each child pay the father the sum of one dollar a week. The son whose union was on strike was to begin payments after his return to work.

Mrs. P.'s children, including a partially blind son, all contributed to her support, except for J., who refused to do so. She approached the Board to obtain the support of J. as well. J. testified that he had recently married and that his new wife would refuse to work if any money went to his mother. After some questioning by the judges, J. began to unfold a list of grievances against his brothers and sister. He told the court that when his father had owned a vacation hotel, he was the only child to assist his family by working there. The other children had been financial burdens. He also felt that if his mother's financial situation were as serious as she claimed, she would not be residing in an expensive apartment, as was presently the case.

The daughter testified that her brother J. had always been very selfish and inconsiderate. He had told his mother that he was getting married only one day before the wedding, and even then he had not invited her. As for the "expensive apartment," she pointed out that her mother had a boarder who helped pay most of the rent.

In response to an appeal from the judges, all the children agreed to continue their support payments, except for the reluctant brother. The judges accordingly fixed an amount which he was obligated to pay.

Mrs. W. asked the Board to order two of her sons, aged twenty-four and twenty-one, to support her. These boys, still single and both employed, had moved out of her house. Five other children lived at home with her, three of whom were under the age of sixteen; one of these children was employed and contributed part of her salary to the household expenses. The eighth offspring, a son, had been married for a year and was at that time separated from his wife.

The eldest son testified that he and his brother had left home because of the mother's bad temper. When angry, she yelled so loudly that all the neighbors could hear. He was employed as a laborer and worked very hard for his living. He rented a furnished room near his place of work in Brooklyn. The other brother also testified that he could not stand his mother's temper. He did not have a steady job, and had moved to the Bronx in order to be close to his girl friend's home. This boy claimed that when his mother found some letters which his girl friend had written to him, she showed them to her neighbors in order to embarrass him.

Giving further testimony, the older brother alleged that their father's death, a year before, was due to an illness caused by their mother "having made his life a misery." He added that when their married brother came to visit them following the separation from his wife, their mother had thrown him out of the house.

The sons refused to offer support voluntarily, even after the judges reminded them that a civil court could order them to pay a substantial amount. The rabbi on the panel of judges advised the younger brother that his girl friend's family would show him greater respect if they saw him making sacrifices for his mother. The sons nevertheless remained adamant in their refusal to assist her.

The judges, recognizing that the sons could not afford to pay large amounts, decided that the older boy should pay his mother $3.50 a week, and the younger boy $1.50 weekly. They also spoke to the plaintiff, urging her to show more love and respect for her children if she wanted their love and respect in return.

Mrs. W. was still not satisfied, however. She said that the previous week her eldest son had promised to pay her $5 weekly, and that she had brought him before the Board because she felt this sum to be inadequate. The son admitted that he had promised his mother the amount stated, but disclosed that this promise had been extracted from him after his mother had threatened to "disgrace him in front of his employer and cause him to lose his job."

The judges did not alter their decision.

There were other cases in which the judges felt that the children were supporting the parent adequately, and that the parent had no good reason bring the matter to the Board.

Mr. R. was living in his son's home. After an imagined insult by his daughter-in-law, he began cooking his own meals. He then approached the Board with a claim for support from his son. The son testified that he was the only one of the children supporting their father. He had brought him over to the United States from Germany, and when his father contracted pneumonia, he had paid all the medical fees. He still wanted his father to remain at home with him.

The judges ruled: "We feel that this son is doing his best for his father, and the father should make an effort to be happy with him."

In a similar case, a father complained that he could not go on living with his son because the latter did not maintain a *Kasher* kitchen. He requested that all his children contribute to his support so that he could live alone.

The son affirmed that he had always kept a strictly *Kasher* home. He believed that "the trouble with Father is that he is a fanatic and is always imagining things." A second son claimed that there was absolutely no justification for the father's suspicions and that he was "merely a crank."

The judges dismissed this complaint and said that the sons need not maintain their father in a separate accommodation as long as the first son continued to keep a strictly *Kasher* home.

There were some cases in which the parents' complaints proved to be unfounded, as the children were actually willing to support them. The children would claim that their feelings were hurt when their father or mother took them to the Board, instead of appealing to them personally for assistance.

In one such instance, the judges ruled: "The Board feels that the children of this plaintiff are reasonable and have proven themselves willing to contribute funds to cover their father's cost of living. We do not find it necessary to stipulate any set sum."

The children, in a similar case, were willing to support their father, but wanted a signed agreement stipulating the amount which each one was to pay.

Often a case involved one son or daughter who had undertaken the entire financial and emotional responsibility for supporting an aged parent. The decision of the judges was necessary to establish what share the other brothers and sisters should pay. In other cases, an aging or sick parent was residing with one child, who requested financial assistance from the other children in order to enable the parent to be admitted to a home for the aged. There were also cases where the parent was welcome to continue living with a son or daughter, who wished, however, to receive monetary assistance from the other children for the parent's support. Most of these cases were settled in a straightforward, amicable way. Some actions might be classed as belonging to the "no-man's-land of human needs in which public relief does not operate." A typical case follows.

A young woman was brought before the Board by her brothers and sisters on the all-too-familiar charge of failing to contribute toward the support of their parents. Her brothers and sisters all agreed that the young woman was perfectly capable of making a substantial contribution, but she stubbornly refused to do so. This particular daughter, it appeared, had been the chief support of the parents for many years, since she had the largest earning capacity of the entire family. Everything would have continued in this way, but for the fact that when she once forgot to send her monthly allowance, and her brothers and sisters reminded her of the oversight, she became outraged. No amount of coaxing or pleading could thereafter induce the daughter to resume her obligations. The family was very reluctant to turn to the appropriate city courts, because of her long record of generosity toward her parents.

When they all came before the judges of the Jewish Conciliation Board, it was at once evident that an unusual personality stood before them, one who required delicate and tactful handling. The judges listened to a full review of the family's past history. Close questioning revealed that this daughter had done more for the parents and for orphaned nephews and nieces than all the others combined.

The judges partly convinced the emotional daughter to reestablish her close relationship with the family, but their task was not fully accomplished until one of the judges and a social worker visited her home and listened again to the young woman's catalog of real and fancied grievances.

Finally, the Board succeeded in restoring the previous friendly relationship and secured a renewal of her support for the parents.

Infidelity

Within the sphere of marital conflict, very few cases of infidelity as such, unrelated to other family problems, came before the Board. In any case, the Board had no authority to grant divorces. Such issues, however, did arise in the context of other situations which came within its purview.

In one such case, the plaintiff maintained that he wished to move back into his home, but that his wife would not allow him into the house. In exchange for the privilege of moving in with her, he offered to pay the rent. The wife said that her husband was often drunk and that he had left home in order to live with another woman. The husband then testified that he had given up alcohol, but he did admit to the second charge.

One of their daughters affirmed that she and the other children had no respect for their father because of the way in which he had treated their mother. Nevertheless, she offered to assist her father financially if he would behave decently. After he had moved in with a strange woman, she said, they had all refused to have anything to do with him.

The judges ruled that the defendant was justified in refusing to take her husband back, but that the children should give him financial assistance.

A husband accused his wife of betraying him with one of his friends. He claimed that he was uncertain as to whether their second child was his own. His wife told the court that her husband was very suspicious and would not even allow her to shop alone. She had avoided seeing the friend in question for over a year because of her husband's suspicions. She had also agreed to have their second child examined in order to assure her husband that it was indeed his. The husband, however, did not trust the doctor, who was a longtime friend of the wife. In his testimony, the husband also stated that in Europe they had been married only by the civil authorities and that, although he wished to arrange a religious ceremony in America, his wife continually postponed such a decision.

The ruling of the judges was that the couple should be married in a religious ceremony, which they should consider symbolic of their new life together.

———————————

The following heartrending case involved a husband who did not believe that his wife's unborn child was his. The wife was in the fifth month of her pregnancy when the hearing took place. The judges suggested that the couple consult an Orthodox rabbi. The latter asked the woman to swear before a Torah scroll that the child was her husband's, and she did so.

Shortly afterward, she telephoned the Jewish Conciliation Board's social worker, saying that her husband still refused to believe her and had several times threatened to kill her. He insisted that if the baby turned out to be a girl, it could not be his own. Though alone and terrified, the woman refused to complain to the police or to initiate divorce proceedings, because she had entered the country illegally from Canada. Her husband had already threatened to report her to the immigration authorities, who would deport her. She begged the social worker to help her find a job so that she could live on her own. The Board's social worker gave her the names of several employment agencies.

One week later, the social worker received a call from the husband, who reported that his wife had left home. He asked whether the Board had helped her to find a job. On receiving an affirmative reply, he demanded the name of the agency which had assisted his wife. The social worker's suggestion that he consult a psychiatrist was brusquely dismissed. This suggestion was pursued during a later telephone conversation with the wife, when the social worker proposed that she enlist the aid of her husband's family in an effort to persuade him to seek psychiatric advice.

The final entry by the social worker in this case indicates that although the wife gave birth to a child resembling its father, and despite two blood tests, one performed by a doctor chosen by the husband, which proved that he was the baby's true parent, the husband still would not recognize the child as his own. He ranted and raved, wishing that the child had been born dead and insisting that it be given away for adoption. The wife was afraid that her husband might try to kill the baby. He finally agreed to obtain a Mexican divorce, following a promise from the wife that he could have all their furniture. Her fear of being reported to the immigration authorities prevented her from demanding support payments. The Board's social worker promised to give the woman every possible assistance in finding employment for herself and day care for the baby.

Mrs. A. was a wife who often dated other men. Her husband, though a non-Jew, brought his problem to the Jewish Conciliation Board.

The woman's latest companion had written to the husband, assuring him that he had no wish to break up their marriage. Nevertheless, Mrs. A. kept a photograph of this man in the apartment. Moreover, she often took her young son along when she went to see him. Mr. and Mrs. A. were employed in the same office, and she had told everyone about the affair.

When Mrs. A.'s sister spoke to the Board's social worker, a new aspect of the case was revealed. She explained that her sister had a history of mental illness, and had been hospitalized following a teen-age abortion. She had also been in trouble with the police several times while in high school. Confirming Mr. A.'s testimony, she said that this was not Mrs. A.'s first "affair" and that her sister always bragged about being unfaithful to her husband. The sister's chief concern was for the couple's son, who was growing up and beginning to grasp the significance of his mother's behavior. In addition, Mr. A. had also been hospitalized once for psychiatric observation. Now the son was also beginning to exhibit signs of emotional disturbance.

The social worker submitted the case for a hearing and made the following proposal to the judges, who later adopted it as their decision. The couple should separate for a period of one to two years, during which time their son would be placed in a foster home. This would offer the boy a chance to live in a more peaceful environment. At the end of this period of separation, the couple would be able to assess their feelings toward each other and in regard to their marriage.

Unhappily, about a year later, Mrs. A. telephoned the social worker in a state of depression, saying that she was three months' pregnant and could not obtain employment. Her male friend refused to assist her, and her husband, from whom she was still separated, also would not help her. The Board's social worker gave Mrs. A. the names of several employment agencies which might be able to assist her in finding a job. The only good news at the conclusion of this entry was regarding the son. Thanks to the Board's wise counsel, he was doing very well in school and liked his foster parents. Mrs. A. reported that she and the boy's father visited their son regularly every week.

Marital Tensions

Many cases of estrangement between husband and wife came before the Board. Despite their commitment to the principle of reconciliation, the judges recommended separation for spouses who were obviously incompatible.

Mr. S. complained that his wife had moved into the home of a married daughter and refused to see him. He wanted her to return home. The wife testified that she could no longer tolerate living with her husband. During the thirty-two years of their marriage, she had never had a moment's happiness; her husband, she claimed, had always mistreated her, often threatening her with bodily harm. Mr. S. denied these charges, maintaining that he had always been a good husband and a good provider.

The daughter with whom Mrs. S. was living said it was obvious that her mother did not wish to be reconciled with her father. "After all," the daughter said, "a mother doesn't usually prefer to live with her daughter rather than with her husband." They both asked only that Mr. S. agree to leave them alone.

The judges ruled as follows: "It is the Board's wish that Mr. S. and his wife live together peacefully, but under the circumstances, it would be advisable for them to remain apart for six months, during which time Mr. S. must stay away from his wife and family. It is hoped that, after that period of time, Mrs. S. may agree to a reconciliation. If not, the couple will have the option of returning to the Board for a reconsideration of their problem."

Quite a few domestic conflicts which came before the Board were not serious ones, and could be alleviated by the friendly intercession of a third party who enjoyed the disputants' respect as a seasoned, impartial, and caring individual.

In one such case, the judges listened to a couple enumerating minor grievances on either side. "Do you love your wife?" they asked the husband.

"Yes, I do," he replied.

"And do you love your children also?"

"Yes."

"Would you like to stay with your wife if the differences between you could be ironed out?"

"Yes."

The judges' decision was, quite simply, that the parties should exert every effort to adjust their problems.

The couple left the hearing in a cheerful frame of mind. Their only wish had been for a disinterested party to hear their laments and to assure them that their problems were not insurmountable.

In the following case, a minor incident became a major source of dissension.

Mrs. M. complained to the judges that she was sure her husband was seeing another woman. This was the only possible explanation, she believed, for the fact that he was suddenly so short of money.

"He was never late paying the bills before," she explained, "but now he is. He must be spending the money on someone."

The husband told the judges that he was spending the money "with friends—gentlemen friends." He then went on to describe what he considered to be the real cause of his wife's complaint and, indeed, the reason for his spending less time at home. It all began one evening when he and his wife, together with his daughter and her fiancé, were watching a movie about a fashion photographer accused by his wife of having an affair with one of his models. Mr. M. jokingly said, "If you can't beat them, join them!" This remark greatly offended the daughter, who then proceeded to ban her father from speaking to anyone at her forthcoming wedding. Mrs. M., instead of realizing that her husband had said it as a joke and taking his part, sided with the daughter. Since that evening, the relationship between Mr. and Mrs. M. had been very tense.

In an effort to bring about a reconciliation, the spokesman for the judges' panel said, "The husband was undoubtedly joking, but the joke was in bad taste." He then congratulated the couple on being good parents and raising a daughter with a fine sense of modesty. "Turn over a new leaf, forget this incident!" he appealed. Stating how impressed the judges had been by the obvious affection between Mr. and Mrs. M., he begged them not to allow one incident to destroy their home.

The following domestic quarrel illustrates how societal values have changed. In December 1944, a husband came to the Board seeking a reconciliation with his wife. Mr. and Mrs. Y. had been separated for two years and shared the custody of their only child. The wife was in full-time employment, and Mr. Y., who worked in the evenings, looked after the child during the day.

Mr. Y. complained that his wife did not care to stay at home and keep house, that she did not like to clean and could not cook. It had been her wish to have a baby, but after their child was born she preferred to pay a stranger to care for it rather than give up working. Mrs. Y. told the Board that she had always been the financial support of their family, since her husband could never earn a good living.

Today, it might not seem so unusual for a wife to work outside of the home while her husband did the chores and looked after the children. In 1944, however, the social worker to whom the judge had referred the case urged that the wife give up her job and remain at home in order to keep the family united. The husband was admonished for being lazy, and he was advised to find a full-time job.

Not infrequently, the ostensible cause of a complaint really masked a different grievance or deeply felt need.

A woman living apart from her husband complained to the Board that he was not taking adequate care of their eighteen-year-old son, who resided with him. During the course of the hearing, the judges realized that the wife had actually come to the Board in the hope of achieving reconciliation. The husband too, it seemed, wished to return to his wife. Neither had known how to approach the other, and they were overjoyed at the judges' decision that they resume life together. In this case, the child was the motivating force for a reconciliation.

Parents and Children

As already indicated, one of the most difficult areas of human life is the parent-child relationship. A key aspect is the failure of children to live up to their parents' expectations. Often this problem is compounded by the human failings of one of those concerned. A number of such cases came to the attention of the Jewish Conciliation Board.

Mr. and Mrs. W. complained to the Board that their thirty-one-year-old son, a college graduate, could not hold down a job. A compulsive gambler, he was constantly involved in "get-rich-quick" schemes and demanded money from his parents for these and other expenses. The couple had worked hard all their lives, but were not people of means. The son now wanted $3,500 for speculation in the commodities market. His previous speculation adventure had cost his

parents $10,000. They were ready to help him again, but only after he
would find permanent employment and cease gambling.

The son alleged that his parents had always discriminated against
him in favor of his brother. There was no mistaking his bitter resentment. He had received good grades in college, while his brother had
failed, yet their parents had given the unsuccessful brother large sums
of money and only handouts to himself.

The judges attempted to reason with the son. "After all, your parents
are not youngsters," they pointed out. "They worked hard for their
money and are entitled to enjoy the fruits of their labor. Even if you
did not receive all the benefits you would have liked, they did support
you through college."

"They also supported my brother," he replied. "There's a great
difference between getting A's and B's as I did, and flunking out, like
him." The son continued to vent his anger against his parents, insisting, even when shown proof to the contrary, that they had a $10,000
bank account. The judges' attempts to reason with the boy were
countered by detailed instances of the favoritism allegedly shown
toward his brother.

Finally, the judges ruled that if this son would find steady work for
a period of six months, and could manage to save $500, his parents
should make him a gift of $1,000. Mr. and Mrs. W. were pleased with
this decision, but the son immediately found reasons for not being able
to secure employment. When one judge suggested that International
Business Machines might well have room for a college graduate with
his qualifications, the son alleged that this company never employed
Jews. The judge then pointed out that the claim was not only inaccu-
rate, but that IBM permitted observant Jewish employees to leave
work early on Friday, the eve of Sabbath. In conclusion, the judges
reprimanded the son for constantly seeking excuses for his own failures.

In the next case, arguments between the parents regarding their
son's future had become so acrimonious that a domestic breakup
seemed imminent. Each parent had a contrasting interpretation of the
son's behavior.

The father claimed that the boy was lazy, refusing to seek employment. To the mother it appeared that he was simply ambitious and
unwilling to accept "just any job." The father complained that the son
had no friends of his own and, perhaps for this reason, always accompanied his parents to the beach. The mother thought it very con-
siderate of her son to spend so much time with her. At this, the

father declared that their boy should leave home and learn to fend for himself. The mother insisted that he was taking an X-ray technology course and that, after completing these studies, he would find suitable employment.

In desperation, the father threatened to leave his wife. "Maybe she prefers my son's company to mine," he said to the judges.

Their ruling was that the son should remain at home until he had completed his studies. They admonished the father for wanting to drive his son out of his home, but they also advised the mother not to allow the boy to accompany them all the time.

Mr. and Mrs. B. brought their son before the Board, complaining that he had left home "to live a wild life." When he suddenly married, they received no invitation to the wedding, and since then they had not seen their grandchildren even once.

The son's testimony pointed to a different kind of situation. He maintained that his parents had always expected more of him than was reasonable and that he had moved out of their home in order to live independently, and not to lead a "wild life." When he decided to get married, he had long been out of contact with his parents. Nevertheless, he had invited them to his wedding, but had not even received a written reply. Now he was surprised to hear that they cared to see his children. This encounter at the Jewish Conciliation Board, he said, was his first meeting with them since before his marriage. On the other hand, he described his relationship with his in-laws as very close.

When questioned, the son agreed that he had a good mother, but felt that she could not be satisfied. He could only offer her the same consideration that he would show to any other human being.

One of the judges turned to him and said, "Your mother has humiliated herself before three strangers in coming to us, merely to get a little attention from you. Don't you feel you should respond?"

"Yes," the son reiterated, "as I would to any human being, not to a mother."

The judges urged the son to telephone his parents occasionally and to invite them to his home. They also advised the parents to be grateful for being able to see their son occasionally, and not to expect more from him than he was capable of giving.

A couple brought their son before the Board in 1944, complaining that this seventeen-year-old lad had lately become disobedient to his parents, apathetic about schoolwork, and disrespectful to his teachers.

He was slovenly in his person, and had begun associating with undesirable friends. The parents, intelligent and in comfortable circumstances, did everything in their power to restore the boy's normal behavior, but to no avail.

After trying to win the boy's confidence, the judges asked him to talk about his problems. He told them that he saw no point in studying because he knew that he would be going into the Army very soon, and it did not matter what would happen to him in the interim.

It was apparent that the young man's state of despair had been brought about by his impending induction into the armed forces. This was a difficult case to adjust in view of the boy's fixed ideas, but the Board succeeded in extracting a promise from him that he would make a serious effort in his studies until the completion of his high school course. The social worker also interested him in a Jewish cultural club where he could find more suitable friends.

Since it was felt that the parents needed guidance no less than the boy, it was arranged that the social worker visit their home and have several talks with them. She saw the boy on a number of occasions and was able to report that there had been a definite improvement not only in the son's attitude toward his parents and toward school, but also in the way in which the parents related to their boy.

In-Laws and Grandparents

Despite the popular jokes about in-laws, very few cases of in-law interference came before the Board. Two instances, however, are worth citing.

A wife complained that her father-in-law constantly interfered in her marital life and would not allow his son any independence. This situation was further complicated by the fact that her husband was employed by his father, who thus controlled him and his finances. The wife wanted her husband to leave his present job and "make something of himself." In addition, she claimed that the father-in-law had tried to estrange her children and husband from her and that he insulted her in front of them.

When the father-in-law testified before the Board, he made it clear that he did not approve of his daughter-in-law and that he considered her to be more interested in money than in his son. The wife countered that she would much prefer her husband to work on his own, even if he earned less money, than to remain under his father's domination. She described her husband as both dependent upon and terrified of his father. The father-in-law insisted that he had only been trying to establish his young son in a good business.

The judges did not render a decision, but they did offer some practical advice. They tried to make the wife realize that a man as stubborn as her father-in-law would never agree to apologize to her, and that she should not expect him to do so. They advised her to try and understand the bond between father and son. They also urged that the husband receive professional counseling.

In a similar case, a wife complained that her husband had given his mother a key to their apartment. The mother-in-law used it freely, walking right in at any time and interfering in their lives. She also frequently criticized the wife's handling of domestic matters, in front of her husband and children.

For his part, the husband complained that his wife saw only the negative aspects of their relationship with his mother and always ignored anything favorable. As an example, he mentioned the fact that his mother would often enter their apartment in order to leave cooked food and baked goods. He considered that what his wife described as interference was in reality a desire to be helpful

The judges proposed that the husband speak to his mother regarding his wife's feelings and help her to understand that she was making them unhappy. They suggested that she no longer retain a key to the couple's apartment, and they stressed that although, as a son, he must continue to show love and respect toward his mother, as a husband, he must devote primary attention to his wife. The wife agreed to visit her mother-in-law occasionally, provided that the latter no longer had the disputed key.

There were also a number of cases involving disputes over matters of child-rearing.

A father complained that his wife and in-laws were too lenient with his son, and that they overindulged him with spending money and tickets for the movies. The wife explained that her husband had been brought up by a very strict father and was now too severe with his own son, believing that a son must literally fear his father. She told the court that on a few occasions, when the son had come home late at night, his father had locked him out of the house.

The son testified that he enjoyed physical training and often came home late because he had been spending time at the gymnasium. He never stayed out late on school nights, however, and always attended synagogue on Friday evenings and Saturdays. In addition, he had been employed during the summer and had deposited his earnings in the bank. The boy admitted that his school grades could be better, but claimed that, when he did receive good grades, his father never praised him. Accordingly, he was not disposed to make a greater effort.

The judges advised the father to be more tolerant of youth and not to demand perfection from his son. They suggested that he learn to enjoy his son's company instead of trying to instill fear in him. "Be sympathetic to your son. Don't use intimidation, but reason and love."

Children as Victims in Family Quarrels

An elderly couple complained to the Board that their son-in-law, who had remarried after the death of their daughter, refused to allow them to see their grandchildren. They also accused his second wife of having told the grandchildren that the plaintiffs were not their real grandparents.

The son-in-law and his wife testified that whenever the grandparents had visited them in the past, they had told the children: "We have regards from your mother; she is alive and sent us here." The children naturally became confused and upset by their grandparents' remarks. The grandparents also told them not to associate with their half-brothers and half-sisters, and not to share gifts with them. The parents were trying very hard to bring up all the children on the same footing, as brothers and sisters, and the second wife affirmed that the children's teachers and their neighbors had all complimented her on the fine manner in which she was raising the family. The couple did not object to the grandparents' visits, but rather to the divisive tactics and the morbid attitude which they adopted in front of the children.

The judges spoke with each of the litigants separately and also with the grandparents' son, who volunteered to act as intermediary. They impressed upon the grandparents that their grandchildren now had two other sets of grandparents and siblings and that, although the youngsters should revere the memory of their deceased mother, they must not be made to feel contempt for their stepmother. Next, the judges spoke with the young couple, urging them to be patient and understanding with the grandparents.

The plaintiffs were given permission to see their grandchildren once a month, alternately at their own home and at that of the children. To insure that all would go well, the grandparents' son was asked to be present during these visits.

A grandmother asked the Board to allow her to retain custody of her grandchildren. Since their mother had been institutionalized, the grandmother had been raising them. Their father had recently obtained a divorce and remarried, and now he and his wife wanted the children.

When they appeared in court, the children were poorly dressed and in a state of neglect. Their father's new wife declared that she recognized the difficulties involved in raising another woman's children and gaining their love and respect, but felt confident that she would prove successful. The children, however, had been turned against their father by the grandmother, and they refused to live with him.

Because of the grandmother's obvious inability to provide adequately for the children's welfare—both financially and emotionally—and despite the children's prejudice against their father, the judges ruled that he should have custody of the youngsters.

The judges concluded this hearing with an appeal. "We trust that, with much patience and a loving attitude, both of you will soon win the love and respect of these children . . . and the children will soon realize how much their father cares for them."

Problems of Stepparents

In the following case, the conflict was between the wife's wish for security and the husband's fear of commitment.

Mr. and Mrs. K. had been married for eight months, and Mrs. K. was expecting their first child. She had two children from a prior marriage and wished Mr. K. to adopt them. Her husband declared that he planned to adopt the children, but preferred to wait until he was sure that the marriage would succeed. The judges reminded him that the moment his wife had become pregnant he had already assumed irreversible responsibilities.

It was apparent that, whereas the wife was concerned for the children's financial security, the husband was reluctant to be burdened with a heavy legal obligation. The judges searched for a compromise solution. They recommended that the husband adopt the children within sixty days, and if he should refuse to comply by then, that the wife withdraw her earnings from their joint bank account and redeposit them in a trust account for the children.

There were frequent instances of conflict and dissension between older persons who had remarried, and who had grown children of their first marriage.

Mrs. T.'s complaint was that, only three months after her wedding, the twenty-six-year-old son of her husband's first marriage came to live with them. The boy was unemployed, a troublemaker, and abusive toward her. She wanted him to leave her home.

Mr. T. testified that, although he did not insist that his son live with them, his present wife had promised before their marriage that he could do so. Mr. T.'s daughter, with whom the boy had been living previously, admitted that her brother was difficult, but confirmed her father's testimony that Mrs. T. was familiar with the boy and his problems and had accepted the situation prior to the marriage.

Mrs. T. denied these contentions, stating that the boy had been discharged for belligerence from a Civil Conservation Corps camp in California and that, at twenty-six years of age, he had a history of unemployment.

The son maintained that he was only twenty-one years old and alleged that his discharge from the Civil Conservation Corps had been inspired by anti-Semitism. Lacking a trade, he had encountered difficulty in finding employment and was dependent on the allowance he received from his father.

The judges opined that Mr. T.'s son was a healthy young man who should have no difficulty in finding employment. They urged that he rent lodgings for himself and that his father continue to assist him financially until he would be able to find a job.

Mrs. H. complained that the stepchildren of her second marriage had told her, "You are the second wife and nothing belongs to you." Describing them as well-to-do, she asserted that they had taken all their father's money and were also the beneficiaries named in his insurance policy. She would therefore be left without means.

One son testified that their father was not the wealthy man that Mrs. H. imagined him to be. Furthermore, he said, his father handed over his entire salary to Mrs. H., who doled out the spending money.

At the judges' suggestion, Mr. H. agreed to rewrite his insurance policy, assigning one-third to charity and two-thirds to Mrs. H. Mrs.

H., in turn, agreed to write a will leaving one-half of her savings to her husband and the other half to charity.

Family Quarrels

Among the cases involving disputes between siblings is the following unhappy story.

Mrs. K. asked the Board to order her brother-in-law, Mr. C., to provide funds that would enable her to bring her sister and his brother, a married couple, to the United States. She claimed that he had hitherto refused to assist their family in Europe, and had indeed caused the suicide of his sister by refusing to send her an immigration affidavit.

Mr. C. denied the accusation, maintaining that he had sent many affidavits to Europe and that the document sent to his sister had not been accepted. He also told the court that he had been supporting a family of fourteen persons in Europe during the twenty years since his arrival in the United States. Some money transmitted recently had been confiscated by "the new government in Austria" (it was a year or two after the *Anschluss*), and he therefore considered his moral and legal obligations to have been fulfilled. He refused to send more money, feeling certain that the family would not receive it.

The judges ruled in favor of Mr. C. "Whatever contributions Mr. C. did make are considered acts of charity. It is not within the jurisdiction of this Board to force persons to make charitable contributions."

Mrs. D. complained that her brother, Mr. G., refused to finance their mother's emigration from France to the United States. Mr. G., however, testified that their mother had on various occasions in the past traveled to the United States at his expense, but had always been unhappy in America and returned to France.

He was willing to continue sending money and packages to his mother, but felt that it would be futile to try and bring her to the United States, since no transportation was even available at the time (1945). Moreover, on her last trip to America, the immigration officials had not permitted their mother to disembark from her ship.

The judges ruled in favor of Mr. G. "He cannot be compelled to bring his mother to this country," they concluded. "The Board is satisfied that he is doing whatever he can to help her."

A man came to the Board hoping to reconcile his two quarreling sisters. One sister lived with their brother, who was an invalid, disabled by several strokes, and she would not permit the other sister to visit the brother.

Sister A. testified that previously she had often visited her ailing brother and had taken him for rides, which he enjoyed. She had a key to his house, but one day found that the lock had been changed by sister C. Sister A had angrily broken a window, but later paid for its repair. She begged the judges to secure permission for her to visit her brother.

The other kin told the judges about the rivalry between sisters A. and C.

The judges ruled that sister A. be permitted to visit her brother outside his home twice weekly, for three hours. After a period of three weeks, if tranquil conditions were restored, she could resume visits to her brother at the home of sister C., notifying her by telephone of the planned visit. The judges expressed the hope that a harmonious relationship would now develop among all the parties concerned.

A young woman requested the Board's help in bringing about a reconciliation between her two younger sisters, both of them over twenty-one years of age. Although they lived in the same apartment and shared the same room, the two had not spoken to one another for over eight years. The estrangement had gradually become intensified.

The woman who brought this matter to the attention of the Board, without the knowledge of her estranged sisters, described a condition of almost unbelievable animosity between them. Not only had it warped their own lives, it had also disrupted the everyday life of their parents and had gradually affected the younger children at home.

The entire family was now on the verge of nervous prostration. They were ashamed to bring the situation to public notice or to any social service agency. Having heard of the Board's work, the older sister felt that this delicate matter might best be handled by the JCB.

Through the social worker's repeated personal contact, kindness, and sympathetic understanding, together with much tactful handling of the whole family, the two estranged sisters were gradually made to realize that their past behavior had been unjustified. The case was brought to an amicable solution.

Parental Interference

Some parents find it difficult to allow their children to live their own lives.

Mrs. W. complained to the judges that her daughter had thrown her out of her home. The daughter testified that she could no longer stand her mother's constant prying and interference. Mrs. W. would go through her daughter's bedroom and read her personal papers and letters.

The judges decided that this mother and daughter could not live together peacefully, and they suggested that Mrs. W. consider entering a home for the aged.

Mrs. K. lived with her bachelor son, who had recently begun dating a Gentile woman. The mother asked that the Board order him to terminate the relationship. "He is a fine boy in every other respect," said the mother, "except that he is in love with this woman."

The son told a more melancholy story. "I will be thirty-one years old in six months' time. I just don't want to be told what to do by my mother. I have to cater to her every whim. I don't want anyone to interfere in my life. I feel I'm old enough to know my own mind." Regarding his relationship with the non-Jewish woman, he explained that he was not interested in getting married to her and did not expect the affair to last long. When asked by the judges why he had never married, he replied, "Whenever I cared for anyone, my mother would interefere and say she did not approve."

The young man went on to describe his mother-dominated life. "Except for two nights a week, I spend every evening at home. My mother insists that I take her everywhere. On Saturday, my one day off, I feel I have a right to do as I please."

The judges turned to the mother with some salutary advice. "You demand too much of your son. You are a widow now, but you lived a full life until your husband died. You ought to make a new life for yourself now, and not cling to your son."

"I have a gentleman friend," the mother replied. "He comes to our house and we all have dinner together."

"Yes," interrupted the son, "and then she insists that I chauffeur both of them around. I even have to sit in the car and wait for them when they go visiting!"

The judges' decision was as follows: "We believe that the son will see the matter in its true light and terminate his present romantic relationship. The mother is not to continue to dictate to him. He will work out the situation by himself."

Mrs. G. begged the judges to order her daughter to stop seeing her boyfriend. "He isn't good enough for her," she claimed. "He's different . . . He isn't normal."

The daughter explained that she was willing to delay the marriage until her friend would complete his studies, but that her mother had totally rejected him. She believed that this animosity stemmed from the fact that he had been born in Germany, and not in America.

Mrs. G. protested, "When he speaks, it's as though he is hiding something." Mr. G. said only, "He seems a little shy." Another daughter described him as an average young man. She could not understand her mother's hostile attitude.

The judges complimented the daughter for agreeing to appear before the Board. Had she not respected her parents, she most probably would not have done so. To the mother they said: "You have no right to stand in the way of your daughter's happiness." They advised the daughter, however, not to rush into marriage and not to harbor a grudge against her mother. Then they turned again to the mother and repeated: "You will ruin your daughter's life if you continue in this way. She is twenty years old and you can no longer make decisions for her."

Mrs. E. came to the Board with the complaint that her son was seeing a non-Jewish woman and had become separated from his wife. She wanted the judges to order him to sever his ties with the woman.

The son maintained that he had not seen the woman for several months. He also insisted that his mother had been directly responsible for the separation between his wife and himself. Eager to break up his marriage, she had attempted suicide, declaring her son's behavior to be the cause of her unhappiness. His wife had recently become aware of his extramarital liaison, but he believed that there was a good chance for his wife and himself to become reconciled, if only his mother would stop interfering. "Please tell her that her forty-two-and-one-half-year old son should be emancipated," he pleaded.

The judges ruled that Mr. E. and his wife should receive marriage counseling. To the mother they said: "You go your way, and he will go his way." When she protested, "If I leave him alone, he will see that woman every day," the judges admonished her. "Let things develop without you," they said. "Allow your son to become reconciled with his wife."

Other Family Dissensions

Gambling sometimes gave rise to family disputes in the Jewish community. The plaintiff in one such case complained that his wife had taken control of his business and refused to give him any money. The wife claimed that her husband was a habitual gambler and, if permitted, would fritter away all his earnings.

The judges ruled that the husband receive a small weekly allowance, but that the wife continue to manage both the home and the business.

Mr. C. complained that his wife had taken a Works Project Administration job which *he* had wanted. He demanded that his wife resign and hand the position over to him.

Mrs. C. testified that when her husband was employed, he gambled away his entire paycheck. He had even pawned her clothing in order to have money for gambling. She affirmed that it was only by being herself employed that she could make sure of a steady income.

The judges ruled that Mrs. C. should retain her position, and that the husband must seek alternative employment. In the meantime, they instructed the wife to help her husband with a small allowance every week until he could find a job.

Certain domestic problems did not fit into any regular category. These usually involved persons who made unwarranted accusations against member of their own families, or who suffered from a persecution complex.

An elderly woman complained to the Board that her daughters and sons-in-law were trying to drive her insane. She accused them of beating and starving her, and even of attempted murder. Her distress had become so extreme that she refused to believe the news of a brother's death, insisting that he was trying to avoid repayment of a loan which he had secured from her in the preceding year.

When the judges recommended that the mother be placed in an institution, one daughter objected. She said that despite all the anguish which her mother had caused her, it would be even more painful to see her mother institutionalized.

The social worker then intervened and suggested that the mother set up house with a woman who had appeared before the Board in another connection, and who had requested at that time that someone share her apartment. The judges accepted this proposal and the social worker promised to make the necessary arrangements.

Cases Involving Israeli Litigants

During the 1950s, actions concerning the State of Israel, in one way or another, began to appear on the Jewish Conciliation Board's agenda. Whether specifically Israeli in nature or involving the new state only marginally, these cases reflected a new dimension in the life of the Jewish community.

A man representing his uncle, who now resided in Israel, complained to the Board that the uncle had given the defendant a Torah scroll when they had both been in Russia, and that the uncle now wished the scroll to be returned to him in Israel.

The defendant testified that, when fleeing from the Nazis, he had lost this *Sefer Torah* along with several others which had been entrusted to him for safekeeping. In the light of this statement, the judges ruled that the defendant submit a notarized letter stating that he had lost the Torah scroll. On the basis of such a letter, they would rule in his favor.

The judges thanked the nephew for his concern and expressed satisfaction over the fact that the name and activities of the Board were known in Israel.

A couple complained that the husband's sister and brother-in-law, who had helped them emigrate to the United States from Israel, had now become insulting and abusive toward them.

The sister and brother-in-law claimed that the Israeli couple had originally agreed to repay the loan which financed their emigration, but that they now refused to do so, maintaining that it had been a gift. This had created a great deal of bitterness between the two families.

Since there was little evidence to prove either side's testimony, the judges explained to the couple from Israel that, whether they repaid the loan or not, they owed a debt of gratitude to their American in-laws for having helped them. They urged both couples to make an effort to restore harmonious family relations.

An indication of the Board's general concern for the well-being of clients was evidenced by the assistance which the judges gave the ex-Israelis in a matter unrelated to the family conflict. In the course of their testimony, the newcomers happened to mention that they had two daughters, aged nine and eleven, whom they wished to place in a summer camp, but that they could not afford the fees. Before the hearing was over, arrangements had been made by the Board for these girls to attend summer camp for two weeks, commencing the following day.

The following three cases introduce the new element of *Aliyah*, immigration to Israel from Diaspora lands.

A father complained to the Board that his son, an Israeli by birth, wished to leave the United States in order to join the Israel Air Force. The father, however, wanted his son to complete his college education in the United States before making such a move.

After closer questioning by the judges, it became evident that the boy's decision had been well thought out. He had already clarified the regulations for entry into the Israel Air Force, and he explained that if he should put off his decision, he would later exceed the age limit. Were the Air Force to reject him as a candidate, however, this young *Sabra* had already thought of alternative possibilities in Israel. He told the judges that he had no friends in the United States and that he had never adjusted to life in New York.

The judges ruled that the father should not refuse his son the right to plan his own life. "Although he will not complete college here," they said, "you have a son who will find his happiness in Israel and of whom you will be proud."

This case was heard in 1965. One cannot help wondering whether the young man in question was one of those Israeli pilots who made history in the Six-Day War, two years later.

In the next case, it was a son who opposed his mother's desire to return to Israel. He refused to pay for her trip, feeling certain that she would be unhappy in Israel and that she would eventually ask for money to finance her return trip to the United States.

The mother affirmed that she had lived in Israel for thirty-three years and had traveled to the United States only at the insistence of her son, who was resident in New York. Asked whether she had any family in Israel, the mother replied, "Everyone in Israel is my family."

When the son remained adamantly opposed to giving his mother the fare back to Israel, the judges urged him not to refuse and declared an adjournment of the case for a few days in order to give him some time to think the matter over. And indeed, a few days later, the son returned and informed the judges that he had been pleased with their consideration and fairness and had now decided to defray the cost of his mother's return to Israel, with the proviso that it could be a two-way trip if, within a short time, she were to decide to come back to the States.

The issue of *Aliyah* was only one of many disputes which divided Mr. and Mrs. K. Their daughter wanted to settle in Israel and her mother approved, but her father wanted her first to earn a college degree in the United States. There were other issues and tensions which beset this couple, to such an extent that the social worker had advised their separating for a while. In the meantime, she suggested that they learn more about Israel in order to understand their daughter's decision to live there.

The social worker had sessions with the couple over a period of several months. The issue of their daughter's *Aliyah* disturbed the father more and more. When the girl finally left for Israel, he claimed that she had done so without his permission and that his wife had paid her expenses. He became insistent on a divorce, while his wife still hoped for a reconciliation.

The daughter's story ended happily. While attending the Hebrew University, she met an Israeli boy of Tunisian origin who was serving in the Army. They were married. Her father objected because the boy's family was poor and "only spoke Hebrew and French." The mother went to Israel to meet her son-in-law and wrote very warm letters about him to her husband.

The parents' story did not have a happy ending. The social worker managed to persuade the husband to await his wife's return before initiating divorce proceedings. His parting complaint was that "Israel is stealing American talent."

A woman filed a complaint on behalf of her sister, who was living in Israel. This sister had obtained a civil divorce, but her ex-husband refused to complete the process by granting her a *Get* (Jewish religious divorce). According to Jewish law, she could not remarry without a *Get* and, if she nevertheless did so, the children of such a union would be considered *Mamzerim* (illegitimate).

Even though the Board could not act as a Rabbinical court, the client hoped that, in consequence of its intervention and persuasion, the husband might be persuaded to grant his wife the Jewish divorce. After

numerous communications and appeals, he consented. The sister
thanked the Board for "bringing about a result which could not have
been achieved by any other means."

In 1939, the Rabbinical court of Haifa referred to the Jewish
Conciliation Board a case of nonpayment of support. A man who had
moved to New York from Haifa had ceased support payments, ordered
by the *Beth Din* a year previously, to his wife, who remained in
Palestine. The report advised the Board that the wife was in dire need
and did not even have enough food to sustain herself.

When called to testify, the delinquent husband stated that he had
married a woman half his age because he had been sorry for her. He
was over sixty now, and his thirty-five-year-old wife had spent all of his
money in the meantime. Now he felt no obligation to continue
supporting her.

The court ordered him to abide by his previous agreement to
support his wife. The judges reminded him that they now had jurisdiction over this case, in accordance with the instructions received from
the Haifa Rabbinical court.

A son brought his mother to see the social worker. The mother had
stopped eating anything except bread and water, and said that she
would not resume eating properly until her children allowed her to go
and live in Israel. The children had said that if first she would agree to
eat, they would send her to Israel, but she refused to trust them.

The social worker, as an impartial observer, was able to find a
solution acceptable to both the son and the mother. The children
should send their mother to Israel only on the understanding that she
would return to the United States within two months, if her condition
did not improve. In addition, the social worker offered to make
arrangements for the mother to enter a *Bet Avot* (residence for the
elderly) in Haifa.

On the following day, the son telephoned and informed the social
worker that he had reserved a ticket on a flight to Israel, and that his
mother had begun eating regularly again.

Clashes of Cultures

Sometimes the conflicts involved cultural differences among
"mixed" American-Israeli Jewish couples.

In one case, the Israeli husband wanted to go home, whereas the

American-born wife wished to remain in New York. The wife also claimed that her in-laws, who were visiting them at the time, had insulted her, and that her mother-in-law had accused her of "stealing" her son. The conflict had become so serious that the husband now refused to support his wife.

The judges admonished the husband, warning him that he was legally obliged to support his wife. They ordered him to begin doing so within five days.

The wife stated that she was willing to visit Israel, but that she could not be sure whether she would remain there permanently. The judges asked the husband, "If she agrees to go, will you have no other complaints?"

"Even if she goes," he insisted, "she will have to live the way I think she should."

Since no final decision had been made by the husband regarding Israel, the judges could not issue a definite ruling. They stated, however, that if the husband decided to return to Israel, and his wife refused to accompany him, they would be prepared to hear the case again. There is no record of a subsequent hearing.

An American-born husband complained that he and his Israeli wife were not getting along together. His wife, who was expecting a baby, had warned that unless he would arrange for her two teen-aged children from a previous marriage to join her in the United States, she would fall ill and lose the baby. He had complied with her wishes, but since the arrival of the children there had been no peace in his home. He stated that the children showed him no respect, insulted him, and, although he knew no Hebrew, absolutely refused to speak English.

The wife testified that her children had been good students in Israel, but were now having language problems in the United States. Although she wanted her daughter to finish her studies in the United States, her husband insisted that the eighteen-year-old girl quit school and find a job. The children now wished to return to Israel. Although their mother had relatives in Israel who could look after them, she preferred that they remain with her since she felt responsible for their upbringing.

The wife told the judges that her husband constantly reminded the children that he had brought them to the United States, and he seemed to expect their unceasing gratitude for this favor.

The judges urged more patience and understanding on the part of both husband and wife. The husband was made to understand that the children were not insulting him when they spoke Hebrew. At the same time, the wife was also advised that it would be helpful if her children would make an effort to speak English at home. The two parties were urged to reestablish harmony in their marriage.

Another case of this type involved a young American girl who had met her husband in Israel, where their first child had been born. While they were living over there, her parents had sent them money. Her husband handled all the finances and would often give money to his own parents. She considered that her husband had taken unfair advantage of her parents, and claimed that the couple themselves were sometimes left without money for food.

After returning to the United States, she had given birth to a second child. This, her husband later informed her, had been planned by him in order to tie her down. She was upset over his attitude because she had not been physically or emotionally prepared for a second child. In addition, not only were her parents still assisting them financially, but her husband refused to give her any money, claiming that she could get more from her parents if necessary. He had also struck her.

The husband testified that he had come to the United States against his will, since the decision had been entirely his wife's. Regarding his parents, he explained that his wife had known that they were very poor and that he had an obligation to assist them. He himself had been employed until recently, but was now laid off. The husband admitted that he had broken objects at home in fits of anger, but denied ever striking his wife. He seemed quite unable to understand his wife, complaining that she always argued with him and refused to do what he asked.

This couple had seen a marriage counselor, who felt that their problem stemmed from the fact that they came from two different worlds. They were told by the counselor that as long as the husband considered himself the master and his wife the servant, they would never have a workable marriage.

The judges proposed a trial separation in the hope that it might eventually lead to a more amicable relationship, but both parties rejected the suggestion for different reasons. The husband insisted that his wife belonged with him. She had no faith in the marriage and accused her husband of marrying her in order to settle in the United States and live off her father's money.

Realizing that there was no way to bridge the gap between them, the Board felt obliged to dismiss this case without taking a decision. It was one of the rare instances in which the tribunal felt at a loss, not wishing to impose a decision and yet not succeeding in having its advice accepted voluntarily. Perhaps the judges hoped that time would be a healer.

Cases Related to the Nazi Era

During the earlier years of the Nazi period, cases were brought before the Jewish Conciliation Board involving monetary transactions, such as loans to facilitate the emigration of relatives to America or donations to relatives still trapped in Europe.

Relief committees were formed through which packages of food and clothing, as well as money, were conveyed to relatives and friends in Central and Eastern Europe. When, however, those areas were over-run by Hitler's armies, and the Jews unfortunately trapped there were robbed of their possessions, the agencies decided that it would be useless to continue sending money abroad and accordingly deposited funds in special accounts, to await the dawn of a better day. This decision of the relief committees was generally accepted. There were a few, however, who insisted that the money should not lie idly in a bank while Jews in Europe went without food or clothing.

One such case came before the Jewish Conciliation Board. It seemed clear to the judges that the member airing his grievance against the committee dealing with the problem was actuated by good motives but poor judgment, and that this was the source of the conflict. It took much patience and understanding, born of sympathy for the conditions in occupied Europe, to bring about an acceptable decision which enabled the particular committee engaged in this work to maintain its activities, subject to the expert advice of duly recognized relief organizations.

A woman claimed that she had dispatched money to enable her cousin in Germany to emigrate to the United States. The cousin now refused to reimburse her. The defendant testified that he had received the money, but had given part of it to another relative. Forty percent of the remainder had been confiscated. What was left had been utilized to purchase gifts for his American cousin.

The judges ruled that the defendant owed his cousin a debt of honor and that he was obliged to repay the amount, but that he could deduct what had been given to the other relative who was still in Germany.

A refugee complained that, after arriving in America, she had tried to claim the possessions which she had sent from Germany for safekeeping by her cousin, but that the latter refused to release them.

The defendant exhibited receipts for over $100 on account of expenses which she had incurred while procuring an affidavit for her German cousin. She refused to release the plaintiff's possessions until she was reimbursed, but had been offered only $40.

The judges ruled that the plaintiff should pay her cousin $50 and that, upon payment of that sum, the defendant should return all the property of the plaintiff.

Mr. L. told the Board that he had paid a philanthropic society for a food package to be sent to his family in Poland. The package never reached its intended destination, and he therefore asked for repayment of his money.

A spokesman for the philanthropic organization testified that it could not guarantee delivery of packages because of frequent acts of confiscation by the Nazis. The organization was only able to ascertain the safe arrival of the packages in Portugal. From that point onward, every effort was made to route the packages to Poland, but while parcel insurance covered the dispatch to Portugal, no company would insure packages destined for Polish addressees.

The plaintiff claimed that he had been assured that his package would arrive in Poland, and he therefore considered that the organization had not fulfilled its obligation.

The judges ruled that the philanthropic organization was not liable for the refund, but that it should make every effort to secure compensation from the insurance company.

Scars of the Holocaust

During the decade following World War II, litigants appearing before the Jewish Conciliation Board who happened to be survivors of the European Holocaust often tended to relate their current problems to what they had undergone in Europe. Even in situations which were totally unrelated to the *Sho'ah*, this type of behavior was not uncommon. Having been indelibly scarred by the Nazi terror, such people could no longer deal objectively with any aspect of their lives. The following case is a typical example.

Mrs. M. approached the Board with a complaint that her husband was "a gambler, an alcoholic, and a liar," and that, though steadily employed as a baker and earning a good salary, he was often in debt, stayed out late, and returned home drunk. In addition, she charged that he had become abusive and had started to beat her. Mrs. M. testified that this had been going on for nine years. She added: "Previously, he was the best husband and father; now he is no father and no husband."

Mr. M. then told his side of the story. "I am not exactly an alcoholic," he said. "I have never been drunk on the job or missed a day's work." He claimed that he did not want a divorce and would agree to any proposal that might help him to stop drinking. He agreed to consult a doctor and even to be hospitalized, if necessary.

When one of the judges, in the course of the hearing, asked if her husband was religious, Mrs. M. replied, "No. He was in a concentration camp and no longer believes in God." She went on to explain that, although they had originally met in a Nazi concentration camp, her husband had always refused to answer any questions about his family.

The Board's consulting psychiatrist testified that Mr. M.'s terrible experience might have contributed to his becoming a partial alcoholic.

Notwithstanding Mr. M.'s promise to stop drinking and to attend a clinic, a note was entered by the Board's social worker five days after the hearing: "Sunday, Mr. M. just got drunk." Following this, however, was a more hopeful entry: "Mr. M. just called and promised to visit the clinic with his wife today."

Mrs. Z., a concentration camp survivor, complained to the Board that her only living relative, a nephew, was trying to deprive her of her money. She explained in Yiddish that he had taken her to a notary public in order to sign some papers which she did not understand. She now demanded: "My signature must be returned to me." Mrs. Z. also claimed that the nephew, Mr. L., had offered to invest money for her in the stock market.

Mr. L. explained that the papers in question were application blanks, issued under the Restitution Laws which had been promulgated recently in West Germany. He affirmed that, after his aunt had signed the correct forms, he had sent them to Germany. According to Mr. L., his aunt had a history of mental disturbance.

He also showed the judges a copy of the letter which he had subsequently sent to Germany in order to appease his aunt, who asked for the return of the application form with her signature. In addition, Mr. L. insisted that he had never suggested to his aunt that she invest her money in the stock market, nor had he ever assisted her in any financial transactions.

It was obvious to the judges that Mrs. Z.'s fears were unfounded, but that only her "returned signature" would set her mind at rest. They therefore promised her the Board's assistance in obtaining its return. They also tried to allay Mrs. Z.'s fears with the following assurance: "Your great fear is that you do not know what you signed. Don't be afraid—your nephew cannot do anything to harm you with your signature. Sleep soundly and don't worry. The rabbi and lawyers here assure you that your nephew cannot do you any harm with your signature."

Mrs. G. contacted the Board after having heard its Executive Secretary speak at her synagogue. She had come to the United States at the age of nineteen. Her entire family had been destroyed by the Nazis, and she herself had escaped detection by attending a convent school. She had now learned of her eligibility for restitution payments, but previously she had encountered difficulties in applying for these as a minor.

The social worker compiled a list of agencies which would assist Mrs. G. in the filing of her claim, and helped her in its preparation.

On another occasion, the Board received a letter from an inmate of a state hospital, asking for help in obtaining his release from the institution, to which, he claimed, he had been confined illegally. His letter indicated that he was a person of considerable education who had undergone much torment in Nazi Germany. After contacting the authorities, the Executive Secretary of the JCB learned that this patient had been properly committed to the hospital upon very strong proof of a chronic mental illness. It was also ascertained that the patient was suffering from a tubercular condition which required intensive hospital treatment. While, under the circumstances, a release could not be effected, the patient was contacted by the social service worker and drew comfort from the knowledge that he had friends who were interested in his welfare.

In concluding this section, it may be appropriate to remark not only that the cases which came before the Jewish Conciliation Board for hearing, or which were settled in its offices without hearings, reflected the times and circumstances in which the JCB's role was cast, but that the JCB played its part, modest but meaningful, in handling and often solving problems which reflected those times and conditions.

Decision Problems

Situations sometimes arose where the judges serving the Jewish Conciliation Board realized that a clear-cut decision could not be rendered or would not be adhered to. Even in cases where the defendant refused to appear, or the evidence was insufficient, or where it was obvious that the decision of the tribunal would not be implemented, the judges did their best not to have to exert their authority.

When one litigant was dissatisfied with the judges' ruling and refused to accept it, recourse to the civil courts was sometimes recommended, even though the judges were entitled to impose their decision, in accordance with the arbitration laws of the state.

Such situations constituted the margin of failure with which every philanthropic or social endeavor is beset.

It would be unrealistic and unwarranted to claim that the Jewish Conciliation Board was always successful in its endeavors. A few of the failures may be worth citing. Even in such cases, however, the mere act of listening to complaints was a humanitarian service, and often the subsequent assistance of the Social Service Department had its own beneficial value.

Mrs. D. brought suit against a home for the aged which had discharged her mother for being unmanageable, and demanded that the home readmit her. The representative of the home testified that, after three years' residence, Mrs. D.'s mother had become argumentative and abusive. Following complaints by other residents regarding her behavior toward them, the resident psychiatrist examined the mother and advised that she be removed from the institution. Accordingly, the home contacted Mrs. D. and the other children, but none of them responded. The home was consequently forced to place the mother in a state institution for the mentally disturbed.

In the light of the evidence submitted, the judges had to inform Mrs. D. that there was nothing they could do for her. It was a rule of this home not to readmit a person who had been discharged for uncontrollable behavior.

An elderly, almost deaf woman kept shouting at the judges throughout the hearing. Her complaint was that her children did not respect her, and that one daughter had beaten her. The woman's son maintained that his mother was senile, imagining a variety of injustices against her. He also stated that she had been institutionalized for a while, and that members of the family were trying to deal with her as best they could. Throughout his testimony, the woman continued to shout and wave a portfolio of old photographs in front of the tribunal.

Although the judges realized that there was nothing they could do, they listened to her complaints, as they did in many such cases where no appropriate decision could be taken. When they dismissed this case, the woman thanked the judges for listening to her.

Mrs. K. and her son complained that Mrs. P. and her daughter were persecuting them. A civil court had determined in a paternity suit that Mr. K. was the father of Miss P.'s child. Despite his insistence that this was not so, he had been ordered to pay Miss P. an allowance for child support. Mr. K.'s appeal against the decision was now pending. The plaintiffs wanted the girl and her family to stop bringing them bills for payment.

Although the judges understood that the case would have to await a decision of the Court of Appeals, they spoke to the two young people in an effort to determine whether there was any love between them. It was soon apparent that they had no ties of affection, and the case was therefore dismissed after the parties had been advised to await the ruling of the civil court.

A man charged his wife and son with a "frame-up," in having sent him to a mental institution. After his release, he returned home to find that his family had moved. He finally discovered his wife living with another man, and she wanted a divorce.

The man's son testified that his father had been committed to the mental hospital after an examination and that he had not been released, but had escaped. The original cause of his hospitalization had been a threat to murder his wife.

The judges spoke to the plaintiff, trying to convince him to return to the hospital. They assured him that he would be released if there were nothing wrong with him. They then dismissed the case on insufficient grounds. The son gave his father some money before they parted.

A daughter brought her mother before the tribunal. Ever since she had moved from home, her mother had hounded her at work in a campaign to force her to return.

"I should have left home years ago," said the twenty-three-year-old girl. "My mother has a violent temper. She constantly throws things at me, and once she almost blinded me with a belt. No boy I date is good enough, and she asks them their 'intentions' almost immediately. She is always calling me an 'old maid' and telling me to jump out of the window because I'm not yet married."

The daughter listed more grievances. "I was engaged at seventeen, but broke it off. My mother kept the ring. She has no understanding, only a heart of iron."

The mother would not reply directly to any question from the judges, but continually bemoaned the fact that her daughter was a liar and did not love her. The judges reminded the woman that her daughter was over twenty-one and self-supporting. They tried to help her understand that there was nothing wrong with a young woman living alone, and stressed the importance of not disturbing her daughter at her place of work, since she might lose her job as a result.

The judges then turned to the daughter and suggested that she visit her mother occasionally. Thereupon, the daughter began to cry, insisting that her mother beat her when they were together.

Finally, she agreed to visit her mother the following week. "The two of you can live separately and try to be friends," one judge advised. They promised the judges that they would do so, and left the room together after shaking hands.

Much to the consternation of the panel, the daughter ran back into the courtroom a few minutes later, saying that her mother had threatened to "take it out on her" for the judges' decision. The girl was advised to wait until her mother left the building. Thus, what had appeared at first to be a successful resolution of the problem actually turned out to be a failure, but the judges had at least tried.

———

A sixteen-year-old boy approached the court, testifying that his parents had lived apart for the past three years. Now he and his brother and sister were interested in bringing about a reconciliation between them. He and his brother resided with their father. They asked both parents to set aside their differences and make a normal home for them.

The mother stated that she would never return to her husband and children. She claimed that for twenty-five years she had been abused, that her children did not love her, and that her husband encouraged them to disobey her. She was now earning a comfortable salary as a nurse and enjoyed living alone.

The father explained that their problems had begun eight years earlier. At that time his wife had taken him to the Magistrate's Court, claiming that he had tried to murder her. The court had then ordered his wife to be sent to a hospital for observation. After ten days, she was released into her husband's custody, at his request. Following this, she had taken him to the Family Court. She subsequently left home and, despite his many pleas, refused to live with him again.

The judges appealed to the mother, saying, "We have discussed this situation and have found something very unusual about the case. . . . Your own child is pleading with his parents to live together so that they can make a normal home for him. It very seldom occurs that a child approaches the Board to beg for such a reconciliation. We feel that any woman with a mother's heart would not refuse her son's plea. This boy is very unhappy and is entitled to have his mother with him. He will become a very embittered person unless you help him. He is now at an age when his character is being formed, and he needs you to help him."

The mother remained adamant in her refusal to consider a reconciliation, saying that she could no longer control her children. The presiding judge again turned to her and said, "This Board cannot compel you . . . all we can do is appeal to your conscience."

Her answer was unchanged.

The judge then spoke to the son. "We have done our best for you. All we could do was to try and appeal to your mother to come home. We feel that she is not well. When such a person is sick, you cannot condemn her. Don't feel bitter or harbor a grievance against your mother. Had she been well, she would have granted your request to return home. Instead, feel grateful that you have your father with you. You are a fine boy, and for that reason you have come to us with your request. If you do well in life, you will make your mother happy."

Collateral Help Given by the Jewish Conciliation Board

There were many situations, as has been made evident in this chapter, where the Jewish Conciliation Board relieved the burden of government courts by adjudicating cases which might otherwise have been brought to them. There were other situations, however, where the assistance of the government had to be invoked and where clients were helped to navigate their way through the American legal processes.

During the Depression, Mr. and Mrs. S. appeared before the Board, the woman accusing her husband of wife-beating and failure to support her and their two children. She also alleged that, at the time of their marriage, he had taken $2,000 of her money which he never used for their mutual benefit. The judges did not rule on this point, but instructed Mr. S. to give his wife and children $15 support money each week.

When Mr. S. refused to abide by the Board's decision, his wife took her case to the Family Court. The social service worker of the Jewish Conciliation Board accompanied her and conveyed the Board's ruling to the Family Court. Not only did the government tribunal uphold the Board's decision, but it decreed a larger settlement, ordering Mr. S. to give his wife one-half of each week's salary for maintenance. It also stated that Mrs. S. was eligible for the city's relief money, including meal tickets and rent. The recommendation of the Board and the testimony of its social service worker were key factors in securing city relief funds for Mrs. S.

In another case, the decision of the Jewish Conciliation Board provided the defendant with protection in the event that the plaintiff would decide to pursue the matter in the Family Court.

Mr. G., an unemployed peddler of fifty-five, brought a support claim against his son by a first marriage. Mr. L., the son, testified that his mother had divorced his father on the grounds of desertion, when he himself had been only one year old. Although, after twenty-seven years of absence, Mr. G. was an absolute stranger to him, Mr. L. was willing to support him to the best of his ability. He proposed the sum of $10 monthly. Although it was a modest amount, even at the time of this litigation in 1940, the Board found it acceptable under the circumstances.

The judges also advised Mr. L. that should his father decide to press this case in the Family Court, in the hope of receiving more money, he (Mr. L.) was to inform that court of the Jewish Conciliation Board's decision.

The following case was referred to the Board by a city court. An entire family had been torn asunder by the bitter disputes between a brother—a former serviceman in the U.S. Army—and the rest of his family. The brother complained that following his discharge from the Army he was refused an interest in the family business, although he claimed to be a partner therein. So fierce were the wranglings between father and children that the matter finally reached the city court, where criminal proceedings had been instituted.

The presiding judge in the city court, after listening to the case for almost a whole day, felt that this was a matter which could best be settled by the Jewish Conciliation Board. Soon after the case had been referred to the Board, a special session was convened for the hearing. After less than two hours, the disputes and claims made by various members of the family were finally settled. What is more important, the judges of the Jewish Conciliation Board managed to remove some of the bitterness which had hitherto soured relations between the parties concerned.

It often happened that litigants, after receiving an invitation to appear before the Board, would settle their disputes among themselves. The Board's offer of its good offices thus served as an incentive for the adjustment of differences out of court. The Board considered this to be the most desirable outcome of its intervention. Two of the many examples are cited below.

Mr. R. brought action against his brother, who was not contributing his share to the support of their mother. Two days before the scheduled hearing, Mr. R. contacted the Board to say that "the receipt of your letter by my brother has expedited an agreement." Everything had been settled peacefully out of court, as a result of the initial action.

A home for the aged had filed a complaint against the children of a resident for nonpayment of fees. Our office contacted the children and set a time for a hearing. A week prior to the hearing, the Board's Executive Secretary received a letter from the director of the home, canceling the action and stating that the defendants had reached an agreement with the institution. The director wrote, "We want to thank you most sincerely for the help you have given us. Your letters to the children were instrumental in settling this matter."

In almost every category of dispute, there were some disagreements which were thus settled by the parties themselves, after receipt of a letter from the Jewish Conciliation Board.

V
Additional Good Offices of the Jewish Conciliation Board

Among the important services of the JCB, as has been indicated, were not only the use of its good name and expertise in assisting many litigants to settle their disputes before the initiating of formal hearings, by airing their disagreements in the offices of the JCB and resolving them with the help of the Executive Secretary or the Social Service worker. Another dimension of helpfulness was the referral of clients to various social service agencies which were in a special position to resolve the particular complaints.

Whether in informal chats or in the more formal hearings, clients were provided with the opportunity to discuss their problems before sympathetic listeners. In many instances, the judges themselves offered their personal help and influence in order to bring about a solution. This chapter will deal separately with such efforts on the part of the Board's judges and Social Service Department.

Judges

Conciliation

The goal of conciliation was always present in the minds and hearts of those men and women who sat as judges. Whether in business disputes, domestic tensions, problems between parents and children, or claims against congregations and fraternal organizations, the judges were ever mindful of their responsibilities, not only as arbitrators and adjudicators but also as conciliators. There were many instances where the situations did not lend themselves to adjudication and where conciliation was the only recourse.

It is difficult to convey the atmosphere which prevailed at hearings of the Jewish Conciliation Board, but a few cases may be illustrative. It should perhaps be added that while the tribunal's sentimental appeals may appear to be somewhat amateurish, this was true only superficially. The judges were often hardheaded businessmen, seasoned lawyers, or veteran judges in government courts, yet they fully appreciated the uniqueness of this tribunal and they acted accordingly. Significantly, it was the sentimental, seemingly amateurish approaches which often proved the most effective.

Thus, in cases involving support, the judges were not content merely to direct the husband to arrange for his wife's maintenance. They would try to bring about *Shalom bayit,* domestic peace and harmony. A bickering couple, when appearing before the Board, were advised to talk as openly and honestly with each other at home as they had at the hearing. It often happened that, though prepared to separate when they first entered court, at the end of the hearing the husband and wife followed the judges' advice and left together, arm in arm.

A few additional examples may be worth mentioning.

A synagogue member, who complained to the Board that he had been unjustly expelled from his congregation, won his case. Yet, after the judges ruled that he be reinstated, they begged the synagogue officers to "please avoid trouble by bearing no grudges."

Mr. T. complained that his stepson was lacking in respect toward him. This boy was his wife's son by a first marriage, and Mr. T. had adopted him. According to Mr. T., the boy, then twenty-two years old and a senior in college, spoke to him disrespectfully, and his mother never reprimanded him for this. Although the boy was engaged to be married the following year, Mr. T. wanted him to leave the house immediately, since he felt the situation had become intolerable.

Mrs. T. blamed her son's behavior on the attitude adopted toward him by his stepfather. "If only my husband would be more pleasant and patient, there would be no arguments," she claimed. Her request was that her son be allowed to remain at home until his marriage.

The judges handed down no formal decision, but rather encouraged Mr. and Mrs. T. to talk their problem over in private. The couple went into the next room and returned an hour later, announcing that they had reached a solution. Mr. T. withdrew his complaint. It was a good human conclusion.

The following case, unfortunately not the only one of its kind, required a large measure of tact on the part of the judges.

A lonely widow, Mrs. S., accused her children of trying to have her committed to an insane asylum. She also alleged that they were poisoning her medication. One of the daughters affirmed that her mother suffered from hallucinations: no one had ever signed any papers committing her mother to any institution, and the doctors who were consulted all insisted that she was in perfect health. Mrs. S. countered with the charge that the doctors were all involved in the conspiracy to poison her.

The judges assured Mrs. S., "It is our opinion that there is nothing the matter with you except for too much time on your hands. You have a lovely family and no one will hurt you. We suggest that you interest yourself in Jewish charities and other Jewish activities, and not think about wrongs which someone may do you. We are greatly interested in your case, and our social service worker will visit you and the other members of your family. We are sure that no harm will come to you. In the meantime, we suggest that no one in your family interfere with the others and we hope that all of you will live in peace."

In her follow-up report, the social service worker recorded that Mrs. S. now seemed much more happy and calm. She had a great deal of confidence in the judges and appreciated and trusted their advice.

A mother approached the Board, complaining that her son had become estranged from her. Life had dealt her a number of severe blows. Her first husband had passed away, and her second husband, both of whose legs had been amputated, was a long-term hospital patient. She felt that she could take no more suffering. When her son's wife developed tuberculosis and went to a sanitarium, she insisted that her son divorce his wife. This, of course, had alienated him from her.

The judges tried to show both parties that they were wrong, the mother for attempting to break up her son's marriage, and the son for not being more patient and understanding with his mother.

According to the transcript of the trial, mother and son left the hearing "in a much happier frame of mind," with the mother promising to visit her daughter-in-law.

A husband complained that his wife spent too much time with her mother. The judges ruled that "both parties are to make a new effort to get along. Each will have to try. The wife must realize that she cannot give her mother all of her time, but has to consider her husband and children. By the same token, the husband must attempt to see his wife's point of view and be much more tolerant. Each side should now feel better for having talked things over . . . "

A wife alleged that her husband spent all his time with his father, while begrudging her the opportunity to spend time with her daughter and the grandchildren of a first marriage.

The judges asked the wife, "What decision do you want from us?" She replied, "I want to see if the home can't be as it was before." The couple heard the Board's plea to meet each other halfway and to compromise for the sake of their marriage. They then agreed to make this effort.

The following case illustrates the "mother-in-law problem" with, however, a successful outcome.

Mr. D. asked the Board to order his mother to stop bothering and insulting his wife. "You can explain to this seventy-six-year-old woman that we don't want to be aggravated. What does she want from us? We've given her three grandchildren. Can't she make peace with herself? What she says to my wife is very wrong."

The mother replied, "I have nothing against my daughter-in-law and I never said anything to upset her. I should drop dead if I'm not telling the truth. I don't mix in their life."

The young Mrs. D. testified that her mother-in-law constantly accused her of insulting behavior, even when she paid her compliments. The mother had finally ordered her son to choose between herself and his wife. He chose his wife. After Mr. D.'s mother told them both to "drop dead," the couple refused to let her visit her grandchildren.

One of the judges said to the old woman, "One thing you must know about human nature is that you must never insult a daughter-in-law. When a man marries, he likes to feel that his wife has been accepted by the family. Remarks like yours will only make your son furious." Turning to the wife, the judge continued, "When you married, you married into this family. If you trade insults with your mother-in-law, it's as though you said these things to your husband."

The Board gave the following advice to the parties concerned. "Grandma, please stop saying insulting things to your daughter-in-law. See that there is peace in the home. You have to set an example to your grandchildren and must use golden words to your daughter-in-law. To the young couple we say, let your children visit your mother, and allow her to visit them in your home so that you can reestablish a rapport. You may learn to stop bickering and to love each other. Forget what happened last year. Plant seeds of love, not hate, in your children."

The transcript concludes with a parenthetical remark. "The mother-in-law apologized to her son's wife, saying, 'If I did anything to hurt you, I'm sorry.' They kissed each other, then the mother kissed her son and they all went out smiling."

Individual Attention

Another aspect worth noting is the "extracurricular" interest taken by the volunteer judges in those who came before them. This kind of personal involvement would never be expected of judges in the government courts. The volunteer judges of the Jewish Conciliation Board were usually prominent members of the community, with many other demands on their time, yet they endeavored to give individual attention to those whose cases they heard.

During the Depression years, an elderly and ailing father asked the Board to obtain support for him from his children. At the hearing, it became evident that the children were themselves in very poor financial circumstances, and unable to provide adequate assistance. Furthermore, none of them had a large-enough apartment to give their father a room.

The rabbi on the panel of judges met privately with the father and persuaded him to enter a home for the aged, where he could receive the best care and attention, as well as financial assistance from the Home Relief Bureau.

Unemployment led to many family rifts. In a number of such cases, the businessman on the panel gave the defendant his card and invited him to come and see him the next day about a job, either with his own or with another firm.

A man was ordered by the Board to mail support payments to his wife, who was still in Poland. When the man, a recent immigrant, explained that he was unfamiliar with the requisite procedure, the rabbi on the panel volunteered to help him send the funds via the Hebrew Immigrant Aid Society.

A distraught couple begged for help in regard to their daughter, who had married a French non-Jew. The girl, who had been raised in an observant Jewish home and who had received a Jewish education, testified that her husband had undergone conversion, following which their Jewish marriage ceremony took place in France.

The rabbi on the panel offered to cable the Chief Rabbi of France, whom he knew personally, for a ruling as to the validity of the conversion and marriage, in order to ease the parents' minds. He also offered to perform a repeat conversion and a religious marriage ceremony without fee, if these proved necessary.

People would often turn to the Board for advice before making a decisive change in their lives. One man, for example, had been employed by his brother-in-law and had been earning a steady salary, though not a high one. Now he had been offered a partnership in his father-in-law's store, and his wife, anxious that her husband improve his situation, was urging him to accept the offer.

The man felt uncertain about the matter. He wanted assurances that he would indeed be a partner, and that he would be respected as such. The businessman judging this case offered to investigate the store and then advise the applicant as to whether the partnership would be a financially sound step.

In a commercial dispute which had been referred to the JCB by the Small Claims Court, the plaintiff appeared three times before the Board, and on each occasion the defendant refused to attend. Since the plaintiff did not want the decision to be made in his favor by default, he asked the judges to certify that he had appeared before them, and to send their report to the Small Claims Court, which would then have the authority to compel the defendant to appear before the civil tribunal.

The Board later received the following letter from the plaintiff: "I am glad that I was referred to your court, even though you could not help me, since I thereby learned that such a wonderful tribunal exists. I am fully aware of the fact that you are not looking for compliments, but I wish to say that I am truly glad to have had an opportunity to observe the splendid work being done by your Board. Not only have you amicably settled many personal or minor disputes, but you have also brought justice and light to far corners of the city which the civil courts could not possibly reach. God bless you all, and may you long continue with this splendid enterprise."

Referrals to Other Agencies

When the judges regarded a particular litigation as too complex to be solved by a simple Board decision, they referred the parties to the relevant counseling or social welfare agencies. If, on the other hand, the issue was not within the Board's jurisdiction, the litigants were directed to the proper authorities—Rabbinic or civil. As from the late 1950s, the judges began to refer clients to psychiatric, marriage, or geriatric counselors, where necessary. These referrals were handed down as formal decisions.

A woman with a history of mental illness came before the Board, asking the judges to dissolve her marriage to a man who was presently in a mental institution. The marriage had been performed only by a rabbi, since they had been unable to obtain a civil license. The woman was now cohabiting with another man who wished to marry her, although he knew of her background. She stated that he treated her well and that she was very happy with him.

The woman's father-in-law, whom she had accused of hiding her *Ketubbah* (Jewish marriage certificate), testified that he had no objection to his daughter-in-law remarrying. He also expressed no objection to her visiting her children, who lived with him. The woman's brother also appeared and maintained that her present relationship seemed to be good for her, as she was taking more care about her appearance.

The judges explained that it was not within their jurisdiction to dissolve a marriage, whether civil or religious. They further advised that the woman consult her psychiatrist before taking any additional decisions, and she agreed.

A client's willingness to consult a psychiatrist was often vital if the judges' advice was to have a successful outcome. The moral influence of the Board was such, however, that most people readily agreed to abide by the decision of the judges.

A woman complained to the Board that her husband had often been unfaithful to her. She was willing to forgive him, if he would agree to consult a psychiatrist. Not only had he refused her request, but he had told her that if she did not allow him to do as he pleased, he would move out of their home.

When questioned by the judges, the husband admitted that he needed help and that his behavior toward his wife had been unjust. He tried to defend himself by saying that his wife was always suspecting him of wrongdoing, even when he was innocent.

The husband agreed to seek psychiatric advice, and his agreement was incorporated in the tribunal's decision.

Marriage Counseling

The judges sometimes realized that any advice which they could give estranged couples would, at best, be only a temporary measure. In order to foster a more permanent reconciliation, they would often recommend that a couple seek professional marriage counseling.

Each of the following two cases involved a religious parent who complained that the spouse and the children were unwilling to follow the Orthodox practices of the parent. In one case, the plaintiff was the father, who was advised by the judges to have more patience and to see the positive side of his children's conduct. (See above, pp. 108–9, and cf. pp. 196–7 below.) In a later case, the judge counseled the plaintiff, who was the mother, to show more tolerance toward her children and more respect for her husband. "You must learn to give way a little," they said, "otherwise your religious beliefs may become an obsession and destroy your family." They also told the father to show more consideration for his wife and her Orthodox beliefs, and to refrain from conducting himself in such a way as to offend her religious sensibilities.

After continued discussion with the couple in the latter case, however, the judges evaluated the problem as one which extended beyond the question of religious dissension. Their final decision, therefore, was that the couple be referred to a marriage counselor. Both parties expressed their willingness to seek professional guidance.

An estranged couple appeared in court with a familiar litany of complaints. She did not know how to live within their means and was a poor housekeeper. He did not trust her with the household expenses and was too dependent on his mother.

"Have you ever had any marriage counseling?" asked one of the judges.

"No," replied the husband. "We were going to once, but my wife objected to the psychological testing and I objected to the expense."

"Marriage counseling aims to reunite all the family and smooth out their difficulties," the judge explained. "I imagine that somewhere along the line something went wrong, and perhaps counseling can be helpful."

After further discussion, the couple agreed to seek such assistance. "You are two intelligent people," the judge declared, "and the fact that you are both here in this court indicates that you want to save your marriage. Both of you are referred to marriage counseling."

A wife complained that her husband, who was the sole support of his mother, also expected his wife to be her constant companion.

When questioned by the judges, the wife made two admissions: first, that her brother-in-law also contributed to the mother-in-law's support, and second, that she herself had not seen her husband's mother for over a year. The judges were unable, however, to convince the wife that it was perfectly reasonable for her husband to visit his mother twice a week, and for his mother to be allowed to see her grandchild once a month. The wife continued to insist that her mother-in-law had broken up her home.

It became obvious to the panel that this couple's problems were more fundamental than the usual "mother-in-law" issue. Accordingly, the unanimous decision of the judges was that the couple seek marriage counseling, and they promised to do so.

Problems of the Elderly

Some couples, having seemingly weathered the storms of decades together, would then separate, usually after their children had grown up and had begun raising families of their own. In such cases, the husband or wife may have been unhappy for years, but the family remained united as long as the children were minors. Once the children left home, however, the underlying problems would rise to the surface. When such a couple appeared before the Board, geriatric counseling was often recommended.

In one notable instance, the couple had been married for forty-six years. Their two children were also married and had children of their own. The wife approached the Board, wanting a separation from her husband. She complained that he beat her and had broken all the dishes in the house. Since his retirement he stayed home all day, insisted on eating every two hours, and abused her when she complained. She insisted that he move out of their home.

The husband maintained that he had not beaten his wife. "I just restrained her by holding her hand, because she throws things when she argues." He then produced a doctor's certificate stating that he had undergone an ulcer operation and must eat bland food six times a day. The wife, however, insisted that the certificate was a forgery.

She also claimed that their incompatibility had begun years before. The husband maintained that he had been trying to help her. "We have been married for forty-six years," he said, "and I don't want us to separate now in the twilight of our lives."

The presiding judge spoke for the panel. "We could say to you, the husband, 'Stop mistreating your wife,' and to you, the wife, 'Stop mistreating your husband.' If you agree to counseling, you both may be able to work out your problems."

The couple agreed, and the judges referred them to a special clinic for geriatric advice.

A similar case involved a couple who had been married for nearly fifty years. In the midst of the wife's complaint, the judge interpolated a query. "You have been living together all these years. Why ask for a separation at this stage of your lives?" The wife replied, "When we were raising our family, the children kept us busy. They grew up and married, and then we became busy with our grandchildren. Now the grandchildren are growing up and I have time to think of my own problems. So I want a separation."

After allowing this elderly couple to air their mutual grievances, the judges persuaded them to make another attempt to live together.

Sometimes, when the judges heard a case which they felt unable to handle, they had no choice but to refer it to the civil courts. For example, if the defendant refused to appear or to sign the agreement of arbitration in a commercial dispute, he would be compelled to respond to the summons of a civil court.

A man complained that his mother-in-law, who had been living with his family for ten years, had now become senile. He felt she should be placed in a home, and he wanted her other children to begin taking over responsibility for her.

The judges decided that they could not order the mother to be placed in a home, since she was not present at the hearing. They also felt that no home would accept her if she were indeed senile. Regarding the unwillingness of her other children to help their brother-in-law support their mother, the judges recommended that the plaintiff take his case to the Domestic Relations Court in order to compel them to assume their responsibilities.

Where matters of *Halakhah* (Jewish law) were involved, the tribunal referred litigants to the Rabbinical authorities. In one such case, a couple insisted that they no longer wanted to live together. After ascertaining that there was no hope of reconciliation, the judges settled the matter of support. They then offered to telephone the Rabbinical Council, which recommended rabbis for the arrangement of a *Get* (religious divorce), with minimal expense and delay.

Family Guidance

The Jewish Family Service, a social welfare agency affiliated with the New York Federation of Jewish Philanthropies and offering a wide variety of services for the Jewish community, was often instrumental in assisting clients of the Jewish Conciliation Board.

In one case, a woman complained that her husband's daughter by a previous marriage was making life difficult for her. The girl, then thirty-seven years of age, had a history of mental illness, and after her release from a mental institution, the psychiatrist had recommended that she live at her father's home—a stable environment which would be of great help to her. The father was very devoted to his daughter, and the wife complained bitterly that he loved the daughter more than her.

During the hearing, the father declared that he did not want a divorce or separation and that he agreed to have his daughter live elsewhere. The judges decided that the father should apply to the Jewish Family Service, which would find accommodation for the daughter in a sheltered environment.

Mr. K. was a *Ba'al teshuvah*, a formerly nonobservant Jew who had become strictly Orthodox in his practices and beliefs. He complained to the Board that his two older sons had already been lost to Judaism and that his wife was now trying to thwart his efforts to "save" their youngest son.

Mrs. K. testified that she kept a *Kasher* home and did not cook on *Shabbat*. She contended that it was the father's beating of their eldest son, when he had been restless in synagogue, that had caused the boy to reject Judaism. Their younger son had decided independently to attend public high school, and not a *Yeshivah*.

Mr. K. asserted that his wife was hoping to "get even with God" because He had allowed Hitler to destroy her family. The wife replied, "I never said that; what I did say was that God had closed His eyes to the murder of six million Jews."

"God didn't close His eyes," the husband countered. "He devised the Holocaust to punish the Jews for eating non-Kosher food and marrying out of their faith."

The Orthodox rabbi on the panel castigated Mr. K. for this statement. "I think that the 'God' who makes us hate other Jews is not the Jewish God. I have never heard a truly Orthodox Jew justify the killing of our six million brethren. God forbid that you should justify such a catastrophe! Those Jews were not bad. Hitler was responsible for their death. We do not understand this, of course, but we still cannot blame God *or* the Jews."

The judges then questioned the son, who testified that his mother had never said anything to prejudice him against attending *Yeshivah*.

As in other cases of this nature, the tribunal endeavored to persuade the father not to impose his own ways on his children: "True love is to love a child even when he or she behaves contrary to what you would wish." However, deciding that the couple needed ongoing professional guidance, which the Board itself was not in a position to provide, the judges recommended the couple to the Jewish Family Service for professional counseling.

In another case of religious conflict within a family, the roles were reversed. Here, the mother wished to maintain an Orthodox home, whereas the father believed that their children should be raised "in the American way." The mother claimed that "he preaches communism to the children," and would not permit them to observe Jewish tradition.

The father complained that the *Yeshivah* which his son attended had a very low standard of secular education. "I am proud of being a Jew," he affirmed, "but I do not hold with Orthodox beliefs." After some questioning by the judges, he admitted that he really did not object to his son attending a *Yeshivah*, but felt that the boy was a poor student and could not keep up with all his studies.

"When you give a boy a Jewish education, you give him the chance to decide for himself," said the rabbi on the panel of judges. "Afterwards, he will at least know who he is, but if you deprive him of a Jewish education, his decisions will be made out of ignorance."

Both husband and wife then said that they felt there was a chance for reconciliation, and the judges recommended that they approach the Jewish Family Service for counseling.

The Social Service Department

Not only was the social service worker responsible for the prior screening of cases scheduled for adjudication, as well as for the follow-up investigations, but her evaluations were also a contributing factor in the judges' final decision. No less significant was the personal conciliation achieved by this department in many cases which were not brought to formal hearings before the judges.

A young couple came to see the social worker with the following problem. They were engaged to be married, but were having difficulties with their respective parents. Both had been engaged previously, but these engagements had been broken off. Now the respective parents felt uncertain about their children's new engagement. In addition, the young man had his own apartment, and the girl's parents objected to her visiting him there. Their parents' lack of faith in them was very disturbing to the couple.

To make matters worse, the parents could not reach agreement over the wedding arrangements. The bride's parents wanted the parents of the groom to share the expenses, but they refused, maintaining that it was traditional for the bride's parents to bear the cost of the wedding. For their part, the couple wanted a very modest ceremony, with only a few friends and relatives present. Their parents, however, continued to make more and more elaborate plans.

The social worker listened to their complaints and agreed to telephone each set of parents and help solve these problems. There is no record of how successful she was, but the case is an example of the friendly intercession of the Board's representative in an effort to solve a family problem.

A young woman called the office asking to speak to a rabbi, but agreed to meet with the social worker. She explained that her home situation was so intolerable that she thought daily of committing suicide. Though willing to consult a psychiatrist, she did not have the money for a private doctor.

The social worker called several hospitals and finally arranged for the young woman to be admitted to one, free of charge, as an outpatient.

A man complained that he had given a large sum of money to a home for the aged, and that it was now refusing to accept his wife and himself because of the wife's almost total blindness. He did not wish to make a formal complaint against the home, however, for fear of antagonizing its officials. He therefore asked the social worker to use the Board's good offices in order to persuade the home to admit them.

The social worker contacted the manager of the home, who explained that the institution did not have the facilities to care for a blind woman. However, after hearing the social worker's plea on the couple's behalf, the manager promised to do his best to influence his administration with a view to approving the application. The complainant left after expressing his gratitude for the social worker's assistance.

When she had not heard from him after a lapse of two months, the social service worker telephoned the manager of the home, who informed her that the couple had been admitted, that they had been given a private room, that the man was caring for his wife, and that they had adjusted successfully to their new life. The manager conceded that the couple had been admitted only as a result of the interest which the Board had taken in their case.

Occasionally, the social worker would assist a client financially by means of the Social Service Department Fund. In one such case, a woman came to the Board asking for help in locating her husband, who had disappeared. They had been divorced for a year, and now she had no maintenance for herself and for her child, who suffered from tuberculosis and needed expensive medical care.

The social worker referred the woman to the Domestic Relations Court, but in the interim she gave her money from the Social Service Fund in order to help pay expenses until the civil authorities could begin assisting her.

From time to time, non-Jews also came to the Board for help.

Mr. P., a young black man, needed an offer of employment in order to obtain his release from prison on parole. He had written to several agencies for help, but most of them had not even replied. After reading a newspaper article about the Jewish Conciliation Board, he wrote for its assistance in finding employment.

The Social Service Department was impressed by this man's initiative and contacted some members of the Board. One of them offered Mr. P. a position in his meat-packing plant, and he was then paroled.

Soon afterwards, Mr. P. visited the Board's offices in order to thank personally those who had helped him.

The social worker received a letter from him two weeks later, describing his progress. "I feel like a new person in every respect," he wrote, "and I am very grateful to you for making all of this possible for me." He had also decided to attend night school in order to improve his prospects.

Some clients, after discussing their problem with the social worker, would admit that they had filed a complaint in order to have the opportunity of talking to someone about their troubles. For example, Mr. Y. filed a complaint against his wife, who allegedly abused and insulted him. A retired man who had been successful financially, he claimed that no matter how much money he gave his wife, she was never satisfied.

"After further conversation with Mr. Y.," the social worker reported, "it seemed to me that he was not really serious about filing a complaint against his wife, but wanted to talk his heart out to an impartial person. There was nothing seriously wrong between his wife and himself, and they evidently still loved each other. He said that he felt much better after relating his troubles to someone, and he thanked me for being patient and listening to him at such length. He then promised to overlook any slight disagreements and to try to live in peace and harmony with his wife, whom he described as 'really a fine woman.'"

One woman, who asked the social worker for advice in 1944, disclosed that her brother, who was then serving in the Army, had written to say that he needed $125 immediately. The sister suspected that a girl was involved, but she had no idea whether the money was requested because he wanted to marry or because he was in some kind of financial trouble.

The social worker advised the woman to send her brother the money, since, if he was really in trouble, she would later regret not having helped him. If he needed the advance in order to get married, he would marry the girl anyhow, but would always resent the fact that his sister nad refused to help.

Reassured and pleased with this advice, the sister immediately sent her brother the money which he had requested.

Mrs. F. filed a complaint against her son and daughter-in-law, who were on their honeymoon. She maintained that she did not object to her son's marriage, even though he had not asked for her consent.

The girl had made a good impression on her, and so, when her son mentioned that he could not afford a ring for his future bride, Mrs. F. provided him with a diamond ring. Mrs. F. now demanded the return of the ring, since her daughter-in-law had not shown enough gratitude for the fine gift.

"After a lengthy conversation with her," reported the social worker, "I was convinced that Mrs. F. wanted to file the complaint only because she resented the fact of her son's marriage and wished to cause trouble between the two young people. I told her that, in my opinion, her attitude toward her son and daughter-in-law was unfair and that, in the long run, she would hurt herself more by trying to stir up trouble between them. She eventually agreed with me and decided not to press the matter. Mrs. F. thanked me for listening to her and for helping her to realize the mistake she was about to make. She promised to tell me how the young couple were getting along, and again assured me that she would do nothing to interfere in their lives."

This mother-in-law theme often recurred. In the following case, the situation had gone almost too far, but thanks to the social worker, tensions were eased and the couple's domestic harmony was restored.

Mr. K. and his wife had quarreled, and she had decided to "go back to mother." He claimed that she was unduly influenced by her mother, who interfered in their marriage. Mr. K. nevertheless felt that his wife wished to be reconciled, as did he, but he had no idea how to behave so as to insure the continuation of their marriage. On one occasion, he had lost his temper and struck his wife, but this action had so filled him with guilt that he could not sleep. Mr. K. also disclosed that he had tried to tell his story to the Domestic Relations Court, but they refused to listen unless he filed charges against his wife. Since he was reluctant to do so, the civil court had recommended that he approach the Jewish Conciliation Board.

The social worker advised Mr. K. to be more firm regarding his mother-in-law's interference and not to let her upset his marriage. She also warned him to control his temper and not to strike his wife.

Mr. K. thanked the social worker for spending so much time listening to his problems, and added that the JCB was the first agency he had consulted which had been so sympathetic and concerned.

A week later, Mr. K. called the social worker and informed her that he and his wife had been reconciled and were living together again. He had taken the social worker's advice and was treating his wife with more consideration, while she in turn was reciprocating. He again thanked the Board's representative for having listened to his story and for helping to preserve his marriage.

A man had sent $3,000 to the Jewish National Fund to have trees planted in the name of his late brother, in accordance with the stipulation in his brother's will. Although he had been sent a receipt from the New York office of the JNF and a Herzl Forest certificate, he was concerned about the validity of the transaction. He did not believe there was a Herzl Forest, and he wanted a receipt clearly marked, "Jewish National Fund, Israel."

The social worker was able to contact the proper authority at the Jewish National Fund, who subsequently assured the man that there was indeed a Herzl Forest in Israel and that his brother's trees had been planted there. The officer also explained that the receipt had been issued by the JNF's New York office, but that the money had been duly transferred to Israel.

Special Problems

Among the cases which came to the tribunal's attention were some involving men, women, and young people who were mentally or emotionally underdeveloped. Every community has such unfortunates within its midst. The problems, in many instances, may not find a lasting solution, yet these maladjusted members of our society move about freely and often make life difficult for others.

The judges and the social workers of the Jewish Conciliation Board, in handling such cases, were fully aware that permanent solutions were often too much to expect, yet they endeavored at least to suggest some temporary measures, in order to avert imminent crises.

The interest of the Social Service Department in its clients was an ongoing one, and it was sometimes maintained in a single case for a considerable period of time. The following was a case which spanned a period of eighteen years, according to the records, indicating the Board's ongoing concern with a difficult, possibly insoluble problem.

In January 1942, the Board's social worker spoke with a mother, Mrs. D., whose daughter had not appeared for the scheduled hearing.

The problem was that B., an underweight and nervous fourteen-year-old girl, was disobedient and willful. Her mother had consulted a number of agencies and had even taken the girl to a hospital, but all to no avail. The social worker was told that B. never shampooed her hair or bathed, but compulsively washed her hands with alcohol. She insisted that the house be spotlessly clean, and she refused to eat together with the family. Not only did her bed linen have to be changed frequently, but if anyone touched her bed, she would demand another change of the linen. The girl also refused to allow her mother to leave the apartment when she was home. Since she had become violent occasionally, the police had made several visits to the home.

It was clear the B.'s real problem was not simply "disobedient and willful" behavior. The social worker therefore agreed to make a home visit. While she was there, B. returned from school in a sullen and uncommunicative mood. The father refused to admit that there was anything wrong with his daughter, except that his wife had spoiled her. He blamed his wife for not letting him spank B. more often. Mrs. D. described these "spankings" as beatings.

The social worker urged Mrs. D. to consult the Jewish Board of Guardians. After having done so, she began to accept the fact that her daughter would have to be institutionalized, at least temporarily. The mother thanked the social worker, since it was the first time that anyone had suggested the Jewish Board of Guardians to her.

There was a long-delayed sequel fifteen years later, in 1957. Mrs. D. again contacted the Jewish Conciliation Board and reported that she was once more having serious problems with her daughter, who was now employed as an assistant buyer and had been sharing an apartment with a girl friend. This roommate had married, and since Mrs. D. had been widowed in the interim, B. asked her mother to move in with her.

B was still suffering from what her mother called her "cleanliness phobia." She would break dishes in the cupboard if they were not clean enough for her, and would not allow her mother to sit on her chair if she had worn the same dress in the subway. When Mrs. D. suggested that B. consult a psychiatrist, the girl retorted, "You are an ugly old woman and need a psychiatrist yourself."

Subsequently, when B. spoke privately to the social worker, she accused her mother of slovenliness and again said that she was the one in need of psychiatric help. Mrs. D. had meanwhile decided to move into an apartment of her own.

The social worker's records for 1960 mention a telephone call from Mrs. D. reporting that B. had been consulting a psychiatrist over the past five months. Her condition seemed to be worsening, and she had quit her job. The mother, greatly concerned for her daughter's welfare, requested that the social worker call B. and "cheer her up." The social worker had to refuse this request, since B. was under the care of a psychiatrist at the time. The records of the case end here.

The last problem in this category also occupied the social worker for a number of years, but fortunately this case had a successful conclusion.

A young Jewish woman, Miss R., was engaged to a black man, and this had caused a rift in her family, which impelled her to leave college and move out of her home. The social worker was asked to speak to the girl, and they met at the social worker's home in the evening.

Miss R. proved to be a shy, withdrawn young woman who explained that she had known her fiancé since high school and that he was presently a college student intending to specialize in psychiatry. Although the young man had at least nine years of training ahead of him, as well as his Army service, the couple planned to marry in two years' time. Miss R.'s parents had legally attached her savings account. Not only did this prevent her from continuing college, but she was forced to work as an office clerk in order to support herself. The social worker, hoping to encourage the girl to become reconciled with her parents and return to college, as well as agree to a trial separation from her fiancé, invited Miss R. to visit her again with her young man.

They did so the following week. Mr. E., the fiancé, is described as "a nice looking, strong-willed boy." Miss R., by contrast, appeared immature and passive, allowing herself to be completely dominated. The social worker persuaded Miss R. to take a Vocational Guidance Bureau aptitude test. For his part, Mr. E. asked for a private consultation with the social worker at the Board's office. During that subsequent visit, he made it clear that any children born of the union would have to be brought up as Christians. Although he had previously described his own family's attitude to the marriage as passive, he now admitted that there was a good deal of prejudice in the black community against interracial marriage. After a lengthy talk, the social worker felt that Mr. E. realized that the marriage would be a mistake, but was too proud to admit it.

The social worker's meeting with the parents of Miss R. took place after they had gone into virtual mourning for their daughter. They described her early childhood as one of parental indulgence, and this seemed to have fostered her stubbornness and weak character. During the years when Miss R had been dating Mr. E, she tried to deceive her parents regarding her boyfriend's identity, but finally left home when the facts came to light. Her parents were upset and angry, and consultations with a rabbi and a psychiatrist had not helped.

Over the next few months, the Board's social worker spent many hours with both young people and with Miss R.'s parents, attempting to find a path through the maze of psychological problems and the emotional family conflict. The situation came to a head when the couple's planned wedding was canceled two days before the event and the social worker found Miss R. at home with her parents. Her father had not only convinced his daughter to postpone the wedding, but had ascertained that the young man's professional hopes had been shattered when he was caught cheating in his examinations. Following this, Mr. E. joined the Army and vanished from the scene. The social worker advised that the family consult a psychiatrist to help them through this period, and the father agreed to the suggestion.

A few months later, the social worker received a letter from the father, informing her that his wife and daughter had gone to Israel, where the daughter was now attending Hebrew-language classes in an *Ulpan*. He wrote that she was dating boys, but still remained reserved with her mother.

The social worker noted in her records that "R will really begin to blossom into a more mature person after this visit to Israel. While I did not believe at first that I would be able to accomplish much, I now think that all my efforts have borne fruit."

About eighteen months later, almost three years after her initial contact with this case, the social worker was able to record: "I have received an invitation to attend the wedding of R. to a young Jew whom she met during her visit to Israel."

VI
Summation

It would be over-optimistic to assume that disputes and altercations which had apparently been resolved by the judges, at sessions of the Jewish Conciliation Board, always remained settled. There were many situations, of course, where the parties to a dispute, who could not agree among themselves, came in good faith to ask our tribunal to make the decision, accepted the decision in the same spirit, and were grateful to the tribunal for rendering them that service.

This was often the case in financial disputes or in litigations where the children accepted their obligation to contribute to the support of an aged parent, but were in need of outside help to apportion the maintenance prescribed. Much the same can be said of disputes arising in fraternal organizations and *Landsmanshaften* with regard to sick benefits or burial privileges.

In all such cases, the good offices of the tribunal were accepted not only with deference, but also with appreciation.

Another area of this kind was concerned with elderly parents whose welfare could best be served by their admittance to homes for the aged. The role of the Board in these cases was to find such a placement and to oblige the children to undertake the financial obligations involved.

Unfortunately, however, there were situations where the good offices of the JCB failed to bring about the desired results. In many litigations, the tribunal handed down rulings which one of the contending parties resented. The dissatisfied party, however, was compelled to abide by the decision, since it was enforceable. Rarely did clients absolutely refuse to comply.

A more troublesome phenomenon was the type of case where

litigants made a show of acceptance and conciliation, which, however, proved to be only superficial and temporary. Often, the judges were left hoping for the best, that their efforts would "hold," but felt a gnawing apprehension that the problem might flare up again.

A well-known columnist, Ernie Pyle, writing in his *Washington News* article of April 7, 1937 (after he had attended a JCB session), summed up his impression as follows:

> The Jewish Conciliation Board seems to me a wonderful thing. It does do good and I can't praise it too highly. But when it comes to genuine conciliation, I'm afraid it has bitten off something that can't be chewed in this world.

Our position in the JCB was that the possibility of conciliation must never be written off and that the appeal to the best impulses in human nature must never be abandoned. We held this kind of approach to be eminently humanitarian and authentically Jewish.

One of the traditional methods of conciliation, especially in the Jewish tradition, is *Pesharah* (compromise)—finding the "golden mean" which lies between the claims made by either side in a dispute. This form of compromise, *Pesharah*, naturally occupied an important place in the decisions handed down by judges constituting the JCB tribunals over the years.

Perhaps the best summation of the work accomplished by the Jewish Conciliation Board is expressed in the following commentaries by two men, both eminent in their respective fields.

Rabbi Professor Louis I. Rabinowitz of Jerusalem, former Chief Rabbi of South Africa's Federation of Synagogues, is an expert in Jewish law and lore. Having become acquainted with the work of the Board, he writes the following evaluation:

> Despite the parallels which have been adduced to provide a framework for the remarkable phenomenon of the Jewish Conciliation Board and to see in it a continuation or an extension of Jewish ethical principles put into practice, it nevertheless stands out as unique in many respects. It contained the elements of a *Beth Din*, but it was not a *Beth Din*. Such sanction as it possessed to enforce its decisions was based on Arbitration Acts in the United States. Arbitration as a basis for settling disputes has a long, continuous, and honorable history in Judaism, yet the Conciliation Board was something different from an arbitration tribunal.
>
> A *Beth Din* is a duly constituted court of Jewish law, which deals with every single aspect of Jewish law, whether ceremonial, ritual, dietary regulations, or commercial law and other aspects of *meum et teum*. There never existed a *Beth Din* which saw it as its *sole duty* to smooth out and settle

differences between individuals. The essence of arbitration in Jewish law is that each contending party chooses its representative who will defend his interests, and both these appointees in turn agree on a third to complete the tribunal. That contending parties should voluntarily agree to submit a dispute to a nonauthoritative body is almost without precedent.

And yet, despite that, not only did the Jewish Conciliation Board embody within it some of the most profound principles of Jewish ethics and social justice, but it was probably a unique experiment which attempted, and succeeded, in putting these principles into an organizational framework, thus providing the channels for their application in practice.

In order to appreciate the truth of this claim, it is necessary to adumbrate some of the principles to which Rabbi Rabinowitz alludes.

Justice versus Conciliation

In an address quoted elsewhere in this volume,[1] U.S. Supreme Court Justice William O. Douglas declared:

> The thing that has interested me particularly about the Board is that it has been more interested in justice than in law. Law and justice are not necessarily the same, as you know. Throughout the centuries, law has been trying to catch up with justice.

No one can doubt the truth of this observation and of what Justice Douglas referred to as "one of the great, eternal struggles of man" to make the two identical.[2] Judaism, however, pays special attention to another and more agonizing conflict of ideals than that between justice and law—the possible conflict between justice and peace. This potential battleground finds its most dramatic expression in a passage in the Talmud where the two brothers, Moses and Aaron, are sharply contrasted. Moses represents the ideal of strict, undeviating, inflexible justice; Aaron regards peace and conciliation as an even loftier ideal. Remarkably enough, the basis of this Talmudical discussion is actually the question of any possible injustice which, from the viewpoint of strict law, is enshrined in arbitration and the compromise to which it usually leads.

The beginning of the relevant passage reads as follows:

> R. Eliezer the son of R. Yosé the Galilean says, It is forbidden to arbitrate a settlement, and he who acts as an arbitrator commits an offense and he who praises the arbitrator scorns the Lord . . . 'For the judgment is God's' [Deut. 1:17]. And indeed, the motto of Moses was, 'Let the law pierce the

1. See Appendix II.
2. Ibid.

mountain!' [i.e. justice must not be thwarted], whereas Aaron loved peace and pursued peace and made peace between man and his fellow.[3]

The subsequent Talmudical discussion makes it clear that the bone of contention is in essence the fact that, from the standpoint of the letter of the law and strict justice, every compromise constitutes an act of injustice, since the legal rights of the plaintiff are reduced by the compromise effected in the interests of harmony and peace.

All those who have had the practical experience of sitting on a *Beth Din* know that to such an extent is there a predilection favoring peaceful compromise over application of the strict law that often an obdurate plaintiff will actually distress the rabbis by saying, "I wish this case to be dealt with according to the letter of the law, and not by compromise."

The essence of the Jewish Conciliation Board's approach was that it gave practical expression to the principle that peace and conciliation take precedence over the strict lines of law and even of justice.

If, as stated, the line of strict justice may be bent somewhat in the cause of peace, so, in the same context, may truth. The rabbis lovingly explain how Aaron, in his zealous pursuit of peace, was not averse even to telling a "white lie," if this led toward reconciliation. In other words, as applied to the work of the Board, it did not matter whether a certain argument held water or not. The criterion was whether it served the cause of peace.

Voluntary Service

Although the two aforementioned principles occasionally found expression in practice, they were never actually embodied in the Jewish legal system. There is, however, a third ideal which *was* written into a legal code, but which became a dead letter. The authoritative code of Oral Law, the Mishnah, actually lays down as a legal principle that "if a man accepts payment for acting as a judge, his judgments are void."[4] Nevertheless, almost from the moment when this principle was established, it was found to be inoperable and for all practical purposes it was never implemented. Not only was a judge (*Dayyan*) permitted to receive payment, but he could demand a fee for hearing a case, provided the respective parties each paid the same amount.

A salaried judiciary is nowadays the established norm, in the State of Israel no less than in the United States or other parts of the world, but this does not mean that, under particular circumstances and for particular purposes, a *voluntary* tribunal may not be empowered to

3. *Sanhedrin* 6b.
4. *Bekhorot* 4.6.

hear and arbitrate disputes. In a sense, therefore, the Jewish Conciliation Board functioned within the sphere of Jewish tradition and in strict
accordance with the Oral Law.

The actual establishment of a body enshrining all the above
principles—the pursuit of harmony and conciliation in disputes over all
other considerations, involving, if necessary, a bending of the strict
line of justice; a completely voluntary service on the part of the
"conciliators" (a more apt term than "judges" or "arbitrators"); a
readiness to listen, consider, and decide on the most trivial of matters
and claims—makes the Conciliation Board a unique example of
specifically Jewish social ethics in practice, for which there are few
precedents, if any. It is this overall consideration which raises the
activities of the Board far above the apparent triviality of some of the
cases with which it had to deal. In case after case, one can see all these
principles activated and all formal consideration of legal niceties vanish
into thin air in the light of four words: "the parties shook hands."
Peace, harmony, and conciliation had been effected. To achieve this, it
was worthwhile for three eminent gentlemen to give up some of their
time to adjudge a dispute which may have resulted in the award of
only a few dollars.

Dr. Howard E. Berk, the psychiatrist who volunteered his services
to attend many of the sessions and to provide valuable advice, ap-
praised the Board's work as follows:

The panel members, rich in skills, often learned and wise, with long and
particular experience, compassionate, gently patient, shrewdly impatient,
and, oh so rarely (perhaps by some turn of the weather) none of these, joined
together in the panels to hear and to heed the angers, the sorrows, and the
aching burdens of Jews of this city; the weary yearnings, all but given up, the
fierce cries of rage from brothers and fathers locked in a family vendetta and
raised to some Jewish power over ancient wrongs and promises, real or
sometimes imagined. . . . Mothers and sisters and wives also, with stubbornly sustained anger over slights and hurts of long ago; still others of
strange and tortuous thought, and so many more. Some looking for *Shalom*,
yet many, not so hopeful, still demanding their day in court to vent the
wrath of many years before the closely attentive judges. To demand a
favorable decision, but to accept instead, smilingly, with a round of hand-
shakes, a fair decision. Justice! Justice! Justice! A day in court! Before a real
court of their own kind—*The Jewish Court.*

I, a physician and practicing psychiatrist in good standing with my fellow
professionals, have seen marvellous things happen at sessions of the Jewish
Conciliation Board—happily marvellous things. Marvellous, because as a
physician and psychiatrist I wouldn't ever, ever have expected *any* resolution, much less one after an hour or hour-and-a-half in a room filled with

fierce anger and recalcitrant bitterness. Yet, in one way or another, I saw this happen again and again.

But if marvellous events took place at the sessions of the court that I haven't seen in my practice or in long years in hospitals and clinics, how can one account for them? I believe it is because the court, wherever it met, was an event of great inherent dignity, despite its frequent informality; and because the quality of the interchange between the court members, with their diversity of backgrounds and experience, was extremely high and yielded insights that are much less likely to occur, or to occur so quickly, with single individuals (e.g. "therapists," etc.). The Petitioner and Respondent—or Client, if you will—in turn seeking "justice" or peace or vengeance or just comfort and advice found (and expected to find, because they had heard of the court) a setting and a reception elevating of spirit and fortifying of courage, enabling these men, women and children to speak more forthrightly and directly than would be true if the same persons were reduced to presenting their intense concerns to caseworkers or "therapists." Of course, the Jewish Conciliation Board's panels and office staff found some petitioners and respondents better suited for or needful of social work or other clinical or specialist assistance, and with great tact and gentle authority regularly and effectively made such referrals. And indeed, the office staff followed up such referrals, and carefully, as might a *good friend,* to better assure their success.

Continuous exposure over the years to the problems which came before the Jewish Conciliation Board has left upon the writer residual impressions which may be worth recording.

It has made him aware of the presence of dire poverty amid the wealthiest Jewish community in the world. This condition is an indictment of the city, state, and national governments, which should feel ever challenged to provide work at a living wage for every able-bodied man and woman.

It has revealed some of the meanness inherent in human nature, an ongoing challenge to all who are concerned with the improvement of the human species, but it has often also revealed traits of nobility in the humblest of men and women, to whom appeals could be made in the name of justice and compassion.

It has demonstrated that there is among many Jews, indeed among most Jews, a sense of Jewish honor which could be invoked as a motivating force in the conduct of daily affairs and relationships.

The Jewish Conciliation Board did not always succeed in its mission. Frequently, the judges were left frustrated when their appeals for reconciliation fell on deaf ears, or when a human problem was too deeply rooted to be amenable to a solution. Yet, on the whole, the successes achieved by the tribunal far outweighed its failures.

This achievement is a tribute to the wisdom and humanity of the men and women who volunteered their time and talent to serve as judges, to the devotion and ability of the Executive Secretary, to the effective follow-up by the experienced social workers, and—in no small degree—to the underlying sense of decency of the great majority of the Board's clientele.

May I close these pages with a word of valediction. The years of my association with this unique Jewish agency brought me intense satisfaction, which was its own great reward. It was a meaningful experience to be helpful to "Reb Yisro'el," *Amkha*—my humble, often under-privileged brothers and sisters, who were in need of help, sympathetic understanding, and guidance. In my mind and heart, all of this remains a cherished chapter of Jewish and human service.

APPENDICES

Appendix I

JEWISH CONCILIATION COURT OF AMERICA, INC.
225 Broadway, New York, N.Y.

SUBMISSION OF ARBITRATION

WHEREAS differences, disputes and controversies have arisen between the parties hereto and they are desirous of submitting all their said differences, disputes, controversies and any and all manner and causes of action, the parties hereto agree that they will submit the same to

arbitrators

selected by the Jewish Conciliation Court of America, Inc. and the said parties further agree that the award to be made by the said arbitrators shall be in all things well and faithfully kept, observed and performed, and that judgment of the Supreme Court shall be entered upon the award which may be made pursuant to the above submission, said judgment to be entered in any county, to the end that all matters in controversy in their behalf between them shall be finally concluded; oath of arbitration and all other provisions as to form are hereby expressly waived; a memorandum in writing signed by a majority of the arbitrators shall be a valid decision for all purposes.

IN WITNESS WHEREOF, the parties hereto have hereunto set their hands and seals this   day of   193 .

..............................L.S.
..............................L.S.
..............................L.S.
..............................L.S.
..............................L.S.
..............................L.S.
..............................L.S.
..............................L.S.

STATE OF NEW YORK ⎫
COUNTY OF NEW YORK ⎬ ss.:
CITY OF NEW YORK ⎭

On this   day of   193 .

before me came
to me known and known to me to be the individual described in and who executed the foregoing instrument and he acknowledged to me that he duly executed the same.

CORPORATE ACKNOWLEDGMENT

STATE OF NEW YORK ⎫
COUNTY OF NEW YORK ⎬ ss.:
CITY OF NEW YORK ⎭

On this   day of   193 .

before me came
to me known, who, being by me duly sworn, did depose and say that he resides in   , that he is the   of
the corporation described in, and which executed the foregoing instrument; that he knows the seal of said corporation; that the seal affixed to said instrument is such corporate seal; that it was so affixed by order of the board of   of said corporation; and that he signed h   name thereto by like order.

215

JEWISH CONCILIATION COURT OF AMERICA, INC.
225 Broadway, New York, N.Y.

DECISION AND AWARD

WHEREAS we have been designated as the arbitrators pursuant to the submission of arbitration bearing date . . . ., now, therefore, after trial and after hearing all the facts herein, we hereby find and decide as follows: . . . .

. . . .

. . . .

. . . .

. . . .

. . . .

. . . .

Dated, New York, ... 193   . . . .

STATE OF NEW YORK
COUNTY OF NEW YORK   ss.:
CITY OF NEW YORK

On this   day of   193 ,
before me came
to me known and known to me to be the individual described in and who executed the foregoing instrument and he acknowledged to me that he duly executed the same.

Appendix II

ADDRESS BY WILLIAM O. DOUGLAS,
ASSOCIATE JUSTICE, SUPREME COURT OF THE UNITED STATES,
at exercises marking the 35th anniversary of the Jewish Conciliation Board
of America and honoring DR. ISRAEL GOLDSTEIN
on the 25th anniversary of his presidency

Held at the Jewish Educational Alliance, January 17, 1954, at 4:00 P.M.

General Sarnoff, Dr. Goldstein, Friends:

The other evening in Washington I attended a dinner in honor of an 84-year-old American, who has given much to this country in the field of sports, Clark Griffith of the Washington Senators. The introduction was a very flattering one, and when Mr. Griffith rose to reply, he said, with a twinkle in his eyes, "I believe every word of it. The only thing I wonder is whether the chairman believed it." In this case, I know that General Sarnoff believed all the nice things he said about me in his introduction. I only wish they were all true.

I thank him and you for your very warm reception.

When Dr. Goldstein visited Washington some weeks ago and asked me to come today, I was happy to accept. But I did not have time to prepare a paper, to put some things to paper that I could leave behind me on this occasion. I am sorry for I had something very close to my heart to say. But Court has been sitting this week and last week, and I did not find the time necessary to write out my ideas.

I have been much interested in the work of Dr. Israel Goldstein. While I have long known him by reputation, I have not known much about the details of the work of the Jewish Conciliation Board, except in a general way. The thing that has interested me particularly about the Board is that it has been more interested in justice than in law. Law and justice are not necessarily the same, as you know. Throughout the centuries, law has been trying to catch up with justice. It has not always succeeded. That is one of the great, eternal struggles of man.

Our Declaration of Independence states "that all men are endowed by their Creator with certain unalienable rights." That which man gets from his Creator no government can take away. Those of you who have lived under a Nazi

217

regime or a Fascist regime or any other type of totalitarian government, as many of you have, will appreciate what the wide gulf between law and justice often is.

The search around the world by people of all races and creeds is basically for justice. One finds it cropping up in many different ways, both little ways and big ways, as one travels around the world.

When I was out in India, I learned something of the tradition of a great lawgiver by the name of Manu. He is as famous out there as Moses is here. Manu produced a great code. And he became a sort of mythical figure when he was transferred to Burmese folklore.

There is a beautiful Burmese story of law and justice centering around Manu. It tells pretty much the struggle of man through the years. Manu was a judge and he was sworn to do justice as he saw it. Two villagers came to him with a dispute. One had planted a cucumber seed which produced a plant. The plant sent its creepers out onto his neighbor's land. Soon the neighbor had cucumbers growing in his yard. There was a quarrel as to who owned the cucumbers—the man who planted the cucumber seed, or the man on whose ground the cucumbers were growing.

Manu held a hearing and decided that the man on whose ground the cucumbers lay owned them. So that man was awarded the judgment. But the problem worried Manu. Manu thought about it and after a few weeks realized that he had done an injustice, that his ruling on the law was not true to the elements of justice. Therefore Manu resigned as a judge and became a hermit. Manu in Burma today is a symbol of humility, a man in search of justice, a man who recognizes his errors when he makes them, a man who moves forward to the ideal of liberty and justice for all people.

I sat with the Supreme Court of Israel. I had some very moving experiences there that I will not stop to tell you about now. It will be a deviation from what I want to say. But there is one thing I should mention in passing. That Court issued a writ of habeas corpus, which, for those who are not lawyers, is the way by which a prisoner is produced from jail, produced before a judge, so that the court can look into the legality of his detention. If the detention is illegal, then he is discharged. The Supreme Court of Israel issued a writ of habeas corpus directing a hearing on the legality of the detention of an Arab. After the hearing, they discharged this Arab on the ground that he had been illegally detained "in protective custody." In a very tense moment of its history, that stalwart little State of Israel stood on the side of justice and truth on behalf of a minority, and said: "We are going to administer justice equally in Israel to people of all races."

It is a great inspiration to see ideas of equality and justice spreading out over a part of the world that has known very little of it in its long, long history.

The work of the Conciliation Board, seeking to find what is the truth, trying to apply justice, is a great experiment in a busy community where there are many problems, local and international. It is important to take time out to make adjustments in the little problems of people. That in the end marks the differences between a society which administers to the needs of people, and a society where sores and troubles fester, where the needs and aspirations of the ordinary man are neglected.

The ideal of America is something I wanted to speak about, especially to those of you who have recently come here. I suppose all of us in this room are either immigrants to this country, or sons and daughters of immigrants. I, for one, had an immigrant father from Nova Scotia who loved America dearly. The great symbolism of America, in the eyes of the peoples of the world, is that this land is a political asylum. Here is where people could come and find liberty and security, develop their own cultures, have their own political views, their own churches and languages, and yet be a part of one people, one flag, and one unity of purpose. That has been the great vision of America in the world.

I was reading the other day some stirring statements that President Grover Cleveland made when he was vetoing some immigration law, some statements William Howard Taft made, and also Woodrow Wilson, pleading that America remain a political asylum, a place where people of all races and creeds could be organized behind one philosophy of Government. It is that system of Government that has given America its great strength.

But for that system of Government, we would not have had General Sarnoff; we would have been deprived of him and thousands of others born in other lands, who have immigrated here, and who have brought great honor and distinction to this country and to the world. That is one of the most important struggles going on in America today—to keep America the symbol of tolerance and fraternity. That is America's greatest strength in the long run. That is the power of America, not only at home but in the councils of nations. We must, in our community activities and national activities, promote ideals of tolerance. We must keep those ideals of America alive in the hearts of the people. Otherwise, we will lose our position of moral authority in the world.

I state this to you from my heart on the occasion of the 25th anniversary of a wonderful man and his wife, who have been doing in a small way what America stands for in the world, doing the thing that I hope America always will do. So when we salute Dr. Goldstein and Mrs. Goldstein, we salute the best in us—the tolerance, the warmheartedness, the deep sense of justice, and the bright conscience of America. Those are real qualities, those are the things we are apt to forget about when we read the headlines, and find nothing but hate and suspicion and distrust.

I am proud to be here and I am very happy to welcome you in paying tribute to a great American and his wife.

Appendix III

THE ETERNAL LIGHT

"COURT WITHOUT A GAVEL"

Broadcast
June 20, 1954

Presented by
THE NATIONAL BROADCASTING COMPANY, INC.
*as a public service and prepared under
the auspices of*
THE JEWISH THEOLOGICAL SEMINARY OF AMERICA
3080 Broadway, New York

"COURT WITHOUT A GAVEL"

Voice:	(ECHO) And the Lord spake unto Moses, saying, Command the children of Israel that they bring unto thee pure olive oil beaten for the light, to cause the lamps to burn continually in the tabernacle of the congregation, and it shall be a statute forever in your generations.
Anncr.:	The National Broadcasting Company and its affiliated independent stations make free time available to present the Eternal Light, a program which comes to you under

the auspices of The Jewish Theological Seminary of
America. Our program today, "Court Without a Gavel,"
was written by Marc Siegel.

(SOUND: TWO SHORT BUZZES ON OFFICE
INTERCOM)

Miss Smith: Yes, Mr. Roe.

Roe: Miss Smith. Please bring in your notebook . . . the one
with my brief to the governor.

Miss Smith: Right away, Mr. Roe.

Roe: Good.
(SOUND: FOOTSTEPS COMING ON)

Miss Smith: I have it here, Mr. Roe. As far as you've gone.

Roe: Fine. Will you read it back to me?

Miss Smith: Yes, sir.
(SOUND: TURNING OF NOTEBOOK PAGES)
Here . . . (READING) Dear Mr. Governor: As a
member of your commission on judicial practices, I beg
to submit the following findings relative to the expedition of judicial procedures and the securing of qualita-
tively better results in the courts of this state.

Roe:

(TOPPING) The words of
my report to the gover-
nor are formal, and the
phrases are legalistic. But
behind the neatly or-
dered paragraphs is the
tumultuous human
striving for a wiser sys-
tem of justice among
men. (PAUSE) This is
the story of one effort to-
wards that end . . .

The average delay (FAD-
ING DOWN) in court
calendars is now two
years and eight months.
Court proceedings are
costly. Judicial functions
overlap. The adjudication
of claims (FADING) and
disputes is encumbered
by . . .

the story of a unique court that meets on New York's
Lower East Side to dispense a kind of justice first developed when the world was young. (PAUSE) It is the
kind of court we need to keep the world young. (PAUSE)
I think of it always as the Court Without a Gavel.

In the interests of discretion, I will call myself Richard

Roe . . . That's not my name, of course, but I ask you to accept this legal fiction. (PAUSE) A few months ago, I walked into the study of Rabbi Israel Goldstein, who serves as president of the Jewish Conciliation Board of America . . .

(SOUND: FOOTSTEPS COMING ON)

Goldstein: Delighted to meet you, Mr. Roe.

Roe: Thank you. Rabbi

Goldstein: I've been wondering, since you called—

Roe: Why I want to see you?

Goldstein: Exactly.

Roe: As part of our survey, Rabbi, the governor's asked me to look into the less official courts, too—the conciliation efforts made by the major faiths, for example.

Goldstein: We'll be glad to be of any help we can, Mr. Roe.

Roe: Thank you, Dr. Goldstein. (PAUSE) Now, as . . . This Jewish

Goldstein: Jewish Conciliation Board of America—

Roe: Yes—this Jewish Conciliation Board—How many cases a year does it process?

Goldstein: Mr. Roe—

Roe: Yes. Rabbi?

Goldstein: We don't quite think of the people who come before us as "cases"—and the world "process" doesn't exactly—

Roe: Of course. I understand what you're getting at. (PAUSE) Well—as we say in the courts—I'll rephrase the question.

Goldstein: It's not really necessary, Mr. Roe. I was trying only to indicate an attitude. (PAUSE) I'd say we hear about a thousand people a year.

Roe: A thousand! That's a tremendous number.

Goldstein: The number isn't so important—

Roe: (INTERRUPTING) Not important, Rabbi? The courts are so crowded that—

Goldstein: Don't misunderstand me, sir. The Board recognizes that it helps to relieve congestion in the courts. But we think of this work as serving a purpose far beyond speeding justice . . .

Roe: Dr. Goldstein, don't write off the question of speed so lightly. My commission would be happy if speed were its sole achievement.

Goldstein: I agree that speed must be striven for, Mr. Roe. But—if I may make an observation—

Roe: By all means, Dr. Goldstein.

Goldstein: The quality of justice is as important as the speed with
             which it is administered.

Roe: Now that the commission's work is complete, I will
             admit that my call to Dr. Goldstein was one which I had
             considered—to that point—routine . . . A very small
             part of the entire, complicated picture . . .
             Yet I soon found myself considering, with him, the very
             heart of the problem . . .

Goldstein: In our view, justice must be more than just the settle-
             ment of a dispute by the application of the law—

Roe: (PUZZLED) More than—? I don't understand.

Goldstein: Mr. Roe. Let me ask you a question (PAUSE) What is
             the purpose of law?

Roe: To provide equal justice.

Goldstein: I agree. But for whom?

Roe: For all, Dr. Goldstein. For all those who would be
             otherwise unprotected.

Goldstein: This is true, Mr. Roe. But in our view the highest justice
             goes beyond the law.

Roe: How do you mean?

Roe: It reaches beyond the letter of the law. (PAUSE) It
             reaches to love for fellow man.

Roe: Rabbi—This is all very interesting. Theoretically. And I
             subscribe to your ideal viewpoint—

Goldstein: But?

Roe: But what practical application has this to the problem at
             hand?

Goldstein: A very practical application. It's the principle on which
             our hearings are held.

Roe: That men should love each other?

Goldstein: Yes. That the highest justice is such that the disputants
             leave the room hand in hand.

Roe: The loser and the winner?

Goldstein: We hope there are no losers and no winners in our
             hearings.

Roe: But how—how can that be?

Goldstein: Our whole effort, Mr. Roe, is to persuade those who
             come before us to come to an agreement—an agreement
             which both can accept as just.

Roe: To persuade, rather than to judge?

Goldstein: Exactly.

Roe:	That's a very enlightened principle, Dr. Goldstein. How long has your court operated on it?
Goldstein:	Our board? Since the beginning, thirty years ago.
Roe:	For that long? (PAUSE) That's remarkable. The idea of conciliation in the courts is hardly that old.
Goldstein:	(PAUSE) Mr. Roe, the idea of conciliation is some two thousand years old. You will find it expressed in detail in the Talmud.

Roe:	The highest justice goes beyond the law . . . That's a curious idea for a lawyer . . . (PAUSE) On a rainy Wednesday afternoon in April, I travelled down to New York's Lower East Side . . . I wanted to see this court in action . . . I call it a court perhaps from habit, or perhaps only because I cannot think of any word that really grasps the feeling of this unique institution— (SOUND: BUZZ OF ARRIVING CROWD UP. THEN DOWN) The litigants—I'm sorry—I should say the people involved—seemed to be of every age and every economic level . . . (SOUND: REGISTER BUZZ BRIEFLY)
Richman:	(SLIGHTLY OFF) Please take your seats. We're going to begin in a minute.
Roe:	A Mr. Louis Richman, the executive director of the Jewish Conciliation Board, was asking for quiet . . . Asking, mind you, not ordering it. . .
Richman:	Please answer if your name is called . . . (SOUND: CROWD BUZZ DOWN TO SILENCE)
Roe:	

(TOPPING) I listened to calling of the calendar. There was something strange about it to a lawyer's ear . . .		Mr. Milton Greenberg and Mr. Samuel Marcus . .
	Voice:	(OFF) Here!
	Two:	(OFF) Here.
	Richman:	Mrs. Dorothy Block and Miss Anne Block . .
	Woman:	(OFF) We're here.
	Richman:	Mr. Abraham Weintraub and Mrs. (FADING) Abraham Weintraub . . .

Voice:	(OFF) Here.
Woman:	(OFF) Here.
Richman:	(FADING UP) Mr. Alvin Katz and Mr. Jacob Friedlander . . . Mr. Alvin Katz and Jacob Friedlander . . .
Voice:	(WELL OFF) Present.
Two:	(OFF) I'm here.

Roe: Suddenly I realized that the names were being called without a familiar little word I've lived with all of my professional life . . . In this strange court, a case was called as Mr. So-and-So *and* Mr. So-and-So. (PAUSE) The word "versus"—which means against, of course— the word "versus" was nowhere to be heard.

Miss Smith: Shall I go on reading, Mr. Roe?

Roe: Please, Miss Smith.

Miss Smith: The judges are chosen from a panel of several hundred distinguished citizens of this city. They serve without compensation, in groups of three—a lawyer, a rabbi and a businessman in each group. Established originally

(FADING)

Roe:

(TOPPING) After the calendar had been called, the judges filed in and took their places behind a small table . . .

as a free court of arbitration for the Jews of this city, it now serves . . .

(SOUND: FADE UP AUDIENCE BUZZ)

Richman: (SLIGHTLY OFF) Mr. Milton Greenberg and Mr. Samuel Marcus. Please come forward.

(SOUND: BUZZ PETERS DOWN TO SILENCE)

Roe: The two principals came forward . . .(SOUND: FOOTSTEPS FORWARD AND TO STOP). . . and the questioning began.

Judge: Now, Mr. Greenberg, suppose you begin by stating your complaint. The Rabbi here, and Mr. Sobel and I will listen to your side of the story first.

Roe:

As the hearings
started. Dr. Gold-
stein slipped into a
seat beside me . . .

Goldstein: Good afternoon, Mr. Roe. Glad you could make it.

         Voice: Yes, sir, About four years ago, (FAD-ING) Mr. Marcus and I became . . . partners in business. At that time . . .

Roe: I am too, Dr. Goldstein.

Goldstein: Well . . . How do you react to what you see thus far?

Roe: It's a little unusual.

Goldstein: Yes . . . No judicial robes. No lawyers. (PAUSE) It must be an odd sight for an attorney.

Roe: Odd, yes—but there are courts where the judges don't wear gowns. I've seen that.

Goldstein: Of course.

Roe: On the other hand, Dr. Goldstein—

Goldstein: Yes, Mr. Roe?

Roe: In more than twenty-five years as a lawyer, I've never before seen a court without a gavel.

Roe: I cannot go into detail on the many cases I watched that afternoon . . . But there are two situations that remain in my mind, for in their disposition I recognized that certain principles, only dimly understood in formal courts of law, were being used to bring about that higher justice which goes beyond the law. The first involved an elderly couple. They faced the panel of judges somewhat self-consciously, but without fear . . .

Judge: (FADING UP) Then, as I understand it, Mrs. Wein-traub, you and your husband have been married for fifty years . . .

Mrs. W.: Fifty-two years next September, Your Honor.

Judge:	Fifty-two years. (PAUSE) And after fifty-one years you left your husband's house?
Mrs. W.:	I left it and I'm glad I left it.
Judge:	But you're not asking him for support?
Mrs. W.:	Thank God I don't need his support. My children will help me. (PAUSE) If I had to depend on him— (BREAKING OFF) Judge—he's the stingiest man I ever—
Mr. W.:	I object, Your Honor!
Mrs. W.:	It's true, Abe. You know it's true!
Judge:	(TOPPING) Just a minute! Just a minute. Mr. Weintraub.
Mr. W.:	(GOING RIGHT AHEAD) I don't think she should be allowed to call me stingy. I object! I—
Judge:	(FIRMLY) Mr. Weintraub, calm down. You'll have your chance to tell your side later. (PAUSE) And please . . . please don't say "I object" again while your wife is talking.
Mr. W.:	You overrule my objection?
Judge:	Please, Mr. Weintraub. You've been seeing too many movies. (PAUSE) Now let's hear what your wife has to say . . .
Mrs. W.:	(FADING UP) I don't want his money, Judge. I just want to live my own life. (PAUSE) Alone.
Judge:	I see.
Rabbi:	May I ask a few questions?
Judge:	Of course, Rabbi.
Rabbi:	Mrs. Weintraub—you've told this board that you and your husband have seven children and thirteen grandchildren. . .
Mrs. W.:	That's right, Rabbi.
Rabbi:	And with a fine family like that, after a marriage of fifty-one years, you want to leave your husband—
Judge:	She *has* left him, Rabbi. He's brought her here for us to tell her to go back to him—
Rabbi:	Oh, I see. (PAUSE) Mrs. Weintraub, can you tell us why you remained with your husband all these years? Why didn't you leave him before?
Mrs. W.:	Why didn't I leave him before? (PAUSE) I was too busy. (SOUND: AUDIENCE REACTION)
Judge:	The people waiting to be heard will please try to be quiet.

Rabbi: Too busy?

Mrs. W.:   Yes, Rabbi. Too busy. First the children came. Then bar mitzvahs, engagements, weddings. (PAUSE) There were troubles, too . . .

Rabbi: (INTERRUPTING GENTLY) Yes, I'm sure there were troubles, Mrs. Weintraub. (PAUSE) And now you're no longer busy?

Mrs. W.:   Thank God, my children are settled. For the first time, I'm free of responsibilities. (PAUSE) I want to live by myself. Independently.
             (SOUND: AUDIENCE MURMUR)

Rabbi: And you feel you can't do that with your husband—the man you've shared fifty years of your life with?

Mrs. W.:   Rabbi, listen to me. For forty years we lived in a little three-room apartment. Every night, six o'clock, supper on the table. (PAUSE) The same supper. Whatever cost the least. (PAUSE) He has a good business. Not a millionaire, but a good business. Did we ever go away for a vacation? Did we ever enjoy life? No. We saved for a rainy day. (PAUSE) Believe me, the rainy day is here. I'm not going back to live with him.

Businessman: Mr. Weintraub, I'm the businessman on this panel.

Mr. W.:   Yes, sir.

Businessman: What kind of living have you made—I mean all these years?

Mr. W.:   A good living. Enough to live on. Enough to raise seven children—

Mrs. W.:   I'm not saying he was bad to the children . . .

Businessman: We understand that, Mrs. Weintraub. (PAUSE) Now let's get to the point.

Mr. W.:   Yes, sir.

Businessman: You've brought your wife here before this board. She's come here. Now what do you want us to do?

Mr. W.:   I want you to tell her to come back to me.

Judge: Mr. Weintraub, do you know that if this were a court of law, you wouldn't be able to bring your wife into court?

Mr. W.:   I don't understand, Judge.

Rabbi: A husband can't make his wife return to him by law—For that matter, we can't make her return to you either. Not unless she wants to . . .

Mr. W.:   Rabbi—you talk to her. Maybe she'll listen to you. (BREAKING) I can't sleep. I can't eat. I have no reason for living—

Rabbi:	Now just a minute, Mr. Weintraub, just a minute—
Mr. W.:	(CONTINUING) Don't you understand? I love my wife. You hear me, Jennie? I'll say it again.
Mrs. W.:	(QUIETLY) It's the first time he's said that in years, Rabbi.
Rabbi:	Do you believe he means it, Mrs. Weintraub?
Mrs. W.:	I want to believe it, Rabbi. But deeds speak louder than words—Why did he deny us everything?—Why—
Mr. W.:	(INTERRUPTING) Maybe I wasn't so free with money. Maybe I was worried about the children. But I wasn't keeping anything for myself—What I was saving was for my family.
Businessman:	You were saving, Mr. Weintraub? All the time your wife was stretching every penny to make both ends meet?
Mr. W.:	Yes, sir. For sickness, or for our old age—
Businessman:	Didn't you realize how difficult you were making your wife's life?
Mr. W.:	I did without things, too.
Businessman:	That doesn't change the situation. (PAUSE) Where were you saving?
Mr. W.:	In a bank.
Businessman:	Do you have the bankbook with you?
Mr. W.:	Sure I have it with me. Here.
Businessman:	(AFTER A PAUSE) This account, Mr. Weintraub . . .
Mr. W.:	Yes?
Businessman:	It's in your wife's name.
Mrs. W.:	In *my* name? The account's in *my* name?
Mr. W.:	Of course it's in your name. For who else was I saving the money?
Mrs. W.:	You never told me that. (PAUSE) He never told me, Judge. (PAUSE) Abe, you foolish man—why didn't you tell me when I could still listen?
Rabbi:	Mrs. Weintraub, you heard before, your husband can't make you go back to live with him—that is, not by law.
Mrs. W.:	Yes, Rabbi.
Rabbi:	But I want to ask your husband some questions, in front of you, and after he's answered them, I want you to consider what you should do—
Mrs. W.:	All right, Rabbi. I'll consider them. But I didn't know he was saving for me.
Rabbi:	We know you didn't know. Now, Mr. Weintraub—if your wife agrees to come back to you for a trial period, will you try to give her a chance to enjoy life—to live a

	little more for herself, than for others?
Mr. W.:	I will, Rabbi. I promise it. She can have the whole bank account. (PAUSE) It's yours, Jennie. It was always yours.
Mrs. W.:	If I come back, Abe, it's not for the money—
Rabbi:	Mr. Weintraub—Understand this. We can't give your wife back to you. You have to win her back.
Mr. W.:	I'll try, Rabbi. It's not so easy for a man of my age to change—but I'll try.
Rabbi:	Well, Mrs. Weintraub. You've heard your husband.
Mrs. W.:	Yes, I've heard him.
Rabbi:	I think you deserve a little peace and harmony in your old age. (PAUSE) What do you say?
Mrs. W.:	What do I say? (PAUSE) Abe, get your hat and coat. Let's go home.

Roe:	There was not even a formal decision by the judges in the court without a gavel on that afternoon . . . And yet, in half an hour a decision had been reached by common consent that would reshape the remaining years of their lives for the people involved . . . That is the quality that I remember—That out of conflict came harmony . . . That out of that courtroom new relationships between people were established—new relationships based on the oldest patterns of man's wisdom. (PAUSE) The second case I remember well was one in which a Mr. Biederman was asking to be reinstated to membership in a benevolent society from which he had been dropped.
Biederman:	(FADING UP) They have no right to do it, Judge. No right at all!
Judge:	Mr. Biederman, please don't draw conclusions for the judges. Let's stick to the facts.
Biederman:	(IN A HUFF) I'm perfectly willing to stick to the facts! The fact of the matter is—
Judge:	(INTERRUPTING) Just a minute, Mr. Biederman. Who is here representing the society?
President:	I am, sir. Mr. Rosen.
Judge:	What's your capacity in the society?
President:	I'm the president.
Judge:	And Mr. Biederman?
Biederman:	I'm the vice-president, Judge.
President:	You mean you *were* the vice-president!
Biederman:	I *am* the vice-president!

Judge:	Gentlemen, gentlemen! Please. Let us conduct this hearing in an orderly fashion.
President:	That's why we came here, Judge. So we could—
Biederman:	Judge—I resent the insinuation that—
Rabbi:	Mr. Biederman—the last thing we want in this hearing is resentment—
Biederman:	Yes, Rabbi.
Rabbi:	Now let's try to approach this problem without bitterness.
Biederman:	Yes, Rabbi.
Judge:	Mr. Biederman.
Biederman:	Yes, Judge.
Judge:	According to these notes, you've been suspended from the society after twenty years of membership? Is that correct?
Biederman:	That is correct. For no reason—
Judge:	Mr. Biederman—we already understand that you feel your suspension is unjust. Now, hold on for a minute, and let us hear from the president of your society.
President:	What do you want to know, Judge?
Judge:	Why have you suspended Mr. Biederman?
President:	For misappropriation of funds, Judge.
Biederman:	(BREAKING IN) So help me, I never—
Judge:	(TOPPING) Mr. Biederman!
Biederman:	But he can't say—
Judge:	Mr. Biederman, you know we're here to listen to this dispute impartially, don't you?
Biederman:	I'm sorry, Judge, I didn't mean to—
Judge:	That's all right. (PAUSE) Now let's proceed. Mr. Rosen—this is a very serious charge—to accuse a man who's been active in your organization for twenty years of dishonesty—
President:	Dishonesty? You think we're accusing Biederman of dishonesty?
Judge:	Well, you said he misappropriated funds, didn't you?
President:	I'll explain that in a minute, Judge. (PAUSE) But let's get one thing straight right away. I know Biederman for thirty-five years. No-one is going to say that Biederman is dishonest. (PAUSE) Not while I'm around to hear it.
Rabbi:	Mr. Rosen. Let's get to the bottom of this question of misappropriating funds.
President:	Yes, Rabbi.
Rabbi:	Just what did Mr. Biederman do?

President: Nothing so terrible, Rabbi. It's the way he did it we object to.

Rabbi: Can't you be a little more specific than that?

President: Certainly. Our society was organized to help the needy on the Lower East Side. Every year we contribute a certain amount of money for that purpose—to help the needy on the Lower East Side.

Rabbi: And we understand that Mr. Biederman is in charge of distributing those funds.

President: Yes, Rabbi. This year, Mr. Biederman gave our money to a fund which helps the needy throughout the city.

Biederman: Is that so terrible? Is that a reason for—.

President: (TOPPING) We don't object to the contribution, Rabbi. It's that he did it without consulting us.

Rabbi: And you consider this a misappropriation of funds?

President: It's not the funds, Rabbi. He gave the money to a perfectly worthy cause. It's a misappropriation of authority. (PAUSE) So we suspended him.

Judge: Mr. Biederman—

Biederman: Yes, Judge.

Judge: This constitution of your society—it says that the purpose of the society shall be to help the needy on the Lower East Side . . . Has this constitution ever been changed? . . .

Biederman: The constitution hasn't changed, Judge, but conditions have changed.

Judge: We know that conditions have changed, Mr. Biederman. But a constitution is a constitution. A society can't run except by its own rules.

Biederman: Look, Judge. My father founded this society. I know what his intentions were—

Judge: Whatever those intentions, Mr. Biederman, this is the constitution of your organization.

Rabbi: Mr. Biederman—

Biederman: Yes, Rabbi.

Rabbi: It seems to me you acted in perfectly good faith.

Biederman: Thank you, Rabbi.

Rabbi: But you would have done better to try to get your organization to amend its constitution first. That's the democratic way to do these things—

President: Rabbi—you've just put your finger on it—

Rabbi: On what, Mr. Rosen?

President:	On the whole situation. You think we suspended Biederman for this alone. Of course not. It's not just this incident—
Rabbi:	I didn't think it could be. Organizations don't usually suspend members on as small a technicality as this one—
President:	For the last few years, Rabbi, he's been doing whatever he wants to. He doesn't ask the membership. He holds a meeting with himself and passes a resolution. Then he acts on it.
Biederman:	Rabbi—if the membership had been more active, maybe I would've been less active—
Rabbi:	I think I understand, Mr. Biederman.
Biederman:	Thank you, Rabbi.
Rabbi:	But I also understand your organization's position. Activity is no excuse for being undemocratic.
Biederman:	Rabbi—was it democratic when they suspended me?
Rabbi:	It may have been unwise, Mr. Biederman—but apparently it was democratic.
Biederman:	Without a hearing?
Rabbi:	They suspended you without a hearing?
Biederman:	At a meeting I wasn't even invited to.
President:	We knew if we invited him, Rabbi, we wouldn't even get a chance to discuss it . . .
Rabbi:	Gentlemen, do you see what's happened?
Biederman:	I see that I'm suspended, after twenty years—Undemocratically.
Rabbi:	Mr. Biederman—when a man inflicts a hurt upon others, he really strikes at himself. We are all part of one another. The society acted unfairly, in my opinion, in suspending you without a hearing. (PAUSE) But would they have acted that way if you had consulted them on other matters?
Biederman:	Maybe not, Rabbi. Maybe you're right. (PAUSE) But the constitution was wrong.
Rabbi:	Mr. Rosen—do you think your membership will agree that your constitution should be amended?
President:	Yes—I think so, Rabbi.
Rabbi:	I think the judges will agree with me then, Mr. Rosen, that two wrongs don't make a right. Mr. Biederman deserves at least the right to be heard by your membership.
President:	Agreed. If he'll just follow the rules.

Rabbi: Will you, Mr. Biederman?
Biederman: Will I? (PAUSE) Of course I will. (PAUSE) You think I
                want to be suspended again?

Roe: In the pursuit of justice, this court without a gavel—this
                court which serves as lawyer to both parties—points a
                way forward towards an age-old goal . . . a standard of
                justice which includes that measure of mercy and good-
                will which makes Justice complete for all. (PAUSE)
                Most of this I cannot place in my formal report to the
                Governor. And yet—yet there is much to be learned
                from the court without a gavel on New York's Lower
                East Side. I am a lawyer, not a scholar, but I know my
                Bible well enough to remember the prophetic injunc-
                tion—"Justice, justice shalt thou pursue."

Ancr.:   If you would like a copy of today's script, please send your
                name and address with ten cents to cover the cost of
                postage and handling to The Jewish Theological Semi-
                nary of America, 3080 Broadway, New York 27, New
                York. And now we take great pleasure in presenting The
                Honorable William O. Douglas, Associate Justice of the
                Supreme Court of the United States. Justice Douglas.

The Hon. W.   The thing that has interested me particularly about the
O. Douglas: work of the Jewish Conciliation Board is that the Board
                has been more interested in justice than in law. Law and
                justice are not necessarily the same. Throughout the
                centuries law has been trying to catch up with justice. It
                has not always succeeded. That is one of the great eternal
                struggles of man.
                    The search around the world by people of all races and
                creeds is basically the search for justice. One finds it
                cropping up in many different ways, both little ways and
                big ways, as one travels around the world.
                    One of the most important struggles going on inside
                America today is the struggle to keep America the
                symbol of tolerance and fraternity. That is America's
                greatest strength in the long run. That is the power of
                America, not only at home, but in the councils of na-
                tions. We must in our community activities and national
                activities promote ideals of tolerance. We must keep

those ideals of America alive in the hearts of the people, otherwise we will lose our position of moral authority in the world.

This problem, like all problems, starts at home and in our own neighborhood. And that is why the work of the Jewish Conciliation Board is so important. The work of the Board, seeking to find what is the truth, trying to apply justice, is a great experiment in a busy community where there are many problems, local and international. It is important to take time out to make adjustments in the little problems of the people. That, in the end, marks the difference between a society which administers to the needs of people and a society where sores and troubles fester, where the needs and aspirations of the ordinary man are neglected.

Anncr.: This has been an NBC Radio Network Production, directed by Edward King. Dr. Ben Zion Bokser, Rabbi of the Forest Hills Jewish Center, is Program Editor.

Appendix IV-A

Resolution Adopted by the City Council of the City of New York
September 16, 1965

RESOLUTION IN HONOR OF JEWISH CONCILIATION WEEK AND RABBI ISRAEL GOLDSTEIN

By Mr. Kupferman—

WHEREAS this is the 45th Anniversary of the founding of the Jewish Conciliation Board of America; and

WHEREAS a celebration will be held to mark the anniversary of this unique social service organization, together with the 35th anniversary of the presidency of the eminent Jewish leader, Rabbi Israel Goldstein; and

WHEREAS the celebration will take place on Sunday, September 19th, 1965, at the Educational Alliance on the Lower East Side where the Jewish Conciliation Board of America had its roots; and

WHEREAS the general theme of the celebration will be the achievements in the area of arbitration, justice and conciliation that have been rendered by the Jewish Conciliation Board of America, without charge, to many thousands of persons; now therefore be it

RESOLVED that the City Council of the City of New York recognizes September 13th to September 19th, 1965, as JEWISH CONCILIATION WEEK; and be it further

RESOLVED that the City Council of the City of New York extends its cordial greetings and felicitations on the celebration in New York City of the 45th anniversary of the Jewish Conciliation Board of America and the 35th anniversary of its distinguished President, Rabbi Israel Goldstein.

Appendix IV-B

*Text of Mayor Wagner's Proclamation
for Jewish Conciliation Week*

WHEREAS the City of New York and its Jewish community have profited in no small measure from the program of the Jewish Conciliation Board of America over the past 45 years, and

WHEREAS this unique organization serving as a free court of arbitration has combined the wisdom of the Torah, the authority of the law and the compassion of humanity in rendering its decisions in many thousands of cases, and

WHEREAS the year 1965 marks the 45th anniversary of the Jewish Conciliation Board of America, and accordingly it is fitting and proper to publicly acknowledge this fact, now

THEREFORE, I, Robert F. Wagner, Mayor of the City of New York, do hereby proclaim the week of September 13th to the 19th, 1965, as Jewish Conciliation Week in New York City, knowing that all New Yorkers will share my sense of pride in the achievements of this outstanding Jewish agency and extend warmest congratulations.

Appendix IV-C

Congratulatory Letter from Vice-President Hubert Humphrey

The Vice-President
Washington
September 16, 1965

Dear Dr. Mark:

For 4½ decades, the Jewish Conciliation Board of America has set an inspiring example in reconciling disputes between individuals, families and organizations. In so doing, you have fulfilled many of the noblest traditions of the "People of the Book"—the advancement of understanding, the strengthening of good will—virtues which should be followed by men and women of every faith. I am so pleased, therefore, to send this greeting to the Board's anniversary celebration, this Sunday.

In a world of discord where tempers are so often heated by irresponsibles, rather than cooled by thinking people, in an age which has been scarred by so much violence, in a time when man possesses ever deadlier means to annihilate the human race, how we do need the type of spirit—with compassion, justice and wisdom—which your noble organization represents. What a splendid pattern it is that men and women, divided often so bitterly, should continue to turn voluntarily to arbitrators whom they respect and bind themselves to the impartial decisions which result.

I send special greetings, of course, to your great spiritual leader, Dr. Israel Goldstein. For 35 years he has served as the Board's President with great distinction. May he enjoy many more years of health and happiness, and may his successor as President carry on—as I am sure he will—with similar devotion and success.

To Chief Justice Sobeloff and to all the other distinguished officials and citizens who will be gathered in recognition of this anniversary, may I express my esteem and regards. All good wishes to you and your association for continued fruitful service.

Sincerely,

(Sgd.) Hubert H. Humphrey

Dr. Julius Mark
Jewish Conciliation Board of America, Inc.
225 Broadway
New York, New York 10007

Congratulatory Telegrams

WASHINGTON,D.C.—WARM GREETINGS TO THE JEWISH CONCILIATION BOARD
OF AMERICA ON THE AUSPICIOUS OCCASION OF YOUR FORTY-FIFTH ANNIVER-
SARY AND TO YOUR HONORED GUEST AND PRESIDENT RABBI ISRAEL GOLD-
STEIN. YOU ARE TO BE COMMENDED FOR YOUR LONG SERVICE NOT ONLY TO
THE JEWISH COMMUNITY BUT TO ALL AMERICANS FOR YOUR EFFECTIVE WORK
ON THE PERSONAL LEVEL. YOUR ORGANIZATION HAS BEEN UNHERALDED FOR
TOO LONG BY THE PUBLIC BUT I AM SURE THAT MANY INDIVIDUALS OWE
THEIR THANKS TO YOU. YOU MAY BE SURE OF MY CONTINUED SUPPORT AND
BEST WISHES FOR FURTHER SUCCESS.

JACOB K. JAVITS
United States Senator
from the State of New York

WASHINGTON, D. C.—I REGRET THAT MY SCHEDULE DOES NOT PERMIT ME TO
JOIN YOU FOR THE FORTY-FIFTH ANNIVERSARY CELEBRATION OF THE JEWISH
CONCILIATION BOARD OF AMERICA. MY WARMEST CONGRATULATIONS ON
YOUR OUTSTANDING HUMANITARIAN EFFORTS. PLEASE EXTEND TO RABBI
ISRAEL GOLDSTEIN MY WARMEST BEST WISHES FOR MANY MORE YEARS OF
DEVOTED SERVICE TO THE MEMBERS OF THE JEWISH COMMUNITY.

ROBERT F. KENNEDY
Attorney General of the
United States of America

NEW YORK, N.Y.—AS PREVIOUSLY ADVISED BY LETTER PRIOR AGREEMENTS
PREVENT MY ATTENDING CELEBRATION OF 45TH ANNIVERSARY OF JEWISH
CONCILIATION BOARD OF AMERICA AND 35TH ANNIVERSARY OF PRESIDENCY
OF MY DEAR FRIEND AND RABBI EMERITUS DR ISRAEL GOLDSTEIN. HE IS AN
INSPIRATION TO US ALL IN THE GREATEST AMERICAN TRADITION OF FREEDOM
AND DIGNITY OF THE INDIVIDUAL. BEST WISHES TO ALL PRESENT.

LOUIS J. LEFKOWITZ
Attorney General of New York

Appendix V

Excerpts from Addresses by Dr. Israel Goldstein

V-A   Dinner, January 27, 1932

Let me welcome you all to this, the first annual dinner of the Jewish Conciliation Court of America. Our gathering was intended for those who have a special interest in the type of work which this court is doing.

Not even the most optimistically minded citizen would claim that our regular courts of law are able to meet adequately all situations which come before them for adjudication. Although, theoretically, the poor man has the same rights before the law as the rich, actually he is at a disadvantage because he is unable to set in motion the legal machinery for the protection of his rights. There is the element of cost of litigation which is frequently so high as to bar the working man from the court. There is the element of delay.

The Jewish Conciliation Court of America exists for the purpose of offering a medium of conciliation and adjudication for individuals and groups who cannot and should not bring their cases to the civil courts. Often it is a problem which does not call for adjudication as much as conciliation. In all cases, whether they be of conciliation or of adjudication, the procedure of the court is simple.

The litigants themselves present their own stories and the witnesses are called directly by the judges. There are three judges at every session—a rabbi, a jurist and a businessman. The litigants speak whatever language they can best express themselves in. The linguistic talent of the judges and the vivid gesticulations of the litigants make all languages equally intelligible. In the course of a single afternoon, as many cases are tried as would take a week or more in the city courts. There is no charge of any kind entailed for the litigants. It is truly touching to see the confidence and ease of these poor people, when they come to our court, knowing that there they will be understood.

There have been in our community a number of sporadic efforts in the organization of such courts. These may, however, have been individual enterprises, sometimes used for individual exploitation. In any case, they have not won the confidence of the community. Our court has succeeded in drawing to itself the best elements in our Jewish public life, and has won the confidence and cooperation of some of the most representative Jews in our community, representing all walks of life and all branches of religious opinion. It is the only broadly communal institution of its kind. I have full confidence that, in the course of time, it will receive the recognition and cooperation which it deserves.

Our society is now at a stage when the regularly constituted courts of law do not seem to meet the needs adequately. We believe that an institution like ours renders a service to the cause of Jewish self-respect and Jewish self-discipline. We believe it renders a civic service to the community. We believe that it renders service to the cause of conciliation and goodwill, and to the cause of better understanding between man and man.

V-B   Board of Directors Meeting, January 9, 1935

During the past year, we have received gratifying endorsement of the public significance of our work. The past year has also witnessed an attempt in many American communities, including our own city, to solve some of the chronic problems of court delays by the establishment of additional tribunals where adjudication can be exercised with a minimum of delay. The agitation for the simplification of court procedure—which leading jurists, from Elihu Root down, have been urging for years as a boon, especially for the poor man—seems at last to be meeting with a response. The improvement, which is still slight and incipient, will take a long time to reach a significant stride, but the trend at least is encouraging.

For the year which lies ahead, we shall endeavor to enlarge the social service aspect of our program. The great number of our cases affect a stratum of society where social service attention is needed, such as proper direction to unemployment relief or work relief, placements in homes for the aged, and skilled intercession in maladjusted family relations.

V-C   Station WEVD, June 26, 1948: "Humanizing Justice"

To radio audiences it is nothing new to be told about goodwill and courts and mediation boards. The broadcasting of people's troubles has become an entertainment feature on more than one wavelength.

I want to talk to you this evening—and others will talk to you on other Saturday evenings—about this problem, from a different angle. The angle is that of sympathetic human service and Jewish dignity. We shall not drag to the microphone miserable men and women, and aggravate their misery by asking them to tell their troubles for public entertainment. Nor shall we put before you a panel of radio judges who, because they have to keep the program going every minute of the radio period, must often give snap judgments instead of well-deliberated decisions.

We shall tell you about cases which come before the Jewish Conciliation Board of America. We shall give you an insight into the problems behind the problems. But above all, we want you to feel—as we do—that by keeping these cases out of the courts we are not only rendering a service to the individuals involved, but at the same time rendering a service to the Jewish community by safeguarding its good name and its dignity.

There is an expression with which some of you are familiar—*yosher,* Jewish justice. You see it in action at every session of ours. Without being bound by technical procedures or precedents, but by the application of common sense, human understanding and feeling for the right, the Jewish Conciliation Board of America not only dispenses justice, but humanizes justice and exercises conciliation in the good old Jewish tradition of *tzedek ve-yosher,* justice and fairness.

V-D   Thirty-Fifth Anniversary of the JCB, January 17, 1954

Twenty-five years of experience in conciliation and adjudicating disputes, far from weakening my faith in human nature, have actually reinforced that faith. I have found relatively few cases of malevolent designs or basic dishonesty. Mostly, disputes arise between parties, each of whom honestly believes that the right is on his side.

I am convinced that a great service could be rendered to every community if, under city auspices, judges would be appointed, not necessarily endowed with legal training, whose purpose would be to conciliate and arbitrate disputes. Attached to every such tribunal should be a social service department with a psychiatrist included in its staff. The services of such a tribunal should be made available without charge only to the substandard income groups. It is an obligation of social security in a broader sense, to strengthen the social security of the community.

The need among the underprivileged for friendly, skilled help in conciliating and adjudicating disputes, altercations and misunderstandings is so widespread that no privately supported agency can cope with it. The Jewish Conciliation Board has been a pioneer in this field, has accumulated a vast amount of experience, and would be glad to make its experience available to any municipally sponsored tribunal which may be established along similar lines.

I strongly commend this proposal to Mayor Robert F. Wagner. The establishment of such a tribunal would add to the human credentials of our great city.

V-E   Forty-Fifth Anniversary of the JCB, September 19, 1965

It has been an extraordinary privilege to have been associated with the Jewish Conciliation Board, as its president, for thirty-five of its forty-five years. This has been reward enough.

In terms of the kind of celebration procedures to which the American public has become accustomed, the Jewish Conciliation Board has been *nekhba el ha-kelim,* most unpretentious: no Fifth Avenue parades, no Waldorf-Astoria dinners, no interviews with Presidents. We preferred to mark the occasion in a manner and in a place which are suitable and characteristic for us. "I dwell among my people." The Jewish Conciliation Board holds most of its sessions here, in the Jewish Educational Alliance. It serves the plain people, of whom Lincoln once said, "God must love them, because he made so many of them."

And yet, under these simple auspices, in this simple program of the Jewish Conciliation Board of America, there are invested human, civic and Jewish values of prime importance.

Every one of you who has served as a judge at one of our sessions will testify that our happiest hours are when two disputants who have come in as foes go out as friends. Nor do we rely altogether on the hour of the hearing to bring about the desired result. Sometimes there are psychological complications which need patient, unhurried attention. Sometimes there are private secrets which need patience to be patiently unlocked. So a great deal of our work is done before and after the sessions by a psychiatrist and a social service worker. I would say that our quality of justice is not strained.

It does not require great perception to understand what our tribunal means to the City of New York, whose courts are clogged up and whose procedures are expensive.

If I may be personal for a moment, it has occupied an important place in my life in the midst of my other preoccupations. Perhaps it was because my other occupations mostly had to do with mass movements in American and Jewish national and international affairs and with ministry to a large upper-middle-class congregation. Working so much of the time for Israel made me the more sensitive to the problems of "Reb Yisro'el," the individual. I have received from this labor of love more than I have given.

I am sometimes asked, "Does this kind of institution have a future?" I see a future for the Jewish Conciliation Board because I see a future for every civic agency which is engaged in the work of arbitration and conciliation, and because I see a special need for a Jewish agency in this field. Jewish families, and Jewish fraternal and religious institutions where disputes arise, will always find at the hands of a Jewish tribunal a more intimate understanding of their problem, a deeper appreciation of the background of their disagreements, and a greater sense of involvement in the solution of their disputes than would be possible in any other jurisdiction. The language may be less and less Yiddish, but the value of the Jewish dimension of the social service rendered will be undiminished. Thus, the ancient *mitzvah* of bringing peace and understanding between man and his fellow man will continue to find uninterrupted fulfillment in the work of the Jewish Conciliation Board of America.

To have a part, however humble, in "bringing peace between man and his neighbor," is a great *mitzvah*, a duty and a privilege in the Jewish tradition. *Shalom*, according to Jewish lore, is one of the attributes and names of God Himself. It is, and it has been, mankind's most desperate need and supreme blessing—locally, nationally and globally. We carry a tiny candle when mankind needs the sun of righteousness "with healing in its wings"—but it serves the same cause, it brings some light into dark corners. Let us do our part as it is given us to do, great and small.

Appendix VI

*Persons Who Served the Jewish Conciliation Board During the Years
1930–1968*

A. OFFICERS AND MEMBERS OF THE BOARD OF DIRECTORS

Rabbi Israel Goldstein ....President (1930–1968)
Mrs. Rebekah Kohut ....Vice-President (1930–1952)
Rabbi Moses Hyamson........................Vice-President (1930–1949)
Judge Jacob Panken ....Vice-President (1930–1968)
Rabbi Leo Jung ....Vice-President (1950–1968)
Rabbi Julius Mark..........................Vice-President (1957–1968)
Charles Frost..............................Vice-President (1966–1968)
Jacob R. Schiff............................Treasurer (1930–1948)
Israel Sachs ....Treasurer (1949)
Nathan S. Sachs ....Treasurer (1950–1957)
William Sachs ....Treasurer (1958–1968)
Jacob Goodman............................Associate
        Treasurer (1958–1968)
Louis Richman ....Executive
        Secretary (1930–1957)
Ruth Richman ....Executive
        Secretary (1958–1965)
        Executive
        Director (1966–1968)
Hon. Bernard S. Deutsch ....Chairman of
        the Board (1930–1936)
Simon Bergman ....Chairman of
        the Board (1937–1939)
Rabbi Israel Mowshowitz....................Chairman of
        the Board (1968)
David A. Brown ....Vice-Chairman of
        the Board (1935–1936)

Board of Directors

Hon. Sol Tekulsky (1932–1968)   Morris Weinberg (1952–1968)
Ludwig Vogelstein (1930–1935)   Rabbi Jonah B. Wise (1930–1939)
Nathan Warshaw (1963–1968)   William Wolpert (1954–1968)

B. PERSONS WHO SERVED AS JUDGES: 1930–1968

Abels, Rabbi Moses S.   Bressler, David M.
Abrams, Hon. Lewis A.   Brill, Rabbi Isaac L.
Agronsky, Gershon   Brodsky, Irving
Alderman, Hon. Israel P.   Brodsky, Hon. Louis B.
Alstadt, Rabbi Philip R.   Broff, Stanley
Altman, Moses   Broido, Louis
Altman, William R.   Brown, David A.
Altschul, Mrs. Jeanette   Brown, Frederick
Apfel, Isidore   Browner, Mrs. Frances
Appelbaum, Rabbi Carl   Buchbinder, Rabbi Jacob T.
Ashkenazi, Maurice   Buck, Bernard L.
Azarow, Arnold B.   Burack, Rabbi Aaron D.
Azarow, Nathan   Burke, John S.

Bachrach, Louis   Cedarbaum, Rabbi David I.
Backer, Hon. George   Chanin, Irwin S.
Backlar, Samuel S.   Claman, Emanuel
Bamberger, Rabbi Bernard   Claster, Samuel W.
Basel, Rabbi A.   Cohen, Rabbi Boaz
Beloff, Judge Samuel W.   Cohen, Charles
Benjamin, Paul   Cohen, Elias A.
Berger, I.   Cohen, Koppel
Bergman, Simon   Cohen, Lawrence B.
Berkowitz, Rabbi William   Cohn, Joseph
Bernfeld, Paul   Cooper, Judge Irving Ben
Bernstein, John L.   Cross, Rabbi Nathan
Bernstein, Hon. J. Sidney
Biben, Joseph H.   Dana, Chaplain Major Max H.
Bienenfeld, Rabbi Jesse   Davidson, Gabriel
Blakensteen, William   Derby, Rabbi Josiah
Bloch, Rabbi Irving   Derfner, Samuel
Bloch, Dr. Joshua   Deutsch, Hon. Bernard S.
Block, Rabbi Alvin   Dingol, Solomon
Block, Hon. S. John   Drachman, Rabbi Bernard
Bloom, Rabbi Maurice   Drob, Rabbi Max
Blumenstock, Louis   Druckman, Abraham D.
Bokser, Rabbi Ben Zion   Dym, Rabbi Aaron
Borg, Mrs. Sidney
Bosniak, Rabbi Jacob   Ebin, Rabbi Nachman H.
Botein, Judge Bernard   Eisenman, Morris
Boukstein, Maurice M.   Eisenstein, Rabbi Ira

Eisner, Hon. Mark
Elder, Judge Morris
Eller, Abraham
Elterman, Leon J.
Epstein, A.
Eskolsky, Rabbi Mitchell S.
Etra, Mrs. Gustava
Evans, Hon. William S.

Fabricant, Louis
Falk, Samuel
Feinthal, Rabbi Morris G.
Feldman, Benjamin
Fenichel, Seymour
Fertig, Hon. M. Maldwin
Field, Samuel
Fierst, Harry P.
Finkelstein, Rabbi Louis
Fischoff, Rabbi Ephraim
Fishman, Jacob
Fishzohn, Samuel S.
Fogelman, Dr. L.
Frankel, Louis
Frankenthaler, Judge George
Freeman, Gerald
Freund, Jules S.
Friedman, Hyman
Friedman, Louis S.
Frost, Charles

Gainsburg, J.
Gair, Harry A.
Gallant, Rabbi Abraham
Garter, Nathan
Genn, Simon
Gershman, Joseph S.
Gerson, Louis
Gerstein, Rabbi Louis C.
Ginsberg, Isaac
Glazer, Rabbi B. Benedict
Godnick, Berton W.
Godnick, Charles S.
Goldberg, Rabbi Joshua L.
Goldberg, Rabbi Morris M.
Goldberger, Leo J.
Golden, Harry
Goldsmith, Lawrence

Goldstein, Mrs. Bert
Goldstein, Emanuel
Goldstein, Rabbi Herbert S.
Goldstein, Rabbi Israel
Goldstein, Judge Jonah J.
Goldstein, Rabbi Morris
Goldstein, Nathan L.
Gollob, Bernard
Golovensky, Rabbi David
Golub, Barney
Goodman, Abraham
Goodman, Jacob
Gordis, Rabbi Robert
Gordon, Rabbi Harold H.
Grafman, Rabbi L. Eliah
Greenberg, Judge Henry Clay
Greenberg, Rabbi Louis
Greenspan, Hon. Benjamin E.
Gresser, Lawrence
Gribetz, Louis J.
Gross, Dr. Solomon S.
Grossman, Rabbi Jacob B.
Gruber, Benjamin B.
Gruenewald, Dr. Max
Guilden, Ira
Guilden, Morris
Guttentag, S. W.
Guttman, Joseph

Haas, Dr. Joseph
Hahn, Rabbi Judah Louis
Halperin, Harry J.
Halpern, Rabbi Harry
Halpern, Irving
Handler, Milton
Harris, Mortimer I.
Hartstein, Benjamin A.
Held, Adolph
Held, Dr. Isidore W.
Held, Max
Heller, Rabbi A. M.
Hershfield, Harry
Hershkopf, Bernard
Hirschorn, Benjamin
Holland, Emil
Hollander, Max L.

Horowitz, Hon. Charles
Horowitz, Harry
Hurowitz, Samuel W.
Hurwitz, Rabbi B. Leon
Hyamson, Rabbi Moses
Hyman, Louis

Ilson, Rabbi Aaron B.
Isaacs, Hon. Stanley M.
Isler, Herbert

Jakobovits, Rabbi Immanuel
Jaretzki, Alfred
Jasper, Seymour
Joseph, Hon. Lazarus
Jung, Rabbi Leo
Junger, Morris J.

Kahan, William
Kahane, Rabbi S.
Kahn, Alexander
Kahn, David W.
Kahn, William M.
Kalmanoff, Jacob
Kalmanoff, Max
Kanner, Joseph W.
Kanter, Gilbert
Kaplan, Rabbi M. A.
Kaplan, Rabbi Mordecai M.
Kaprow, Barnett
Kassin, Aaron Z.
Katz, Ernest H.
Kauff, Hy
Kessler, Mordecai
Kirshblum, Rabbi I. Usher
Klaperman, Rabbi Gilbert
Klein, Rabbi Edward E.
Klein, Jacob
Klein, Joseph J.
Klein, S.
Klein, William
Koenigsberg, Jacob
Kogan, Nathan B.
Kohn, Henry
Kohn, Rabbi Jacob
Kohut, Mrs. Rebekah
Kopelman, Barnett E.

Korkus, Edwin F.
Korn, Dr. Harold
Krakauer, Gabriel M.
Kramer, Charles P.
Kramer, Joseph
Kramer, Samuel,
Kramer, Rabbi Simon G.
Krasne, Abraham
Krass, Rabbi Nathan
Kroll, Charles
Kross, Judge Anna M.
Kuflik, Samuel
Kwalbrunn, Rabbi Moshe

Lande, Louis
Landman, Rabbi Isaac
Landow, Sam
Langer, Rabbi C. Simon
Lauer, Hon. Edgar J.
Lawn, Rabbi Jerome M.
Learner, Ben
Leeman, Irving
Lefkowitz, Hon. Louis J.
Levin, Maurice
Levine, M. Carl
Levine, Judge Max S.
Levinthal, Rabbi Israel H.
Levy, Benjamin J.
Levy, Hugo
Levy, Judge I. Montefiore
Levy, Jacob
Levy, Judge Matthew M.
Levy, Meyer
Levy, Hon. Samuel
Lewis, Judge David C.
Lewisohn, Adolph
Lewitt, Charles Howard
Lipman, Samuel
Lipschitz, Rabbi Chaim
Livingston, Hon. Jacob H.
Lookstein, Rabbi Joseph H.
Lubell, Morris M.
Lurie, Dr. Abraham
Lyman, Hon. William

Mack, Major William J.
Maier, Rabbi Reuben

Maisels, Judge Israel A.
  (South Africa)
Mandelbaum, Joseph
Manecher, Irving
Manson, Hon. Julius J.
Marcus, Henry
Marcus, Rabbi Joseph E.
Margolis, Rabbi Elias
Margolis, Rabbi William
Margoshes, Samuel
Mark, Rabbi Julius
Markewich, Judge Arthur
Markewich, Hon. Samuel
Marks, Isaac
Mayes, Aubrey
Meckler, David L.
Medalie, George
Mekler, Rabbi J. H.
Melniker, Jerome
Miller, Mrs. Frances
Miller, Rabbi Irving
Miller, Rabbi Joseph
Miller, Michael A.
Miller, Samuel
Minkin, Rabbi Jacob S.
Mintzner, Hon. George J.
Morgenstern, Morris
Morris, Hon. David
Morros, Boris
Moss, Hon. Paul
Mowshowitz, Rabbi Israel
Muney, Samuel D.

Naitove, Moe
Nathanson, Alexander S.
Neumann, Hon. Ely
Newman, Rabbi Jacob J.
Newman, Rabbi Louis I.
Norman, Edward A.
Noveck, Lawrence
Null, Samuel

Orenstein, Rabbi Jehiel
Orr, Hon. Samuel

Pack, Hon. Carl
Paley, Harry

Palitz, Clarence Y.
Panitz, Rabbi David H.
Panken, Judge Jacob
Paull, Julius
Paznik, Sam
Pearce, Samuel
Perilman, Rabbi Nathan A.
Perlman, Hon. Nathan D.
Perlman, William M.
Plotkin, Rabbi Benjamin
Polachek, John
Pollak, Milton
Pool, Rabbi David de Sola
Popkin, Louis
Posner, Louis
Prager, William
Predmesky, Rabbi L.
Pressman, Jack
Propp, Mortimer J.
Propper, Karl
Pulvermacher, Joseph

Rabbino, Maurice
Rabin, Hon. Benjamin J.
Rabinowitz, Jacob
Rabinowitz, Rabbi Simcha
Rackman, Rabbi Emanuel
Ranen, Hon. Ellis
Ratnoff, Dr. Nathan
Recht, Charles
Reichman, Gerson
Reichman, Rabbi Solomon H.
Rheinstein, S.
Richards, Bernard G.
Rittenberg, Louis
Rocker, Louis P.
Roden, Samuel
Rosenberg, Alexander
Rosenberg, Fred
Rosenblatt, Judge Bernard A.
Rosenblum, Rabbi William F.
Rosenfeld, Max
Rosengarten, Isaac
Rosenthal, A. M.
Rosenthal, Henry
Ross, Arthur
Roth, Louis K.

Rothenberg, Judge Morris
Rothfeld, Saul
Rothman, Henry
Rubin, Rabbi Henry H.
Rubin, William
Rubinger, Charles
Ruskay, Cecil B.

Sachs, Israel
Sachs, Nathan S.
Sachs, William
Sacks, Rabbi Maxwell L.
Safian, L. A.
Salit, Rabbi Norman
Saltzman, Rabbi Manuel
Samet, Shimon
Samler, Louis
Sandler, Bernard H.
Sandrow, Rabbi Edward T.
Sarachek, Rabbi Joseph
Sargent, Samuel L.
Sarnoff, General David
Sarnoff, Irving
Sarnoff, Simon
Scharfman, Isidore
Schenk, Rabbi Max
Schenkman, David A.
Schiff, Jacob R.
Schildkraut, Eugene
Schlein, Robert
Schlesinger, Emil
Schlossberg, Joseph
Schmer, Max
Schmulowitz, Nat
Schneider, Max J.
Schneiderman, Ms. Rose
Schoenfeld, John
Schoenfeld, Rabbi Lazar
Schoenstein, Paul
Schorr, Rabbi Henry A.
Schulman, Rabbi Gabriel
Schwartz, David
Schwartz, Max
Schwartz, Mrs. Rose
Schwarz, Julius
Schwefel, Rabbi Louis J.
Schweitzer, Isidor S.

Segal, Rabbi Bernard
Segal, Rabbi Samuel M.
Seligson, Rabbi David J.
Semel, Bernard
Shafferman, Maurice
Shaine, Maurice L.
Shalleck, Hon. Benjamin
Shalleck, Milton
Shapiro, Leon J.
Shaw, David
Sheinkman, Jacob
Sherman, Carl
Shore, Samuel
Shulman, Rabbi Charles
Siegel, Hon. Isidore
Silberberg, Abraham A.
Silbert, Theodore H.
Silver, Hon. Charles H.
Silver, Julius
Silver, Rabbi Maxwell
Silverstein, Rabbi Israel
Simons, Murray
Sincoff, Jacob
Singer, Rabbi Howard
Singer, Jacob
Smith, Joseph
Sobol, Benjamin
Sobol, Ira J.
Solomon, Rabbi Elias L.
Solomon, William
Stackell, Judge Harry
Stein, Barnet M.
Stein, Dr. Joseph
Steinbach, Rabbi Alexander A.
Steinberg, Rabbi Milton
Steuer, Max D.
Stolz, Irving
Strahl, Hon. Jacob S.
Straus, Donald
Sussman, Louis
Sussman, William S.

Tarshis, Morris
Taub, Emanuel
Taussig, Ms. Frances
Tedesche, Rabbi Sidney S.
Teitelbaum, Isidor

Tekulsky, Hon. Sol
Teplitz, Rabbi Saul I.
Tintner, Rabbi B. A.
Tokayer, Rabbi Marvin
Tolkoff, Jacob S.
Tyler, Gus

Umansky, David

Vladeck, Hon. B. C.
Vogelstein, Ludwig

Wagner, Charles
Waldman, Louis
Warburg, Mrs.
Warshaw, Nathan
Wasservogel, Judge I.
Weber, Simon

Wechsler, Philip
Weil, Victor L.
Weinberger, Rabbi Bernard
Weisman, Max
Wiesel, Elie
Wiesen, Max
Wilk, Abraham S.
Wise, Rabbi Jonah B.
Wise Tulin, Judge Justine
Wolf, Emanuel
Wolf, William F.
Wolpert, William

Yankauer, Alfred

Zahavy, Rabbi Zev
Zaritsky, Max
Zeitlin, Rabbi Joseph

C. SOCIAL SERVICE DEPARTMENT

Friedlander, Miss Sadie
Maxine, Miss G.
Richman (Bornstein), Mrs. Ruth—coordinator
Saller, Miss
Silver, Miss Esther
(with the assistance, for the first few years, of ladies of the B'nai Jeshurun
Sisterhood: Mrs. Samuel Elbaum, Mrs. Shepard Goldberg, Mrs. B. J. Levy,
Mrs. Yolan Lubin, Mrs. Jacob Schwartz, and Mrs. William Wolff)

D. VOLUNTEER CONSULTANT PSYCHIATRIST

Dr. Howard E. Berk

E. PATRONS

Altman Foundation
Altschul Foundation
Camps, Lee and Jane, Foundation
Congregation B'nai Jeshurun
    Sisterhood
Congregation Emanu-El
Frankenthaler, Judge George
Friedsam Foundation
Hurowitz, Sam, Estate
Metzger Price Fund

Blumenstock, Louis

Browdy, Benjamin
Druckman, Abraham D.
Field, Samuel
Frost, Charles
Guilden, Ira
Godnick, Berton W.
Goldstein, Judge Jonah J.
Goodman, Abraham
Goodman, Jacob
Kahn, David W.
Kahn, William M.
Kohn, Henry

Mandel, Milton
Mark, Rabbi Julius
Miller, Michael A.
Morgenstern, Max
Morgenstern, Morris
Mowshowitz, Rabbi Israel
Reichman, Gerson
Sachs, Nathan S.

Sachs, William
Schiff, Jacob R.
Schlechter, Mrs. Louis
Schwartz, Mrs. Rose
Shapiro, Leon J.
Singer, Jacob
Teitelbaum, Isidor
Warshaw, Nathan